American Half Breed

How a bi-racial kid from the hood was saved by the U.S. Navy and its Special Boat Teams

By

CWO5 Ron Carpenter U.S. Navy SWCC (Ret)

Forewords by Retired Navy SEAL Captain Kenneth Niederberger and Jean L. Becker, former chief of staff to President George H. W. Bush

Copyright

This publication is provided for informational and educational purposes only. The views expressed are those of the author and do not necessarily reflect the official policy or position of any government agency, organization, or institution.

First Edition: 2026
Published by American Halfbreed Publishing
Saint Petersburg, Florida, USA
Library of Congress Control Number: [To be assigned]
ISBN: 979-8-9952080-2-0

""The views expressed in this publication are those of the author and do not necessarily reflect the official policy or position of the Department of Defense or the U.S. government."

Contents

Dedication

To my mom, who showed true grit against insurmountable odds. Despite being so young, raising so many children with little support, relying on Uncle Sam for a welfare check with the stipulation that no man could live in the house and enduring the many times she was victimized while protecting us, sacrificing the very essence of her womanhood she will always be my hero.

We often questioned why she remained in the prison she was in, and why she did not leave. All these years later, I realize why. The system is designed to keep poor people in place to keep them poor. It replaces hope with the law of scarcity, making us believe we never have enough of what we need to escape. They give you just enough to survive, never enough to thrive.
For all of you mothers out there like mine, you are the true heroes in every man's life. Without you, there would be no me or we.

To my wife, for your steadfast love and support. Without you, I would have no one to brag to. I love you and thank you.
To all the nobodies who will soon realize they are somebody, as this life places them in the positions they were always meant to be in. We are born as a success story. We just have to write it.

To our future generation, who will take the torch from ours, I wish you discernment, empathy, and a love of country.

Acknowledgements

I would like to thank my good friend, Dava Guerin, author of many books, for helping me tell my life story. Her ability to help me recall so much about my life and things I had long kept in the vault has been essential in making this book a meaningful narrative.

In addition, having expert readers review the manuscript and provide their insights and suggestions has been invaluable. They include Retired Navy SEAL Captain Ken Niederberger and Jean Becker, a New York Times bestselling author, who wrote heartfelt forewords and shared their thoughtful perspectives. Ken dedicated most of his adult life serving our country. Jean, an author herself and former chief of staff to George H. W. Bush, knows firsthand the power and importance of service.

Without my brothers and sisters Sheri, Pinky, Angie, Tommy, and Tobo (Hunk) who have made and continue to make my life special, I would not be where I am today. I love you.

I also want to thank Uncle Sam and the City of Chicago for teaching me that even the most insurmountable obstacles in life can be overcome with grit, determination, and honor. To the USS Pyro (AE-24) (1987–1991) and all my shipmates who helped this half-breed become whole and forced a change in me by giving me numerous opportunities to return to honor. I am forever in your debt.

Finally, to my Gunnersmates in Third Division, especially Bossman and Lou Singleton, who helped me grow and excel as I got out of my own way and started drinking the Kool-Aid of success. Thank you all.

To the United States Naval Special Warfare Command United States Navy SEALs and Special Warfare Combat Crewmen, as well as members of other service branches who helped me grow and never looked at me as black or white, but simply as a "Boat Guy," I offer my deepest gratitude.

A special shout-out to Boat Troop Five and Riverine Task Unit Five. What a ride we were on. We went through a lot together and adapted to the enemy, the mission, the terrain, and the environment. Thank you all for mentoring me and helping shape the SWCC I became.

To Navy SEAL officers Mike Lumpkin, Dave Pittlekow, Rob Newsom, John Jones, Chuck Herbert, and Ken Niederberger who consistently helped shape me and trusted me even when I was not sure of myself, thank you.

To my SWCC Warrant Officer brothers, and to all the enlisted leaders who set the bar high in my life; George Anger, Mark Presson, Mark Martin, Harold Fannel, Mike Lore, Mario Martin, Eric Mimms, Gabe Lopez, Angel Arauz, Dave Strachan, Dan Synder, Dave McCoy, Dave McClain, Hank Taylor, Kris Carini, Gary Luna, Justin Ackerman, and many others I am forever grateful.

To my closest confidants and brothers Bob Daniels, Ivan Tancredi, and George Turak thank you for your love and guidance over the years. Without your support, teamwork, friendship, and brotherhood, I would not be where I am today. For all of you, I owe my deepest gratitude. You will always be my family.

I love you all.
Hooyah.

Foreword

By Navy SEAL Captain (Ret) Kenneth Niederberger

This book is required reading for anyone that believes life's obstacles are too much for them to overcome. Ron Carpenter's story is an amazing journey of overcoming unbelievable circumstances growing up in inner city Chicago to rise to the top of the Naval Special Warfare Combat Crewman leadership. His frank style holds nothing back. His story will bring some of us to tears but woven throughout Ron's colorful style of prose, is a tale of winning, of continued resilience, of not allowing oneself to become or to remain a victim. It is inspiring and I believe it will inspire future readers, especially young people looking for purpose in life.

I have known Ron for over a decade, and we met at the sunset of his storied NSW career. In one of many adventures, we worked together to bring a previously unutilized capability to a reliable mobility and collection platform for the US Special Operations Command that today plays a significant role in US military operations in the Middle East today. I assigned Ron this task without sufficient resources, people and limited funding. It was not his primary and certainly not his desired job. This was easily something that he could have allowed obstacles to stop its progress. However, true to his character he overcame those challenges in his own unique and sometimes unauthorized way to deliver roses out of manure. As I read American Half Breed, I now see where Ron's grit, determination and desire to achieve arise from…and reading it I believe you will also find hope in it.

I have spent 28 years in NSW serving at commands that selected its people not just simply receiving them from the Navy's personnel assignment bureau. In Naval Special Warfare, there is a difference between wearing a uniform with a patch and earning your place in the team. Ron is one of those select Special Warfare Combat Crewmen who earned it. As you read the story, you will see he led his people while operating worldwide in almost any sea state, under any conditions and at any given time. While their job is simple to describe you will see it is difficult to execute; deliver special operators into hostile environments and bring them home. That sounds straightforward. However, it is not.

As you flip the pages of this book keep in mind where Ron started. He did not grow up on the water. He did not come from money or a long line of Naval Service. He came out of inner-city of Chicago, from a world where the choices were narrow, the margins were thin, and nothing was given. In that environment, most young men learn to survive. Ron learned to fight forward and excel… more importantly he led and inspired others around him to do the same.

There is another thing you should know about a SWCC warrant officer. The rank comes with authority, but authority alone will not move a boat team one inch. What moves them is credibility. Ron carried the scars, the stories, and the skills of a man who had done the job in bad places and terrible conditions for a long time. When he spoke, people listened not because he was required to be heard, but because he had already proven he was worth following. As you read this book and remember Ron's origins, you can see why he was good at operating in challenging times.

In the end, this is what matters: a young man who had every excuse to aim low chose to step into the hardest water the Navy has to offer and stayed there long enough, and performed well enough, to carve his name into SWCC history. The rank on his shoulder—CWO5—is proof. The pages that follow explain the cost.

You are about to read how he did it, in his own colorful words and uniquely entertaining style. My hope is that as you do, you see what I saw and still see today… a man who humbly shouldered more than his share, inspired those around him, while succeeding in meeting our country's most important maritime security goals. I find the story inspiring and I believe you will too.

—Captain (Ret.) Kenneth Niederberger
United States Navy SEALs

Foreword

By Jean L. Becker

Ron Carpenter has a story to tell that every single American needs to hear.

This inspiring, often breathtaking account of his life takes the reader on a wild and fascinating journey from the rough and tumble streets of the South Side of Chicago, where he risked his life almost every day simply by existing, to his years as a sailor in the United States Navy, where he risked his life for God and country.

Ron's story is one of the best examples I have read of how good can triumph over evil, hope over despair, and determination over all else.

He accomplishes all of that by being a powerful storyteller, sharing with readers both the darkest moments of his life and the moments that made him realize I can do better. I can be better.

I was honored when Ron asked me to write this foreword but also a bit confused.

After all, I am a farm girl from Missouri whose life experience is about as far removed from Ron's as one can get. But I couldn't shake two thoughts that kept coming back:

- My former boss, himself a Navy veteran, would love Ron's story and would indeed consider him a hero.
- One of the problems in our country right now is that we tend to spend time with, talk with, and agree with people who look like us, think like us, and are us.

It is long past time for the farm girl from Missouri and the boy from the mean streets of Chicago to get to know each other to listen to each other, and to learn from each other.

I know I learned a lot from American Half Breed.

So will you.

Read it. Absorb it. Appreciate its honesty. Then think about how we can all do better and how we can all be better.

Jean Becker
Chief of Staff to George H. W. Bush (1994–2018)

Introduction

It was another crazy day in the hood. I had no idea how crazy it was about to become.

Growing up on welfare on the South Side of Chicago forced my brothers, sisters, and me to grow up far too fast. We became calloused, lost empathy, and buried parts of our humanity as our world revolved around welfare, poverty, drugs, prostitution, alcoholism, death, gun violence, and incarceration. It should surprise no one that we eventually came to see this as our strange version of normal.

My biological father left me and my four siblings when I was five years old. Not long after he vanished, my mom had a new boyfriend named Fred. Everything was going about as well as it could in the hood. Fred even offered my mom a job at his restaurant so she could make a little money until one evening my father unexpectedly returned to our apartment.
When he saw Fred standing next to my mom, he pretended to be thirsty and asked her for a glass of water. Then something snapped. It was like a switch flipped and unleashed the beast.
My father became enraged. Completely out of control.

A normal person might get angry even act out but not my father. With me and my sister Sheri hiding under our bunk bed in the living room, trying to understand what was happening, he pulled out a handgun and shot Fred right in front of us.

The image of a man lying dead shot and bleeding out on our living room floor haunted me for years. As I grew older, that moment, along with others, subconsciously gave me the kick in the butt I needed to move on and get out.

To this day, my sister still does not remember me being under the bed with her. Who knows? Maybe she is right. But traumatic memories have a strange way of reshaping themselves over time. No matter how hard we try to block them out or believe what we want to believe they linger until they become part of our fractured reality.

After all these years, and after the trauma my family and I endured, our reunions can still feel dysfunctional when we get together. Talk about "today's nightmares becoming tomorrow's memories."

When we recount our past experiences, it sometimes resembles a special operations team discussing how they survived a firefight or an ambush. But fortunately, there is also plenty of laughter and love.

Somehow, I believe that its part of our family's continuous and sometimes contentious healing process.

Like many other young people growing up around gangbangers, pimps, and drug addicts in one of the toughest neighborhoods in the country, I was programmed for failure. Our choices were simple: stay out of jail, stay away from drugs or fall into both and become another statistic. No one was pushing hope our way.

And to top it all off, my father who, as I mentioned, abandoned me, my three sisters, and my brother was Black. My mom, of Italian descent, was White. Hence the title of my book, American Half Breed, and my lifelong struggle to figure out where I belonged.

You may wonder why I wanted to tell my story.

The answer is simple.

I wanted to share the lessons I learned from growing up with nothing. I often joke that we were so poor we would eat the peas one day and drink the juice the next.

Ironically, we became so accustomed to a routine that most normal people would find incomprehensible. Our biological father abandoned us and was a murderer who got away with it. Our cruel, alcoholic stepfather was also a pimp and drug dealer. He was a violent man who abused my mom and us kids to the point that we believed it was normal for men to abuse their families and for kids to go to school with black eyes and bruises. To me, that was business as usual.

The lessons I learned came through triumph and disaster, while I adapted my behavior to treat those two imposters just the same. Most of my troubles were self-inflicted and, as I mentioned before, were the result of the poor examples I had growing up as a biracial city kid with a "South Side Chicago attitude."

For example, when I was thirteen years old, I helped steal a kid's bike with no concept of the consequences. I was shocked when I was caught and arrested a few days later because the kid whose bike we stole was the son of a Chicago Police Department officer. Lucky me, right?

But that experience made me realize I did not want to be a loser or keep breaking my mom's heart. My solution was simple: I got a job selling the Chicago Tribune City Edition newspapers on Saturdays and Sundays at sporting events. Even as a young kid me Angie and Tommie would walk a few blocks to the OK Supermarket and help older folks carry their groceries to their cars or homes, then used some of the money we earned to buy my mom her favorite strawberry shortcake, play pool, and grab a cheeseburger and fries at Jim's Arcade, six wings for a dollar at the Chinese restaurant, or rib tips at Jet Way.

It felt good to be good. I liked making money without having to do it illegally.

Despite my early trauma, I was determined to escape the crazy and deadly streets of the South Side of Chicago. I just had no idea how to make that happen.

But I knew one thing for sure: I was not going to college. I did not have the money, and I had no idea how college even worked. Plus, I was graduating high school in the top 10 percent of the lower 1 percent of my graduating class which did not help either.

(I literally made a career out of going to summer school and night school to make up for the classes I failed during the school year.)

So, I took a step that very few people in my neighborhood would even consider. I joined the United States Navy and eventually landed where I was destined to be my entire life United States Naval Special Warfare.

I will describe how special operations professionals do the basic things extraordinarily well. You will see how we conduct dangerous and clandestine missions from start to finish and how we always debrief afterward, focusing on what we got wrong, not what we got right.

There is always room for improvement in the military and in life.

You will learn about the "What? So what? Now what?" concept a framework that allows you to take ownership and create your own vector, meaning your speed and direction.

Most Americans have no idea what Special Warfare Combat Crewmen (SWCC) are. We are special operators who are experts in high-speed boats and maritime operations on any body of water. Our boats carry enough firepower to execute and complete dangerous, secretive missions around the world in support of Navy SEALs and other Special Operations units. You will come along with me during some of my special operations missions to Kenya, Iraq, the Philippines and Pakistan, and learn the lessons I incorporated into life, leadership, emotional intelligence, and business.

But a dangerous job like ours is bound to have a downside. What none of us special boat operators could have predicted was that the time and sacrifice required to hone complex technical skills would take a toll on our personal relationships, families, and bodies. Using humor as a coping mechanism especially dark humor was one of the ways I dealt with many dangerous missions, injuries, and the loss of friends over twenty years of combat. You will read about some of those experiences in future chapters.

I will also show you how our training workups for deployment are designed to replicate realistic combat operations or as we often say, "We train like we fight and fight like we train." But despite some of the most arduous training in the world, we SWCC suffer from a range of serious, lifelong injuries as a result of being struck by waves in boats that can produce over twenty g's of force on our bodies.

Traumatic brain injuries, spine issues, nerve damage, reduced mobility, impaired mental capacity, endocrine problems, suicidal ideation, and PTSD are just a few of the injuries sustained onboard boats while we are on active duty that follow us into civilian life.

It has been one of my primary missions since retirement to advocate for making high-speed boat human factors the number one priority for active-duty SWCCs and SEALs whose bodies continue to be destroyed onboard these boats.

On the positive side, there is no discrimination when you are a special boat operator. No "half-breed" labels there. My experiences in Naval Special Warfare will shine a light on how society often gets race wrong. We are not simply colors in this country. We are not the red, white, or blue in our flag. We are the thread that holds the flag together, and it took many nationalities to create our Republic. Patriotism is on steroids among SWCC and SEAL members in Naval Special Warfare.

Though small in number in Special Operations there are only about 850 SWCC in the Navy many multiracial, Black, and brown operators have nevertheless excelled in Naval Special Warfare.

When I served on a ship in 1987, it often felt somewhat segregated by race; Asians hung with Asians, Whites with Whites, and Blacks with Blacks. But when I joined the Boat Teams (Special Boat Unit Twenty-Six), I finally did not stand out among the mostly young white men on the team and within the community.

We depended on one another not only to complete the mission but to literally have each other's backs. Unlike shipboard life, in Naval Special Warfare I was more than just a number. My opinions and input mattered. It was one of the few places where being bi-racial, Black, or brown was rendered meaningless. You were judged on merit and capability no matter what God you worshipped.

The fact is that when people are shooting at you, trust me, no one is an atheist. As a result, there were nothing but God-fearing special operators praying for one another's safe return during some of our most dangerous missions. I loved that about my teammates that they wore their faith on their sleeve and loved me as their brother.

Even though I was finally in an egalitarian environment, I still believed I had to work fifty percent harder than my peers. Especially since I talked more crap than a North Korean radio station. (My nickname in the Boat Teams was "Minigun." At least it was not Zebra or Half-Breed.)

But that pressure forced me to develop a stronger work ethic, a skill that had been completely foreign to me growing up without mentors or role models in the hood.

It was during my four years on a ship the USS Pyro (AE-24) and my early years as a Navy SWCC that my life truly began to change. Those experiences eventually led me to become a commissioned officer.

Through all the setbacks and comebacks, losing friends in Chicago to gun violence and drugs, and losing others in the military during combat operations, as well as witnessing the human condition around the world, I grew to love our country even more.

That love motivated me to share my life story. I hope that anyone living in unthinkable conditions will find inspiration in it and realize that their life is a gift no matter what obstacles they face.

As we often say in the Boat Teams: "CHARLIE MIKE." Carry on with the mission. Have an attitude of action. Never quit.

The truth is, in my humble opinion, your past is not your prison. We need to learn to look at life through other people's lenses so we can learn from their mistakes and avoid making the same ones ourselves.

It saddens me that our country does not realize that one of its greatest untapped resources is the kids growing up in underprivileged neighborhoods regardless of color, race, or gender.

My ultimate goal in writing this book is to motivate young people and anyone experiencing trauma or abuse to embrace the life lessons that can change the trajectory of their lives.

Embrace the simplicity of life's journey without becoming obsessed with money. Because in the end, love is the currency that truly pays off.

Just remember you may be mixed up, but you sure as hell ain't messed up.

I hope you become the person you were born to be faster and with far less trauma than I did.

My hope is that my story will inspire you and show how a multiracial kid from a four-block radius we called our hood could eventually look beyond that environment and shed the negative programming that comes with it.

There is a saying that has always stuck with me: "In that moment of clarity, you achieve clarity of consciousness." From being a troubled eighteen-year-old who enlisted in the U.S. Navy just thirteen hours after graduating from Kenwood Academy on June 14, 1987, to the struggles I initially faced in the Navy, and ultimately becoming part of Naval Special Warfare Special Boat Teams, I experienced many moments of clarity.

Those revelations helped turn my life around and shape me into the citizen of the world I aspire to be today.

We all deserve opportunities to return to honor.

Even a rock, when exposed to extreme heat and pressure, becomes a diamond.

Thank you for taking the time to read my story. I could not wait any longer to share it with you.

CWO5 Ron Carpenter
U.S. Navy (Retired)

PART ONE

SURVIVING THE HOOD

Chapter One

Not White Enough/Not Black Enough

"There is no such thing as race. None. There is just a human race scientifically, anthropologically."

Toni Morrison

The address: 1001 West Sixty-Eighth Street, Chicago, Illinois, between 68th and Morgan and Carpenter Streets. That is where I grew up. (One might think I had some special influence with a street named after our family, but of course, that was not the case.) Our neighborhood was known as Englewood, located in Cook County the most populated county in the state and the second most populous in the country. It is often referred to as the South Side of Chicago, now sometimes called "CHIRAQ." Confused yet? The South Side is one of four major sections of the city, along with the East Side, West Side, and North Side. Englewood is one of the neighborhoods that comprise the South Side. (Chicago is often known as "the Loop," because the city has roughly concentric circles where White, Black, and Latino communities live.)

Our neighborhood was like many others in underprivileged areas. Unfortunately, there were more liquor stores and fast-food restaurants than grocery stores. Buying a piece of fruit or a vegetable was expensive, while unhealthy alternatives like honeybuns could be had ten for a dollar.

Oddly enough, Morgan Street was surprisingly beautiful, with huge oak trees lining the street on both sides. Carpenter Street, however, was the opposite. Many houses were run-down and dilapidated, with two flat apartment buildings and a few vacant lots scattered along the block. On the far corner at 69th and Carpenter was Julius Tavern, where local alcoholics, pimps, and drug dealers congregated. One block further down was Aberdeen Street, where our local grocery store, Okays, provided our sustenance through food stamps and by letting us kids help elderly customers carry their groceries home for a tip.

As with most things in the hood, unpredictability was the name of the game. One day, we were shocked when Frank and Charles the owner and manager had security run us off the premises because one of us had shoplifted. Funny thing was, if they knew that their decision would push us deeper into hustling and other illegal activities, maybe they would have allowed us to continue helping the old ladies with their groceries? Looking back, it's tragic that people like them, who already had a leg up, felt no obligation to encourage us to be better. They could drive home to a different neighborhood after work, while the rest of us hood-dwellers remained in our prison. But can you blame them? How much could they take from kids who were a pain in the butt? And so, the paradigm of despair perpetuated itself.

The building we lived in was a brown, two-story structure owned by my step-grandfather, "Big Tony." He was a generous man who gave my mom a deep discount on rent so that we could at least afford a roof over our heads.

Our neighborhood's claim to fame? When I was a child, it had a reputation for crime, drugs, and prostitution, and it was primarily Black. It was hard for me to believe that in the 1920s and 1930s, the South Side was racially segregated. But in 1940, when the U.S. Supreme Court heard the housing case Hansberry v. Lee which challenged racial restrictions in the Washington Park Subdivision Black families began moving to the South Side in droves. Those who were educated eventually tended to move away, but not our family. We were lifers. And trust me, it could have been my own life sentence. Why? Because the "careers" on the streets were often being on welfare, gangbanging, pimping, or becoming an addict. The main products of those careers were selling drugs and beating up anyone who dared challenge them or, God forbid, snitch. Not exactly the kind of work that provides job security.

Do not get me wrong. It was not all bad. Many older residents were from the Deep South; they became our "village." There were some interesting and caring people. For example, Madea (Mrs. Hall) and her family became very close to us. They were just like family. While they were poor as well, they were not as poor as we were. Regardless, they always offered us food and invited us to their home for a sandwich, cookie, or cold drink in the summer, as well as holidays like Christmas and Thanksgiving. Then there were Mrs. Pratt, Mrs. Allen, Ann, Les, and Martha our go-to folks whom we could always count on to have our backs. Families like the Rheas, who lived across the street, were unique as well. Mr. Rhea worked for Dolly Madison (a real job), was a committed husband, ensured his kids were well-dressed, serious about school, and attended church. Examples like these were there, but they were often drowned out by the poor influences that constantly pulled us in the wrong direction.

And it sure did take a village to raise kids like us from the hood. Mrs. Pratt and Mrs. Allen would see us do things good or bad and became a huge spy network. How they could dial those old rotary phones and get the message to our parents before we even reached the house is still beyond me. My mom gave them full authority to discipline us with a belt or a switch if we were acting out. It was as if they knew we were up to no good and just preempted the call.

But it was punishment with love. If they could have given us the world, they would have, but the system itself had a way of keeping us below the poverty line. Even with our village of support, there were very few options to glimpse life beyond our bubble of despair or to see what a "normal" life looked like. Back then, we accepted our fate; we had no choice. Poverty was programmed to determine our destiny. Today, society often frames it as a racial issue, but I truly believe it is socioeconomic. That class divide is compounded by a system that gives us just enough to survive, never enough to thrive.

It was always an odd contradiction to me that most Black neighborhoods, like the one I grew up in, welcomed everyone with open arms. It didn't matter your color, race, or creed. Yet, despite that hospitality, other neighborhoods particularly white ones rarely reciprocated it. I recall countless times being chased out of the Marquette Park area by angry white men. We could never win. Even when we ventured beyond the hood, we were not welcomed and pushed back to ours.

So our fates were mostly sealed at a young age. Many underprivileged neighborhoods in Chicago, and across the U.S., became conveyor belts feeding the juvenile and prison systems.

By way of family history, my grandmother Nellie was born a coal miner's daughter in West Virginia to Matilda and Pancrazio Centara. They came to the United States from Zagarise, Italy.

In 1948, she moved from West Virginia to Chicago after marrying Louis Biano. Both were seeking better opportunities. Nellie had four children; my mom was the youngest. I never knew my biological grandfather until years later. That is a story for another time.

In the 1950s, my grandmother fell in love with a well-known Black musician named Tony Smith. Talk about courage under fire: a Black man and a white woman married when societal norms made it difficult, yet they stayed together through thick and thin. His band, Tony Smith and the Aristocrats, made enough money to buy an apartment building. Since I never knew my biological grandfather, Tony whom we called "Big Tony" became the closest figure to a grandfather I ever had. He was a big man, not physically, but because of his overwhelming presence and booming, raspy voice.

Big Tony carried himself like a seasoned businessman. Always well-dressed and respected in the neighborhood, he came from nothing but built everything through his own work ethic. A caring man, he tried to guide me, my brothers, and my sisters to become useful members of society, but there was never enough time to reinforce those lessons. Big Tony had his own kids and a full-time job managing his building while booking his band for gigs across the city. So, the few times he offered advice, it felt like lessons from an old kung fu master never fully satisfied with anyone's performance. He had a habit of scolding us, giving a slight smack on the back of the head when we didn't listen, or admonishing us for dropping tools too hard during building repairs. Ironically, it often made us less likely to conform, because we weren't afraid of him.

As I mentioned, my mom was the youngest of four sisters. Like many young women of her era, her main goal was to find a man, get married, and have children. As a teenager, she met my biological father, Ronald E. Carpenter Sr., a Black man from Chicago of German, French-Canadian, and Native American descent. They married after only a few months and started having children almost immediately: Sheri (now sixty), Pinky (fifty-nine), Angie (fifty-eight), me (fifty-seven), and Tommy (fifty-three). Go figure, it took so long for DOD to approve the book that I had to update our ages.

Even at an early age, I sensed my dad was not a good man. His constant smirk made us feel unwanted, clearly an annoyance. Over time, I realized he likely detested us because he felt we took away his "freedom." He did not want to be a father or a husband, for that matter. To my mom's surprise, and with no warning, he walked out one day, returning only sporadically. I remember one visit when he picked me up in a two-door Corvette Stingray with his girlfriend and took me to the zoo. As the oldest boy, I represented his last hope of remaining tied to his kids, of retaining any shred of fatherhood. He failed miserably.

After that day, I saw him only twice more. One day, when I was nearly five, he returned to our apartment one last time and it was a day we will never forget.

Our family's ramshackle apartment had a living room, dining room, two tiny bedrooms, and a bathroom barely large enough for four people, let alone seven. The brownstone, two-story building had eight apartments divided into two sections by separate entrances; we lived on the first floor. Two hallways divided the building into four apartments, and ours was on the left side. The only white person living nearby was a Polish woman named Miss Martin. She had moved into the neighborhood before Black families arrived and never left. No one ever messed with her. We called her the "creepy white lady" because the white powder makeup she wore made her look like a ghost. (Miss Martin lived there until the day she died.)

The walls in most of the rooms had plaster peeling off, the linoleum floors were worn thin, and the bathroom was in desperate need of renovation. Yet, interestingly, the dining room boasted three small stained-glass windows, each patterned with colorful flowers. But no matter the faintest hint of artistic charm, our mundane apartment life was both our sanctuary and, at times, our prison.

Take the roaches, for example. When the lights went out, they staged their nightly parade, hundreds of them, almost moving in formation, especially through the kitchen.

Even while we slept, it didn't surprise us to find roaches crawling up our arms, legs, or anywhere our bodies were exposed. No amount of spraying made a difference; they were permanent residents. Roaches will definitely outlive us all. You get the idea.

My mom slept in one room, while we kids shared the second room. My sisters Sheri, Nellina, and Angelic shared a proper bedroom. My brother Tommy and I slept on bunk beds in the dining room. Those bunk beds became our refuge. They were an improbable escape, yet we preferred them to the floor. They also provided a measure of protection from Mom when we misbehaved.

Hiding under the bottom bunk was our safe haven, even though Mom occasionally used a broom to enforce her discipline when we darted beneath it. Getting a good night's sleep in that apartment was a challenge, especially knowing that beyond our four walls lurked absolute chaos and uncertainty.

Because I was so young, I didn't fully understand the gravity of the situation. Here was my mom, with no one to count on or to protect us, suddenly having to raise five kids alone, with no husband and very limited financial resources. In fact, her only income came from welfare, and navigating its challenges was overwhelming. For example, any presence of a man in the household meant losing all financial support. Go figure how do you weaken a household? By taking the man out of the house.

Many families in the neighborhood were crippled by these welfare laws because it often made more financial sense for fathers to leave than to stay. With no one to protect us, my mom and we kids were vulnerable to being victimized. Twice, men broke into our home and raped her. I have no memory of these events, but my sister Angie recalled one instance vividly: a man broke in through a window, locked us in the bedroom, and assaulted our mom while we could only hear her fighting and screaming for help. That was the first time.

Tragically, there was a second time as well. Even worse, both men were from our own neighborhood. The events were profoundly traumatic for Mom and for us kids, yet somehow, we blocked them out. How could we forget something so horrific? Now, as an adult, it begins to make sense.

There were so few male role models for boys or girls, which was devastating in the neighborhood. We had no way to defend ourselves, and constant victimization left us with few options. Our mom could never be blamed; her choices were always about selecting the lesser of evils in an impossible situation.

In addition to all the problems of living in the hood, it was made worse by the fact that none of us siblings looked like the other kids in the neighborhood. When I dust off my elementary school photo now, I am still reminded of how awkward and uncomfortable it was being biracial. And kids can be cruel especially when you are different.

Throughout my childhood, I was called every name in the book: white boy, half-breed, zebra, and cracker. I was the only biracial kid in a class of all Black students. I tried to get used to it; I had no choice. At least, in my mind, I had none. Being on welfare and biracial left me retreating into my own shell. It worked for a while, but as I got older, rejection especially from the girls in my neighborhood became painful. Every single one of them dismissed me because, they said, I was not "Black enough," as if it were an unwritten rule. Not one Black girl would date me until high school, when I finally got away from the hood.

And even aside from race, there was reality: what girl in her right mind would date a guy with nothing to offer, growing up on welfare? Maybe, at the time, I was blaming my lack of dates on not being "Black enough" when, in actuality, I was just a knucklehead. Something to ponder for sure.

Though we were born and lived in a Black neighborhood, I did not want to be singularly Black because of my multiracial roots. I did not feel I had to choose a side, especially when I looked more Italian. Unfortunately, that often became my Achilles' heel.

As I got older, aside from substandard living conditions, peer rejection, and a father who had left us, I often wondered if life could get any worse.

Even though I was very young at the time, I would witness the horror of death not on the mean streets of Englewood, but right in my own living room.

It was a Sunday night. Sheri and I had just finished eating dinner if you could call it that: a piece of bread with mayonnaise, or a ketchup sandwich. Mom's new friend, Fred, was at our apartment. We actually liked him, so his presence was no problem. He may have had a chance to become Mom's boyfriend. He was thoughtful, generous, and cared enough to even offer her a job at his restaurant.

Just as we were finishing our meal and heading to bed, my father, Ronald, unexpectedly opened the door, walked in, and asked Mom for a drink of water. She got the water, though she was shocked to see him after such a long absence. This was supposed to be just another booty call for him but that didn't happen because Fred was there.

I remember the yelling. Sheri and I hid under the bottom bunk, terrified and unsure of what our dad was doing. Ronald saw Fred in the living room and became enraged, cursing and yelling every name in the book.

Then, our dad pulled a gun from his pocket. Fred backed away, but Ronald moved closer and shot him twice execution-style.

As Fred collapsed on the living room floor, Sheri and I clung to each other for dear life. Mom ran into the living room, screaming, "What did you do?" She was in shock, seeing our dad standing there like a deranged maniac. Then he pointed the gun at her head for a moment to scare her, to put her in her place before shoving her almost to the floor. I remember him running out of the house and bending over the sewer to dump the two guns. Mom was pale as a ghost, tears streaming down her face. It wasn't long after that the police arrived.

So, there we were: hiding under the bunk bed with a dead man lying in our living room. As with most murderers in the hood, Ronald had a story. He never took responsibility. It was no surprise he got away with murder, claiming self-defense, knowing Mom could not testify against him because of spousal testimonial privilege. The bastard got away with it.

After this life-changing experience and many others as I grew older, I decided I had to get out of the hood. I needed more from life than witnessing murders, living among pimps and drug dealers, and being in constant fear. I did not want to become a gang banger or drug dealer.

Because of the hood and seeing what happens to young Black men recruited into gangs, forced into drugs, I wanted nothing to do with it. Even back then, I realized every bad thing was tied to poverty. It didn't matter if you were White, Black, Latino, or mixed. Poverty dictated your treatment. We never received the benefit of the doubt. Even school offered no encouragement. Graduating from the eighth grade did not prepare us for high school. Our lives were prescribed to fill the lower rungs of society. For me, it was metastatic emotional torture, growing up as an outcast in my own neighborhood.

To make matters worse, I was terrible at basketball, the sport most young guys in the hood played. That made me even more of an outcast. I mostly hung out with Tommy and my sisters, who couldn't play either. There were countless unwritten rules.

It was a constant cycle: family members fought, then we fought back. The rules were bizarre, but survival depended on obeying them.

We also feared the gay guys on Carpenter Street. They could fight, and you gave them a wide berth. They always came in pairs. If you got on their wrong side, you risked serious injury. After the first altercation, their families might track you down for round two.

Even kindness came with complications. Once, we helped a drug dealer push his car off the street. Instead of a thank-you, he handed us a bowl of opium. A bowl of opium! We thought it was cool, but in reality, he was recruiting new clients. Everything in the hood had an agenda.

We were free to run and play unless on punishment. The hood was our proving ground: makeshift basketball hoops, street football dodging cars, snowballs with rocks for impact. We even learned to buy what we wanted with food stamps.

The worst part? Many of these dangerous people were in cahoots with law enforcement. Cops drank and smoked weed with the bad guys, sometimes even in our apartment. Being on welfare, poor, and biracial was living hell. To survive, you had to embrace the life around you. A life I never fully did.

Despite all the trauma and what Mom endured, I had no idea what awaited us until she met Stan or as the neighborhood knew him, "Cadillac Stan."

Chapter Two

Cadillac Stan

"There is no faculty of the human soul so persistent and universal as that of hatred."

Henry Ward Beecher

You might wonder what a luxury vehicle like a Cadillac could possibly have to do with Stan. It's actually an oxymoron. Why? In 1906, Cadillac became the first manufacturer of a fully enclosed car. Stan, on the other hand, thought he was the total package, but he was never wrapped too tight. His brain floated somewhere in outer space, among the debris, with no real connection to Earth. The luxury pimp with a deviant pauper's core. Meet Stan Maddox.

Stan Maddox was a behemoth of a man. At six foot six and 260 pounds, he was intimidating as it gets especially to me and my siblings. His story defied normalcy. When we first met him, he seemed tolerable, even a good guy, but we could never have predicted the havoc this pimp, alcoholic, and drug dealer would bring into our lives.

To understand how my mom Geraldine even considered dating Stan, you need to know more about her own early life and struggles. Growing up poor and without influential role models, her only ambition, as I mentioned, was to get married and have children. She never finished high school. Even though she wanted to attend summer school, there wasn't enough money to entertain the idea. Years later, she had to settle for a GED.

"I never knew anything about the world or my future except getting pregnant," Mom said. "So, when I met Ronald Senior, all I could think of was being his wife and having babies. You could say it was the welfare mentality at the time. That was going to be my career."

Mom had three siblings from my grandmother's first husband, Louis Biano: Bette, Delores, and Matilda. Louis came to America from Italy. Like many immigrants whose status was "WOP" (without papers), his name was likely changed to sound more American. They lived in West Virginia before moving to Chicago.

During World War II, my Louis enlisted in the US Navy and was deployed overseas for several years. My grandmother, lonely and missing her husband, sought male companionship regardless of her marital status. You can imagine what happened next. With our family history, no story is ever typical or "normal."

After a few years of managing a home and raising three young daughters, my grandmother ran into a handsome man named Frank Cerise. I'm not sure why he returned to the States after serving in the 82nd Airborne, but he and my grandmother began a secret affair. Back then, relationships outside of marriage were forbidden but such stories are as old as humanity itself.

When Louis returned from deployment, surprise my mom, Geraldine, was born. He had no idea she wasn't his biological child. Grandmom Nellie never told him the truth. Secrets in the hood, and in life, are always double-edged swords. They feel right at the moment, but they have a way of coming back to haunt you.

To make the situation even more complicated, once my grandparents divorced, Frank made the decision to marry my grandmother's sister, Rosie and still had no idea that my mom was his daughter.

Frank Cerise and Rosie had five "official" children and, of course, the sixth daughter, my mom, whom Frank still did not know was his. You could say Rosie, though kind and quirky, clearly had a few screws loose. In fact, she had a nervous breakdown and was hospitalized in a mental institution for years during their marriage. But she had the freedom to come and go from the hospital and would often visit our house, sit in the kitchen, and talk to my mom.

Rosie drank coffee and chain-smoked cigarettes, which would infuriate Stan. I heard him cursing Rosie many times; Mom took it in stride, and Rosie didn't give a damn.

Some of their conversations revolved around secrets and confessions. "Geraldine, I have something to tell you that you won't believe," Rosie said, puffing on her cigarette. "I can't imagine, Rosie, what is it?" Mom replied. "Well, your dad is not your dad." Mom kind of blew off her comment, since we all knew Rosie was a little coo-coo. But Rosie pressed her to explain. "It's a long story, Geraldine, but Frank is your real father not Louis, as you thought all these years." Mom never took her seriously, assuming it was Rosie's mental illness creating a vivid fantasy world. They moved on from the conversation, but Rosie repeated the story over and over.

Then, from 2000 to 2003, my grandmother became very ill and was hospitalized again. This time, everyone feared the end was near. The family gathered in her hospital room to say their goodbyes, and my grandmother made a stunning admission: she came clean and told my mom the truth. Frank Cerise was her biological father. We were all stunned, though my mom was less so. After hearing Rosie tell the story for years, Mom had always suspected it might be true.

After learning the news, my mom called me. "Ronnie, I really didn't believe Rosie, and now I'm blown away Grandma just told me Frank is my father, not Louis. Can you believe it?" she said. "Mom, that's nuts, but nothing surprises me," I replied, knowing full well my family was wacked.

And do you want to know the craziest part? My grandmother didn't die after all she lived for many more years. Now the secret was out for the whole family to absorb. And the irony of ironies? Crazy Rosie turned out to be the sanest one after all.

Back to Mom's childhood. She always loved music, and if her life had been different, she might have stayed in school rather than becoming a breeder and might have pursued a career in the arts. She loved playing guitar; music was her escape. Being poor left no time or money for makeup, hair appointments, or dining out beyond the local fast-food joint. Mom handled most chores herself mowing the lawn, making minor home repairs. Though she never finished high school, she could read and write fairly well. But when my grandmother moved the family to Chicago, Mom's life took a dark turn.

She felt like an outcast in the hood and, like me, never fit in because she wasn't black enough. With no diploma, money, or vision for the future, she set her sights on finding a man. Ronald Carpenter Sr., unfortunately, was it. Little did my mom realize at eighteen that she was headed for disaster with a man she thought was "acceptable."

Almost immediately after marrying my father, babies began making their grand entrance into the world. Ronald, on the other hand, crept in and out of her life, leaving her vulnerable to poor relationship decisions principally, her involvement with Stan Maddox.

"I was heartbroken when Ronald first left me," Mom said. "He would stay for a month or two, then leave again, only to return for a booty call which led to four pregnancies."

"Ronald was selfish and lazy," she continued. "Even though he was a talented mechanic, his drinking and poor choices got him fired. With nowhere else to go, we moved in with his mom. But soon after, I was about to deliver my first child, and he was nowhere to be found. I ended up calling the police, almost having my oldest Sheri in the paddy wagon. I was terrified. The officer saw how scared I was and said, 'Don't worry. I've been delivering babies since 1960.' I suppose he was kind enough, but it didn't make me feel any better being in labor and without Ronald, even though he was a rotten husband."

After my wayward father left my mom again, she moved in with his mother for a while. But soon, Mom's mother-in-law had enough of one screaming baby, another on the way, and my mom's difficult attitude. She took the crib and all of my mom's meager belongings, threw them in the car, and drove her to my grandmother's house. My mom was abandoned once more. I guess bad behavior runs in the Carpenter family.

Despite her trepidation, Mom stayed at Nellie and Big Tony's house for nearly a year. (Big Tony was also the one who drove Mom to the hospital to deliver my second sister, Pinky.) Not long after, my grandmother and Big Tony grew weary of Mom wandering the house at night with two babies crying nonstop. Their solution: let Mom move into the building they owned on the South Side of Chicago, on 68th Street.

Clearly, Englewood was not the safest place for a single white mother and her children. But Mom did her best, first adjusting to life with my grandmother and then to living alone in an apartment in Big Tony's building. She spent a few years there, but it wouldn't be long before violence came knocking or, more accurately, breaking down her door.

"It was the worst time in my life," Mom said. "There were two times when men from the neighborhood broke into my apartment through a window and raped me. I had no way to defend myself, and all I could think about was protecting my kids. If this had to happen, I wanted them to hurt me, not the children. One of those times, they dragged the kids into another room before they attacked me, I was out of my mind!"

"The guy knocked me down, and after they finally left, I called the police. It was a joke. Do you know what they asked me? 'What did you have on?' It was humiliating to think that being raped in my own home might have had something to do with my clothing. But I had to put it out of my mind to survive," Mom said.

Mom was literally scared to death, day and night. One of her neighbors thought she needed a man in the house to protect her and us kids, so she introduced her to Stan.

That, in my opinion, was the worst possible introduction.

Stan Maddox was born in Bessemer, Alabama, and had fifteen brothers and sisters. You could say he was far from a model citizen. He was arrested for selling baseball tickets in Alabama for teams that didn't exist. Instead of going to prison, he was sentenced to a chain gang, a group of prisoners chained together while working outdoors.

Stan's claim to fame? He escaped the chain gang and got away without the police ever tracking him down. What a role model!

But Stan was a product of his own living hell. His mother one generation removed from slavery, who, believe it or not, was bigger than him would beat him, as well as her husband, who stood only about five foot four inches tall with his shoes on. She would tie Stan to the bed and beat him until he was unconscious, as if she were the slave master herself.

His three nephews and nieces all died violently at young ages. Stan was programmed to continue the cycle. Sadly, we often perpetuate what our parents taught us unless we consciously reprogram ourselves to break the destructive pattern. Of course, that's easier said than done, and it can take many years to change such a destructive dynamic.

At first, Stan seemed like a nice guy. My mom wasn't completely sold on him, but little by little, he weaseled his way into her heart along with his clothes and personal belongings, which he slowly packed away in our house.

"Stan made sure we had food on the table and was a great cook. He even taught mom how to cook soul food. He was very nice at first, but it was obvious he wasn't a Chicagoan," Mom said.

Stan soon discovered the lure of city life: bars on almost every corner and the wild nightlife on the South Side. Before Mom knew it, his personality changed dramatically. After one night of heavy drinking, he became violent, trying to strangle her and yelling nonstop. We were terrified.

Soon thereafter, Stan grew his nappy hair down to his shoulders, permed it smooth and straight, and started hustling for money. He bought garish velvet jackets, wide-leg bell bottoms, a fedora hat, and even his first Cadillac Coupe de Ville. But Stan's Cadillac was far from the classic pimp mobile. You could say Stan Maddox looked like he stepped straight out of central casting for "Pimp of the Year"! (Pimpmobiles were part of 1970s popular culture, often appearing in films targeting urban Black audiences, typically set in the ghetto with stereotypical portrayals.) Thus began Stan's career as a drug dealer and pimp.

The worst part for me was Stan insisting that I dress just like him even in elementary school. (There's actually a photo of me looking like I'd seen a ghost, wearing wide collars and bell-bottom pants.) In fact, my mom made me lie to him, telling him I had won the "best dressed" contest in eighth grade. Yes, I was a pimp in training, complete with my pimp starter kit!

But beyond his garish demeanor, Stan was an excellent con artist. Everyone in the hood had a hustle, and one of his ways was exploiting others: he would find girls on the street, offer to pimp them out, give them a small cut, and pocket the rest himself.

My mom grew increasingly frustrated with Stan's violence and "career" choices, but she felt she needed protection despite his abusive behavior. She swallowed her pride and sense of morality, deciding to keep Stan around and remain trapped in the vicious cycle of violence. She chose Stan's version of evil rather than risk being raped again or worse, having me or my siblings harmed. Looking back, who could blame her?

I remember Mom telling me a story that revealed just how deranged Stan really was. He had a sick way of making a point. One day, he decided to take her downtown to observe his emerging enterprise.

"You want to see what I'm fucking doing, bitch?" Stan demanded. Mom didn't want to go, but he literally forced her, grabbing her arm and hustling her into his Cadillac. She feared he was going to kill her. They drove to Clark and Division Street, where Mom noticed a nice-looking Black girl going in and out of a rundown, dilapidated building.

"What's that girl doing?" Mom asked.

"She's making money, and you don't. You're just stupid. See, I'm the one with the brains," Stan said, thinking he was the boss. Mom was humiliated and told him she would never do that.

Stan was also a stickler for rules. Nothing escaped his notice: a crumb on the kitchen floor, garbage left out, specs of food on the dishes, or a speck of dirt on the floor. One time, he placed a matchstick on the bathroom floor as a "test." If it was still there when he came home, we would be beaten. If we made too much noise and woke him before noon, all we'd hear was: "I'm going to whoop your asses when I get up."

Stan always made sure the house was quiet as a church mouse when he was sleeping. As you can probably guess, beatings were the norm in the hood, and Stan was becoming the master.

As Stan became more deeply enmeshed with gang members, drug dealers, and pimps, his violence escalated dramatically. He would beat my mom, throw us kids across the living room and dining room, and on one occasion even try to toss me out of the window. As I grew older, I would sleep with a butcher knife under my pillow, waiting for him to come in so I could defend myself. I never understood why he never appeared while I had that knife beneath me, but I am certain that if we had more than one, I would have kept them all under my pillow at all times.

As my mom often said, living with Stan was a roller coaster one that, for me, would never slow down. We never knew which version of Stan we were going to face at any given moment.

To me, the hood was paralysis. You were literally numb from being poor, biracial, living in the equivalent of Section Eight housing, being on welfare, and having to go to the grocery store with only food stamps to buy what little you could afford. Rest assured, it wasn't organic. The mindset in the ghetto, which Stan fully embraced, was to do anything even if it was illegal to survive. Trust was a drug deal away from oblivion, and everyone hustled to survive. Looking back, we were predators ourselves. Our "hustle" was not against the people who kept us in the prison we called the ghetto. It was not against the system that created prisons and juvenile halls to house us as our lives of crime escalated or place us on the conveyor belt rotating in and out of these facilities. It was against one another stealing, robbing, raping, drugging, swindling and killing our own neighbors, friends, and family. Cadillac Stan was not helping us veer away from that downward spiral.

So, after living with Stan at a young age and going to bed every night in fear, I thought I had seen it all until one early morning when I witnessed another act of violence perpetrated by my pimp, drug-dealing, alcoholic stepfather.

Apparently, there had been a confrontation at a local bar on Clark and Division Street. Stan and a guy named Slick had words about a woman most likely a prostitute and Stan was stabbed in the eye and almost lost his earlobe. He went to the Emergency Room, and once discharged, he sought revenge. A few days later, Stan found out that Slick and his friend were staying at our neighbor Brenda's apartment, two doors down from us. Stan decided to confront Slick, and they got into a fight. He beat up the first guy and then turned his rage toward Slick.

The two were wrestling when they leaned on the banister on the rear porch of the second-floor apartment. Both fell to the ground, and the 260-pound Stan Maddox landed on top of Slick. The force was so great that Slick died at the scene. Tommy and I witnessed the aftermath. We heard them yelling, saw them fall, and watched the police question Stan and place Slick in a body bag. Even as ten-year-old kids, we could not believe what we had witnessed. The next day, we saw Slick's hair stuck to the blood on the cement sidewalk where he died. It was another gruesome image I will never forget.

Sadly, this was not my first experience with a violent death so close to home. Looking back at my military career, I think my life in the hood and witnessing so much death and violence made me numb to combat. As a result, I could use my dark humor as a coping mechanism when dealing with death and war. War oddly never affected me except for the smell of a decomposing, decapitated body that we pulled from a river in Iraq while searching for kidnapped American service members. More about that later.

I bet you were wondering if Stan was ever arrested for murdering Slick.

Well, since the cops often came to our house to watch pimp movies, Chicago Bears games, smoke weed, and drink beer, they were predisposed to cut Stan some slack. Stan's explanation: "It was self-defense." No charges were ever filed, and Stan was free to continue his abuse both on our family and himself.

With the continued violence, near misses, and constant fear of Stan, my teenage years were turbulent and unpredictable. Would I repeat the same patterns of the ghetto I grew up in? Would I end up in jail and fail at any attempt to turn my life around?

I would have to endure a few more years of the hustle getting one over on the next guy and preying on each other like animals. It was my South Side sickness, but I was more determined than ever to survive.

In 1977, my mom got pregnant once again this time not by my father but by Stan. Nine months later, my stepbrother, Stanley Maddox Carpenter, was born. We called him Tobo. Since this was Stan's biological son, he made sure to let us know all the time. Unlike any of us Carpenter kids, Tobo had power over Stan. When he cried, Stan would punish us, believing we were the ones mistreating Tobo. After all we had been through with Stan, now we had to deal with another disturbing part of the saga: walking on eggshells around Tobo, just like we did with Stan.

The only difference was that we actually loved Tobo and treated him as our biological brother, not a half or stepbrother. But Stan would still blame us anytime Tobo cried, so Tommy and I had to act. The little brat had to learn.

Even though we all got along, we noticed that Tobo would cry just to get us in trouble and to get his way and as a result, we were going to get punished by Stan. So, we started giving Tobo something to actually cry about. Tommy and I would beat Tobo up or throw rocks at him. Boys will be boys. But after a few weeks, Tobo got the message. He quit being a crybaby, and we stopped getting extra beatings. He is still considered our Hunk. Life in the hood was improving.

But Ronald's mother, Zaleta, would continue to come in and out of our lives out of guilt or some sense of moral obligation that allowed her to feel less guilty about abandoning us. Stan, however, was a constant presence and an imminent threat in our lives. Like many kids in the neighborhood, we all drank from the same cup of misery and despair, with far too few happy moments that lasted long enough to make us feel normal and sober. There is nothing worse than people who have lost hope and resigned themselves to their current situation as their fate.

Zaleta would make her once-a-year visit with her mother my great-grandmother on Christmas Day. They never quite grasped that what we really needed were not toys, but a grandmother who actually cared. Still, every Christmas, there she was, standing in the hallway with huge garbage bags full of toys. While this was an annual ritual, on this Christmas Day, something was about to change.

When Tobo was about four years old and could understand what was going on, he realized that Zaleta never brought him a bag of toys. One Christmas, after Zaleta handed out all the garbage bags of toys and did not give one to Tobo, Stan became infuriated because Tobo was crying, seeing that we all got our bags while he got none.

Stan grabbed all five bags of toys, dumped them on the ground, found another bag, and made six with an extra one for Tobo. He made sure Zaleta would never neglect Tobo again.

Low and behold, Zaleta stopped bringing us presents and slowly faded out of our lives. We did not see her much after that Christmas Day, but in 1981, when I was twelve, my grandmother wanted to visit my father in Los Angeles. Since she did not want to go alone, and since I was the oldest boy, she asked my mom if I could accompany her. I think my father probably favored me for that reason alone.

It was exciting to have an adventure without getting in trouble, far away from the hood. This was the first plane ride of my life. When we boarded, the flight attendant let me look out the round window on the emergency exit door and explained that what I was seeing was the horizon. I was mesmerized. When we arrived at the airport, my grandmother took me to a restaurant at LAX that I swear looked like a flying saucer. She ordered a Shirley Temple for me and an alcoholic drink for herself. We must have sat there for hours waiting for my father to pick us up. He never came.

We jumped in a cab and drove to his house, which was very close to the airport. We could hear planes fly directly over it, and inside, the entire house seemed to rattle.

My father had a live-in girlfriend named Peggy. She had blonde hair, was very skinny, and we all thought she was a model. Clearly, not a role model, though.

My father's greeting lacked any warmth you would expect from a parent seeing his son or mother after so long. It seemed he was just going through the motions.

The sleeping arrangements were far from luxurious, though luxury was something I never knew in the hood anyway. My grandmother slept in the spare bedroom, and my accommodation was a musty, lumpy couch. Every night, I would knock on the window very hard then make it seem like I was asleep. Why? Because I wanted to witness my father's reaction. It was always the same. He would walk out of his bedroom in his boxers with a shotgun to investigate the noise, then call out my name to see if I was awake. Little did he know, I was the one staging the false alarms. You can see how the hood travels with you.

Peggy would take me to a high-end condominium and let me play in the pool while she worked her hustle on the older men who lived there. Of course, only the ones with money. I thought I had left the hookers and hoes behind with Stan in Chicago. I imagine she did not like manipulating the old men but did what she had to for the illegal tender.

One time, while she was in the hot tub with an old man, she ordered me to bring her pair of suede high-heel shoes. I pretended not to hear her. "Ronnie, get the hell over here and give me my damn shoes!" she yelled. I jumped in the pool with the shoes and carried them across to her while holding them underwater the entire time. Big mistake.

She yelled at me, got out of the tub with her suede shoes dripping wet and brown water running down her arm. She was furious and let me know it. When she took me home, she immediately ratted me out to my father. Ronald stomped into the bathroom, took a leather strap off the wall that he had sharpened on his straight razor, and began to whoop me. "You son of a bitch! You disrespected Peggy and destroyed her shoes," he shouted. I was defiant. "Don't tell me that! You're not my dad. You abandoned us years ago and have no right to whoop me," I said, surprised at my own courage. To my amazement, he stopped, took the strap away, and left me alone.

Since I was there for a few weeks, things settled down. My father told me he wanted me to live with him and not return to Chicago. Wow. Where did that come from? I told him I wanted to go back to Chicago with my brothers and sisters. That night, as I went to bed, I thought about how different my life would have been without Stan and his abuse, and the hood where hope was scarce. But the reality was, I would be no different than my mom choosing one evil over another. So, I told my father I would go back to Chicago.

I had no regrets about returning home to live with my brothers and sisters. Unfortunately, that was the last time I ever saw my father. Zaleta moved to Las Vegas and disappeared from our lives. Of course, she lied, blaming her move on "health reasons."

It amazes me as an adult how easily people make excuses for not doing the right thing. If we were doing the right thing all day, every day, there would be no need for excuses.

Chapter Three

Surviving Stan and the Hood

"Our deepest fear is not that we are inadequate. Our deepest fear is that we are powerful beyond measure. It is our light, not our darkness that most frightens us. We ask ourselves, 'Who am I to be brilliant, gorgeous, talented, and fabulous"

Marianne Williamson

Surviving Stan's abuse as a teenager and young adult was like standing on the bow of a boat in a raging storm, with twenty-foot waves crashing around you and little hope of making it to shore unless you learned to hold on for dear life, to brush it off, and to rinse and repeat. Survival in the hood, and dealing with degenerates like Stan and Ronald Senior, was the unfortunate by-product of a culture that glorified violence and the hustle, while women often became the victims. My mom, brothers, and sisters were not programmed to expect more from life than what we were constantly exposed to; welfare checks, drugs, alcohol, and poverty. On a brighter note, none of my sisters ended up on welfare and, like me, they were late bloomers. Pinky even completed her bachelor's degree. Tommy, on the other hand, will always be a hustler, but unlike Tobo, he has a way of bringing out the best in everyone with his perpetual positive energy.

Sadly, Tobo carries the demons of Stan's misbehavior, and like his father, when alcohol enters the equation, his Frankenstan emerges. Fathers and stepfathers coming in and out of our lives wreaked havoc on our emotions with every unplanned visit, perceived injustice, or fleeting hope for a better day. Though my mom did her very best as a single mother to keep food on the table, there were many times when we had none. That is one of the reasons we developed an affinity for ketchup and mayonnaise sandwiches.

Without a consistent father or role model, Mom certainly had her hands full. When I was about ten years old, she took us clothes shopping with money she had hidden from Stan. Out of nowhere, a well-dressed Nigerian man saw Mom struggling to manage her brood and began telling his sob story: "I'm having trouble with my car but don't have the money to pay for the repairs, ma'am. I'm expecting a large sum from Western Union, and if you lend me the money, I'll repay you double." My mom walked a couple of blocks to the mechanic shop, dragging us along, and gave him the money. We waited there for what seemed like an eternity, only to learn from the owner that the Nigerian man did not have a car at the shop for repair at all. Clearly, we had been scammed.

Long story short, the money meant for our new school clothes was gone. Given Stan's penchant for flashy attire, this was a particularly sad day for us kids. Growing up in the hood with scammers both strangers and those who were supposed to be role models ironically helped us stop being suckers very early in life and became our training ground for the hustle. One way my mom coped with this roller-coaster life, especially dealing with Stan, was by attending church.

When I was around twelve years old, Mom became a member of the Seventh-day Adventist Church. It resembled Protestant Christianity in that it combined elements of Protestantism with twenty-eight fundamental principles. The church emphasizes the second coming of Jesus Christ as well as the observance of the Sabbath. Every Friday at sundown, Mom tried her best to observe the Sabbath until Saturday sundown. She would even put on her best dress, which was usually a hand-me-down, and take the 69th Street bus to Shiloh, located at 7000 South Michigan Avenue on the South Side. But Stan was not having it. He hated her going to church and made sure that as soon as she came home, he would beat her. I would hear her recite the Lord's Prayer over and over. For some strange reason, Stan feared those words and sometimes even backed down; religion forced him to relent.

As the beatings after church became less frequent because God was winning and wearing down the evil to mere insignificance Mom decided to hold a Bible study group in our apartment. Her friend Shirley was the main participant. The two women internalized the power of the church and the Bible's teachings, and, low and behold, while they knew Stan was inherently evil, they became less afraid of him. They realized they had the helmet, shield, and sword of God, and Stan just had to tolerate it.

I never witnessed anything like the power of faith overcoming a lunatic like Stan, the meanest person on the planet. Faith forced him to back away from fights to the point that when Shirley came over, Stan knew to just get up and leave. I remember times when my mom even convinced a sinner like Stan to attend church on Saturday. But do not get your hopes up it did not last long. Despite a few remorseful tears and moments of repentance, Stan always reverted to his old, evil ways.

As a pre-teen, I was not so optimistic about religion. It freaked me out hearing all the prayers, chants, and Bible verses. I swear, when I glanced at the wall in our bedroom, I frequently thought I saw demons. I would scare the heck out of my siblings with my visions. One time, when Shirley and my mom were holding Bible study in the kitchen, I broke a window and pounded on the door, yelling and screaming, "Stop! I can't take it anymore; get out of my house!" Of course, Stan was not there, or I would have gotten my butt whipped for making all that noise and breaking windows. You could say it was akin to Stockholm Syndrome, where a hostage develops a psychological bond with the captor. In some strange way, I felt I was being loyal to Stan by fighting against religion. Go figure, as if I were an abused animal seeking validation from my abusive owner.

Nothing stopped my demons. I did not want them in the house anymore, with all the religion nonsense and incessant praying. For a moment, I even thought Stan might have had a point. Ironically, it took a crazy character from the neighborhood to scare those demons away, even if only for a short while. As a result, my hustling and trying to fit in the hood took an abrupt and unanticipated turn.

There was a guy in the neighborhood we called the "Son of Satan." His real name was Craig, and he was one weird dude. We would see him driving around on his Harley-Davidson motorcycle, wearing pantyhose and a blue jean sleeveless biker vest. What the hell? And I thought I was the outlier. Everyone in the hood knew this dude was crazy, and all the scary movies we used to watch only elevated his status on the creepy scale. Not only did he own a Harley, but he also had a black hearse with a coffin inside. And we all knew he was not in the funeral business. This was the stuff of every young child's nightmare. Even the Son of Satan had unalienable rights in the hood to roam freely and scare the hell out of us.

One day, Tommy, our friend Man, and I caught him performing religious satanic rituals in a vacant lot. We were hiding in some tall grass, watching, and wondering what would happen next. Suddenly, Son of Satan pulled his coffin from the hearse. We were scared as hell. Two dudes on stilts yes, stilts were part of the ritual. They looked in our direction, saw us peering through the grass, and started chasing us. We jumped up and ran home as fast as we could, as if our lives depended on it. I swear we must have broken some track records that day.

Tommy busted open the kitchen door, and there was Mom holding her Bible study; Shirley was there too. We told them what happened, and Shirley piped up: "Boys, you might want to know about Jesus. He will protect you." We were so relieved to believe. Son of Satan had put the fear of God in us, and at least I was ready to do whatever it took to save my soul and all of our lives, really.

I never asked Tommy if he believed, but he did go to church. So, God does have a sense of humor and uses others to push us toward Him. It just took a Harley, a hearse, a coffin, a dude in pantyhose, and two dudes on stilts to change our minds.

That was the turning point in my life. I started going to church and got baptized. No joke everything changed for me that day. All the negativity of living in the hood, all the fear and evil, vanished. I saw the light really; I saw a light and felt the clearest I have ever felt in my life. I became the little preacher man, pushing God's word like nobody's business.

Even though I found religion, I was still acting stupid. Mom found freedom through religion, and I tried, but the hood was still embedded in my soul along with God. At least we had some sort of moral compass to reduce the trouble we got into. We still had to go along to get along, and sometimes that influence landed us in more trouble than I can remember. Mom would say we were good kids, for the most part. We often shielded her from everything we did in the streets until the moments when it blew up in our faces and we needed an adult to represent us or bail us out of jail. The hood is a metastatic cancer. But the experience of being in church, getting older, and having a stronger sense of who I was made me stick up for myself and protect my mom and siblings from dealing with crazy Cadillac Stan.

As Mom and Shirley got more into religion, Stan seemed to take an abuse hiatus. Tommy and I were getting more involved in things we shouldn't have, but we learned how to play the game in the hood. Unfortunately, some of that knowledge came directly from Stan.

For example, every summer the community pool would open at Ogden Park. It was a glorious day for us kids. To my surprise, one afternoon Stan took Tommy and me to buy new gym shoes a rare gesture of kindness.

"Ronnie, tell Tommy that you niggas better not wear those gym shoes to the pool. Got that asshole?" Stan said, clearly not joking. So, of course, we wore our new sneakers to the swimming pool just to show off.

After our swim, we went back to our lockers and guess what? Our gym shoes were missing. The only person who could have taken them was the locker attendant. We were terrified to come home wearing the plastic shoes left in place of our new ones, but we had no choice. What did Stan do? The pimp slapped us, as usual, and in his characteristic rage, headed for the bedroom where he kept his gun.

He opened the drawer, grabbed his gun, and the three of us drove back to the park. He stormed into the locker room with the gun drawn and the trigger cocked. Stan slammed the garage door shut, pointed the gun at everyone there, and yelled, "I'm gonna kill you motherfuckers if you don't return my kid's shoes!" We watched the faces of the people in the locker room turn pure white. Within ten minutes, our new sneakers miraculously reappeared. But Stan, being Stan, still made us wear the plastic shoes all summer. He was still just a mean son of a bitch.

In 1983, things began to change for my mom. She got a job at Asia Chop Suey on 69th and Halsted Street, cooking fast food for about $3 an hour. She made Italian beef and sausage sandwiches, Vienna beef hot dogs and polish sausages, Asian dishes, super tacos, and more. The restaurant was owned by two people from Thailand Nida and Sear who became our second family and always looked out for Mom. Back then, Asia Chop Suey was the biggest craze in the neighborhood because you could get a cheeseburger with fries for one dollar. Along with hustling, Tommy and I helped them buy as many blocks of government cheese as we could also for one dollar a block. Of course, we all knew the cheese blocks were really Velveeta, not Havarti or Pecorino.

The store made thousands of dollars every day thanks to its location near the intersection of Chicago Transit Authority buses. Almost everyone who got off the buses quickly bought their food and made their connecting bus just in time. It was a transformative experience for Tommy, Mom, and me but things with Stan never really changed much.

My sisters were already in high school, doing everything they could to get by, just like me. But they were not prepared for the rigors of higher education. Sheri attended CVS High, Pinky went to Lindblom, and Angie went to Whitney Young. Unfortunately, they had to change schools a couple of times when they could not keep up academically, eventually ending up at local high schools closer to our neighborhood. It wasn't that they weren't intelligent it was that the school system failed to prepare them and millions of other low-income families for success.

As I was ready to enter high school, I was slated to attend Paul Robeson High School, just down the street. I knew I wouldn't graduate if I went there; my destiny would have been gang banger and drug dealer. The school was populated by the Black Gangster Disciples, and being pasty as hell, I didn't think I'd fit in. I said a few prayers, and by some twist of fate, my teacher told me about a lottery program designed to bus kids like me to integrated schools.

I put in my application, and to my astonishment, during the summer of 1983, I received a letter from the Board of Education stating I had been selected to attend one of three schools offered. I chose Kenwood Academy on 5015 South Blackstone Avenue. A huge burden was lifted off my shoulders. Kenwood was about thirty minutes by car and ninety minutes by bus, but I accepted it. I was about to embark on my escape route, a way to leave behind the emptiness and hopelessness of the hood for a new beginning. For once, I had the opportunity to show everyone I wanted to be different and to become a success story. Well, they say the road to hell is paved with good intentions. I soon found out that was all I had.

Every morning, my mom gave me a one-dollar food stamp, which I used to buy a Snickers bar for forty cents at the 69th Street liquor store. The change was enough to get a bus transfer so I could ride from 69th and Morgan and board two more buses to get to school. The trip took almost two hours each way for four years, but it wasn't a big deal I traveled on buses and the "L" all the time in the hood.

You could say the buses were microcosms of life in the city. Fights broke out, fueled by gun violence and alcohol, and drug addicts became even crazier. The unwritten rule: do not fall asleep on the bus or the L. I often saw people nod off, only to have someone sneak up with a razorblade, cut their pocket, and steal their wallet without them even flinching. That was back when criminals had class. In today's Chicago, there are no subtleties shootings aside, people now rush high end stores from poorer neighborhoods, grabbing whatever they can in seconds.

On the bus, you sat where you could. One time, an addict in the back had a case of cough syrup he stole from Walgreens. He opened the box and started chugging it, one bottle at a time, right in the back of the bus. When anyone offered me drugs or other junk, I politely said, "No thanks, homies." Even on the bus, you had to keep your head down in gang neighborhoods. The colors of their clothing and the tilt of their hats were your clues; even gangs had their own fashion hierarchy.

Often, followers of Louis Farrakhan, the leader of the Nation of Islam, were on the bus, asking for money or selling their bean pies. Their mantra: "Ma Brotha, would you like to purchase a bean pie?" You could spot them by their bow ties, white shirts, and neatly pressed black pants I could never afford one. We never disrespected them. We left them alone because we knew they were militant, and where there was one, there were many. It was displaced respect, similar to what we had for Stan, born from perceived fear and violence.

Being on the bus each way to school was like clearing enemy territory in the military. Every section felt like a different stage of a military operation that you had to navigate. It was exhausting. I wasn't safe until I got to the 69th Street L station to change buses. Life on the South Side was just that way.

As both Stan and we kids got older, the abuse became less frequent. I don't think it was because he respected or feared us, but because he sensed our defiance and that puzzled him. He probably knew one day we would repay the favor. But he was still an asshole, and we never felt completely comfortable around him. Even with our newfound independence, we still found curious ways to get in trouble.

One day, Tommy had the ingenious idea to break into an Illinois Bell Company truck parked in the alley near our house. Apparently, the guy left it unlocked. We ransacked the truck but found nothing of value except his cigarettes and a lighter. Tommy and I wandered the neighborhood and went to the vacant lot with an abandoned two-flat and garage, used to disassemble stolen cars and chop them up to sell the parts. Oil and gas covered the floor, but we were too ignorant to connect the dots.

We thought we were cool, smoking the stolen cigarettes and playing with the lighter. Before we knew it, the ashes from the cigarettes landed on the gasoline-soaked floor, and the entire garage caught fire. The blaze grew huge, even igniting trees and electric poles. We panicked, trying to put out the fire, but it was too big.

Tommy and I ran home as fast as we could and told Stan and Mom that someone had lit a garage on fire. The smell of smoke on our clothes was a dead giveaway. We were lucky that no other houses nearby were occupied; otherwise, it would have been a real tragedy.

Stan wasn't buying our story. "It was probably you two motherfuckas that did that fire," he said. Little did he know, he was right for the first time in his life. An hour later, the Fire Marshal knocked on our door and told Stan and Mom that the neighbor across the alley identified the only two white boys in the neighborhood as the culprits who set the garage on fire. We were having none of it.

"It wasn't us," I said emphatically. "It was Baybay; he did it." Since Baybay was always getting in trouble, we figured he would have considered it another feather in his cap. It was a prime example of odd hood logic.

The Fire Marshal nonetheless put Tommy and me on the firebug list until we turned eighteen. When he left, Stan hauled off and slapped us around. "I'm not mad that you did it, but you snitched and named dropped someone else," he said. How's that for logic? After the beating, Tommy and I were punished and stuck in the house for a week.

"You won't be leaving this house for shit! I don't give a fuck if the house is on fire you motherfuckas will stay!" Stan implored. On the brighter side, we had destroyed a chop shop location.

Because of the fire, stolen cars could no longer be taken there, dismantled, and sold for parts. Being the only two multiracial kids in the neighborhood was a drawback; we would always be the first picked in the lineup. I convinced myself that I did good and thought, "I didn't do it! Baybay did! That's my story and I'm sticking to it."

Despite our escapades, Mom still believed we were trying to be good, even though we were still bad. She stood her ground, never letting us out of punishment unless it was to attend church.

Once we served Stan's house arrest, it was widely known in the hood that the Carpenter boys were still causing trouble and now we were pyro maniacs. That wasn't far from the truth.

We sprayed graffiti on walls, stole food stamps, car parts, and anything that looked appealing. We broke into vacant homes and sometimes garages that weren't abandoned. We opened fire hydrants, letting the water shoot out at us. Tommy even developed an addiction to stealing hood ornaments from local residents' cars. He amassed a huge collection until Stan found out and forced him to return them. But Tommy had no idea where the cars were located or how to reinstall the ornaments, so his effort was half-hearted; he only returned a few of the ones stolen in front of our house.

During the summer, Chicago Mayor Harold Daly had a way to temporarily curb crime in the hood. His staff delivered free lunches, hosted block parties, and donated ice cream. He was ahead of his time at least temporarily; the crime rate went down. We were preoccupied with something positive for a change, or maybe he was pandering for votes. Things that make you go, "hmmm."

As I moved into my teen years, more changes were coming some positive, others not so much. My programming was tough to shed. It wasn't that we were born to prey on our neighbors or cause problems; we just had no other way to channel our rage, energy, and boredom. We had no role models to say, "Hey, idiot boy, let me show you a different way of thinking."

When I turned sixteen, I got my driver's permit, passed the test, and finally got my license. As you might imagine, I was far from Mario Andretti. Hell, I barely passed, nearly running into a fire truck on an emergency run.

I knew very little about driving, especially when Stan got a new Cadillac and gave me his 1974 Cadillac Coupe DeVille. It was white with worn paint, an eight-track tape player, and red velvet seats. As

Tommy would say, the tires were "bald as his nuts." I had to sit on an extra phone book to see over the steering wheel. At least for a poor kid, I had my "pimp starter kit."

Though I could drive the car to school and work, I still had to put $5 a day in gasoline to keep that eight-cylinder gas guzzler running. The car had all kinds of issues: intermittent power steering, a crooked wheel alignment, rust everywhere, and peeling paint. What a looker!

Naturally, Tommy and I did what we did best hustling and relocating parts from other people's cars to make mine work. We scoured the city and located seventy-four Cadillac Coupe DeVille's. Stan's hand-me-down Cadillac began to look a lot better. After stealing parts from cars unknown, we thought we had created the best-looking Coupe DeVille in the hood especially after Mr. Baker fixed all the dents and painted it primer brown.

Even with the car tricked out, I still couldn't drive worth a damn. I remember pulling up to a flashing red light and coming to a stop. Just then, a Chicago police car pulled up behind us. I waited at the light for what felt like an eternity, convinced they were setting me up. I refused to budge, but the horn-beeping persisted, so I finally decided to go.

Just as I suspected, the police turned on their lights and siren and pulled me over. "I fuckin' knew it!" I shouted, rolling down the window. "Sir, why did you pull me over?" I asked, as the officer almost stuck his head through the window.

"Because you're driving like a fucking idiot," he barked.

I handed him my license, sitting there in fear worried he might issue a ticket or question why the car was so tricked out.

"Get your ass home, learn how to drive, and fix that fucking exhaust leak before it kills you, son," he admonished. Boy, did I dodge another bullet.

Just another day in the South Side of Chicago, where the police back in the day were respected, feared, and the only real source of law and order in the hood.

And believe it or not, after all those years of driving the Caddy, I never knew I needed auto insurance. I'm lucky I didn't have any serious accidents, though I did scrape a car or two because of the poor wheel alignment. To drive straight, I had to rotate the steering wheel almost 180 degrees. I even sometimes took my sister Pinky's car to show off and, predictably, wound up in trouble.

I still owe Pinky a car for attempting to "Tokyo drift" in hers, and as I acted stupid, I rear-ended another driver. What made it worse? Pinky spent her student loan money on that car, and I wrecked it. Pinky, I promise I'll one day buy you a 1986 Chevy Chevette to replace the one I destroyed.

Tommy and I both loved cars. Tommy took it to another level he even stole Stan's car while he was sleeping and joy-rode around the neighborhood with his homie, Gary. I was devious too. One time, Stan had a Buick Electra 225 we called "Deuce and a Quarter." My homie Man and I met two girls and decided to take Stan's car to impress them. Tommy had a similar idea and beat us to the punch, driving off with Gary and leaving us stranded. Ergo no girls.

We weren't dissuaded. Man, and I ran two blocks trying to catch Tommy and Gary. Low and behold, Tommy slowed at a red light. We made it just in time. I grabbed Tommy, Man locked onto Gary, and we gave them both a little beatdown before taking off in the car, leaving them on the side of the road. I guess that was our neighborhood's first carjacking. We knew we'd get in trouble with Stan, but youthful defiance and hood programming were our drivers. Thanks for the car, Tommy the date went really well.

Meanwhile, Stan continued to get drunk as hell. We never knew when he'd come home from a night of drinking, wake us up, and start talking shit. When he could no longer beat us, he tortured us with his drunk diatribes. He never understood he had to change. Narcissists never do.

Strangely, even though we did not respect Stan, we still craved his validation. Sometimes, Tommy and I would start a fight just so Stan could see us acting tough in the hood like him. We mistakenly believed that showing aggression in front of him would earn his respect.

But no matter what I did, I was constantly surrounded by trouble. Almost every block had gangs protecting their slice of the pie with violence and intimidation. There were the Elizabeth Boys the prototypical gang bangers who laid the foundation for larger gang influence. They were our neighborhood rivals, and we battled them constantly over the OK Supermarket turf. Four or five of them, four or five of us, including my sister Angie, who was always down with us.

Looking deeper, Chicago's gang influence goes back many years. The Black P-Stones and Black Gangster Disciples were the largest, comprised of displaced and angry young men who only knew how to intimidate rivals while protecting their blocks. But for many, gangs provided a tribe, protection, validation, love, and respect. Things most of us didn't get at home consistently. Eventually, some homies became drug dealers and gang bangers. When crack cocaine hit the streets, gun violence followed.

The South Side of Chicago was not a place that inspired bad people to be good. It was about survival. The Black P-Stones, founded by Jeff Fort, had huge "sets" including the Bloods, Black Disciples, Vice Lords, Four Corner Hustlers, and Latin Kings. They even had a Muslim militant branch called El Rukn. The Black Gangster Disciples, founded by Larry Hoover, commanded 25,000 to 50,000 followers, with alliances including the Latin Disciples, Spanish Gangster Disciples, Ambrose, Two-Two Boys, Two Sixers, Simon City Royals, North Side Insane Popes, Latin Eagles, and more.

Given the size and influence of these gangs, it's easy to see that the cops were more perception than reality when it came to keeping the peace. The gangs themselves had a strict chain of command and rules. Violate them, and punishment came fast, sometimes "fifty to the chest." They were effective. Despite being tied to drugs and crime, this system would have persisted with or without police intervention. In many ways, these gangs were like countries within the United Nations constantly forming alliances, controlling territories, and limiting violence so profits weren't disrupted. In that sense, they worked, much like the Mafia did in Al Capone's time.

The federal government eventually stepped in to dismantle the Black Gangster Disciples and Black P-Stones, likely because of their influence over neighborhoods, prisons and the black vote. Think about it: criminals policing the hood better than the cops. Perhaps. But one thing was certain what you fear is what you respect. During my childhood, the shootouts between police, FBI, and gangs often felt like my time in Iraq during a gun battle.

The feds incarcerated gang leadership, taking a victory lap, only to fracture the fragile peace. The once-organized gangs splintered into over 1,600 factions. Though statistics vary, today Chicago is considered the most gang-occupied city in the U.S., with roughly 150,000 members spread across more than 1,600 gangs.

For years, Tommy was a Gangster Disciple. He often recalls how respect and control in the gangs were tied to the chain of command. Young members were indoctrinated on the dos and don'ts of life in the "set." Their rules, while giving an illusion of order and discipline, masked hopelessness and bad intentions under a veil of purpose.

Tommy was right. Chicago was, and in many ways still is, a war zone. Communities across the country, regardless of race, experience similar violence. Being poor, and without proper role models like Ronald Senior or Stan, forced Tommy and me to do the best we could to survive. We endured far more than abuse from Stan, yet we still tried vainly to curb our enthusiasm for trouble.

The boys I hung out with were just as poor as I was. We thought that if we went into another neighborhood to steal something, we weren't victimizing our own hood. Little did we know, a mile away was still our zip code. One day, a kid in our group didn't have a bike, so naturally we decided to steal one. We spotted a kid riding, snatched his bike, and made our escape until one of our friend's aunts called the police.

I was thirteen when I found myself chained to the wall of a police station next to a man strung out on drugs. He was crawling on the floor, searching for something. A cop walked in and asked what he was doing. The addict looked up and said, "I'm looking for a misdemeanor." That moment hit me hard. I swore I never wanted to end up like him. From that day, I started listening to my instincts a little more.

One of the ways I tried to stay on the right path was by going to church. Even that didn't stop Tommy and me from misbehaving. Thankfully, we weren't full-blown gang bangers or drug dealers yet, but we were certainly headed in that direction.

When I was fifteen, Stan, in a rare moment of clarity, tried to set an example though in his own twisted way. He wanted to prevent me from drinking or doing drugs, but unlike a normal parent offering guidance, Stan had his own methods.

One evening, he called me into his bedroom chair the one he used for watching pirated cable TV. Usually, being summoned to that room meant trouble, slaps, or beatings. That night, however, he had a different plan. Spread before me were several pints of alcohol, a pack of Newport cigarettes, and a dime bag of weed. He forced me to drink from the pints, smoke cigarettes, and inhale enough weed to make an adult lose their mind.

"Nigga, you see how fucked up you are? You want to be like this for the rest of your life?" Stan asked, as I struggled to comprehend his words, barely coherent from the drugs and alcohol. When I woke the next day with a pounding headache, the lesson hadn't worked. Stan never realized he had become my gateway to more drugs and alcohol.

Before that night, drinking beer with my homies had been a minor transgression. Afterward, it escalated to hard liquor like E&J Brandy what we called "Irk and Jerk" smoking weed and experimenting with anything my boys could get their hands on, like wicked stick. Stan had unknowingly left his alcoholic, pimp imprint on me just as I was trying to start at a new high school and build a new life.

I was mortified on my first day at Kenwood Academy because of my attire. Remember, my role model was Cadillac Stan, with his permed straight hair, fedora, and velvet jackets. There I was in my moccasins, Lee jeans, and a light blue tuxedo shirt with lines running from the collar to the bottom.

The Black P Stone gang members walked up and said, "What's up, Lil Ron?" I shrugged and replied, "What's up?" not knowing what was happening or how they even knew my name. That day, I immediately made friends with them.

This continued until the real "Lil Ron" confronted me, calling me a "False Flagging Booty Wagger" and claiming I was a "fraud." I explained my actual name was Ron and that I was new, but of course I knew what he meant. He laughed, and we soon became fast friends. Go figure. I had left the South Side to attend a better school, only to affiliate with Latin Kings and Black P-Stones. Walking that tightrope hanging with these gang members while living in a Black Gangster Disciple neighborhood was my new reality. There was no normalcy in the hood.

The other kids still called me "Little Ron." Living up to the moniker, I smoked weed, cut class, and hung out with them. I even failed Italian class, third period right before lunch. While the school was interracial, very few students were lower-class. Most had money, drove cars, dressed well, and got whatever they wanted from their parents. I had nothing. At times, I even stole my sisters' jeans to make it seem like I had more pants than I actually did.

Pinky would be furious because I ripped up the seams that she sewed to make her pants fit tighter. Imagine me, Little Ron, in her pants so tight I could barely breathe, walking around with my testicles pushed up into my stomach. My dumbass could have at least gone to a secondhand store. Why didn't I think of that back then?

At least I had the looks not that I was a snob. I remember the choir teacher grabbing me in the hallway and making me sing "Somewhere Over the Rainbow" repeatedly.

"Ron," she said, "I want you in the choir, but clearly you can't sing. So, you'll be on stage with the choir and lip-sync for the concert with Andy Williams." I couldn't believe it. "Why me if I can't sing?" I asked. "Because of your looks," she said. "You'll add a lot to the performance." Humiliating yet self-affirming. Just what a young, nearly gangbanger needed!

As I got older, walking downtown Chicago, I saw people entering old hotels in formal attire and thought, I would never walk up those stairs. In the hood, we Carpenter kids never imagined what was possible or what we could realistically achieve only what others made look easy.

Desperate to make money legally, I applied at Walgreens on 63rd and King Drive and became a stock clerk. The store was in a different neighborhood, but still in the hood. I wasn't afraid of working late nights there, after all, I was one of the Carpenter Boys.

That's where I met Jackie Thornton, a student at the Academy of Our Lady Catholic School. Her mom noticed me at Walgreens and insisted we meet. Jackie was mixed-race too probably French, Black, and Indian or something similar and we soon started dating, if you could call it that. Without a car, I took the bus to her house, sat on the couch with her for a few hours, and went home.

Jackie was a good girl, and her mom was a gem, trusting me with her daughter. I was too embarrassed to bring her to my house especially because of Stan. I had tried once, and it was a disaster.

Stan remained a monster, earning the nickname "Frankenstan." His beatings, though less frequent, were still unpredictable. We never expected apologies he was too drunk to remember the next day. Over time, with God and the Bible protecting her, Mom learned to leave the house before Stan returned drunk. With Frankenstan, you never knew which version you would get.

As I moved through high school, I joined the Industrial Cooperative Education program (ICE), which gave you credit for working outside the classroom. I always felt it was a cop-out for dummies that weren't really expected to excel academically. The hood mentality of low expectations was alive and well. Even now, I joke that high school was the best fifteen years of my life.

Even in the program, I struggled. I still had to attend summer school and night school every year just to graduate. At least my social life was improving junior girls were starting to notice me. Finally, I scored big! But, as usual, my good fortune didn't last.

I was a sophomore, and some juniors and seniors asked me to go to Senior and Junior Prom with them. I would say "yes," thinking I'd figure out how to get a tux, a car, and money for dinner. I had my date all lined up and was excited until reality hit. How could I take a girl to prom without a proper suit, no car, and not enough money to take her out like the other kids?

So, I stood her up. My excuse: I was poor. The worst part? No one could help me but me. I really blew it. If someone had just shown me how easy it was to get a tux or work out a ride, I would have gone. I'm not blaming anyone just embarrassed and insecure. This, my friends, is the crap from the hood coming back to haunt me. In the hood, it was obligatory to make excuses, betray others, and avoid consequences. It would take a few more incidents and an arrest to finally set me straight.

One of those near misses happened downtown. Me and my boys, Man and Wando, would take the subway to go to the Underground, a club beneath the streets where DJ Ron Hardy mixed house music. Those parties were epic: the beat pounding, weed in the air, and nothing but chaos.

One night, riding the subway there, a drunk man kept staring at Wando. Words were exchanged. The man got in Wando's face. Wando, being a boxer, punched him, and the man fell into a seat pulling a gun as he landed.

I yelled, "He's got a gun!" and jumped on him, placing my finger between the trigger and the guard to prevent him from shooting. Thank God for a Soldier of Fortune article I had read the day before on disarming someone and preventing a gun from firing by placing your finger between the trigger and the trigger guard. I held him down with his arm behind his back. The train stopped, and the doors slid open. Man, and Wando ran off, while I yelled, "He's got a fuckin' gun!"

They returned and started pounding the guy, but he wouldn't let go of the weapon. My finger felt like it was being cut off. Wando wrapped his belt around his hand and punched him in the face. Just then, the conductor intervened, slowing the train and opening the doors. I shoved the guy back into the seat and ran off. I hid behind a turnstile as he ran past me. If he had seen me, I'd be dead.

Looking back, my luck ran out a few weeks later. I was drunk one early morning after partying all night with Man and had to take the subway home. Stumbling to the token counter, I decided to talk some smack to the CTA agent.

"Lady, you look like death on a dirt road, you old crabby bitch!"

She called the police immediately. Both Man and I were arrested and put in separate cells on the North Side, freezing on steel slabs with no blankets in the dead of winter. After eight hours, we were released on our own recognizance, expected to make our court date. Of course, with our South Side wisdom and youthful defiance, we didn't.

That arrest was another wake-up call. I thought to myself: I'm done with this crap. Absolutely the last time I'll be drunk and disrespect a woman or anyone. What was I thinking? How do I get out of this mess I keep landing in? That arrest, combined with previous ones, finally gave me a moment of clarity. I meant it this time.

When the smoke cleared, I was still facing the realities of my hood upbringing. Even though Mom never knew about most of our minor run-ins because the police often released us on our own recognizance, life had more lessons waiting. One of those would happen downtown by Navy Pier and it would be transformational for me.

I heard jets flying overhead and a lot of commotion. I told my boys, "Let's go check it out." We ran over and saw a Black man at a podium with a microphone. He wore blue coveralls with an American flag on his left arm, a unit patch on his right chest, and two yellow racing stripes down the left side. He had a gold tee-shirt under the coveralls, and a khaki garrison hat the Navy calls it a "piss cutter."

I listened closely, and then he started yelling:

"And all you troublemakers out there, causing all kinds of issues in the city and drawing resources from places where they're needed. Do you think you're in a gang? I am in a gang! I am in the biggest gang in the world, and you mess with me, you mess with all of my homies!"

Right then, fighter jets roared past in formation. My heart pounded. I thought, I am definitely in the wrong gang. That was the moment I decided to join the military.

A Marine recruiter came to our school, and his pitch made me sign up on the spot for Marine Force Recon. A few weeks later, a Navy recruiter also came to Kenwood and convinced me I'd have a better career with the Navy. He showed me pictures of Navy SEALs, their powerful boats, and said there were more people in the Navy "just like me" meaning half-breeds. I had signed up for both the Marines and the Navy, which caused tension, but the Navy recruiter handled it. Go figure I didn't even join the military in a seamless way.

I was placed in the Delayed Entry Program for a year until I finished high school. I could not wait; I wanted out of the hood and away from trouble. I had already taken an oath to stay out of trouble and was determined to fulfill it a behavior far from my comfort zone.

Of course, life in Chicago didn't pause for me. I still fought the Elizabeth Boys, went to all-night underground house parties listening to Ron Hardy, and smoked "wicked stick" marijuana joints laced with formaldehyde. I even met a girl during that time who turned out to be psycho: writing letters in her blood and giving me weed laced with cocaine. Despite her dad being a cop, I ran for the hills.

I finally decided I wasn't going to take Stan's crap anymore. One night, I got home late from a party. Mom opened the door, and I said hello, stumbling straight to my bed. Somehow, I ended up lying unconscious on the bathroom floor, one shoe and sock off, foot hanging over the tub like a crime scene.

Mom, who stayed up all night worrying, burst in and screamed, "Ronnie's dead! Ronnie's dead!" Stan ran in, looked at me, and shouted, "Woman, that nigga ain't dead; that nigga drunk." Only the second time Stan was right since being my stepfather. Stan's said he probably doing drugs too. My mom questioned me and I responded, "I don't fucking want to hear it, I am going to fucking bed". Mom responded, and "And he curses too!" We shielded mom from our street side, unlike these kids today.

I had to go to the Military Entrance Processing Station (MEPS) for interviews, exams, and blood tests. We were put in a hotel the night before, told to stay off the women's floor and out of trouble. Of course, I found my way onto the women's floor, drank alcohol, and did things I dare not mention. The next morning, they asked if we'd used drugs or alcohol. I smiled and said, "Of course not!" Somehow, God was watching over me.

I graduated from Kenwood Academy on June 14, 1987, in the top ten percent of the lower one percent of my class. Only thirteen hours separated me from civilian life before my recruiter picked me up for Navy Boot Camp. That night, I stayed up drinking again. I even started a gang fight at Jetway Ribs on Racine Street.

Little Mikey, weighing barely 115 pounds, reminded me of a little dog that never got the message he was small. His bark was bigger than his bite, and he strutted around like he owned the neighborhood. That night, I realized if I survived this life, the military would be a whole new world.

Of course, I envied that trait. So, he and his boys walked up to me and my boys, and I just hauled off and punched Mikey square in the face. Naturally, a big fight broke out, spilling into the street. Traffic came to a standstill. Soon, the police arrived, and we were arrested on the spot. Life as I knew it was over. I couldn't believe I had done this again, right before joining the Navy in the morning. I told the arresting officer that we hadn't started it, the Elizabeth Boys did, but I threw the first punch. I explained that if I were arrested, I would miss my pickup to bootcamp. Thankfully, the officer was an Army veteran; he arrested the Elizabeth Boys and let me and my crew go.

Thirteen hours after my graduation and narrowly avoiding incarceration, Navy Petty Officer Gregory picked me up to take me to bootcamp. I was excited about my options I thought they were San Diego or Orlando. I asked him to stop in front of Mrs. Hall's house, where I knew Man and Raymond slept on the porch. Madear sold eggs, so I grabbed an entire rack, opened the door, and dumped them on top of them. I ran back to the car and told Petty Officer Gregory to floor it.

Now for the exciting part: all Gregory did was drive me to a bus stop, give me a bus token and a Metra train ticket, and tell me I needed to check in at Navy Recruit Training Command in Great Lakes, Illinois, by 1300 hours. I arrived at the train station, boarded, and was on my way to Boot Camp

I boarded the train and was on my way to Boot Camp in Illinois. "Navy it's not just a job, it's an adventure," the slogan said. So much for the adventure they promised.

When I boarded that train, I knew my life would never be the same. I already missed my mom and my brothers and sisters. But at least I was free of Cadillac Stan the stepfather no child should ever have in their life. A drug-dealing, pimping alcoholic who seemed to find his purpose in taking his rage out on our family.

I was saying goodbye to my life in Englewood. But Frankenstan would still be around for many more years. Thankfully, I wouldn't.

I thought I was leaving everything behind. Little did I know the scars and negative programming would try to destroy me for years to come. Welcome to the Navy full steam ahead.

By the way, Stan was murdered in the early '90s, supposedly beaten to death while trying to stop someone from stealing his Jordans.

Rest in peace, Cadillac Stan… Live By the sword, die by the sword.

PART TWO

THE NAVY, FULL SPEED AHEAD!

Chapter Four

You're in the Navy Now

"In some ways suffering ceases to be suffering at the moment it finds meaning, such as the meaning of sacrifice."

Victor Frankl

So, there I was, a South Side Chicago boy with a bus token and a Metra train ticket. (At least you know I was an expert at riding the bus.) But despite my excitement and enthusiasm for beginning this new adventure, I could not shake the fear that somehow, being bi-racial and having spent my entire life in the hood, I would end up right back where I started.

When I finally arrived at the train station, I had little time to contemplate my choice to join the Navy or wonder whether I would fit in and, most importantly, succeed. I did not even know what Petty Officer Gregory saw in me that made him take the time to personally drop me off and trust that I would follow through and show up at boot camp. Every fiber of my being was telling me to run and figure things out later. But my curiosity won the day. I had to discover what the Navy was like and whether I would belong.

I boarded the train and arrived at boot camp in just forty-five minutes. The train stopped at Great Lakes, home of the Navy Recruit Training Command. As I stepped off the train, there was no one waiting for me and no fanfare. From everything I had read about the military, I was surprised that no one was yelling at me or making me shout, "Yes, sir!" at the top of my lungs.

Hell, what did I know?

Unlike many recruits who arrived by bus, I was the anomaly walking through the gate alone with only my suitcase and no clue what I was supposed to do. Of course, being me, I walked up to the wrong gate. It was the academic school side, not boot camp. There was some irony in that, given my own academic challenges.

I was immediately directed to walk under the bridge and check in on the other side. I had a cordial conversation with the gate guards and began to think this Navy thing might actually be okay.

The base felt like a college campus, only with older buildings scattered throughout the grounds. The Navy personnel at the entrance somehow immediately knew who I was.

"Carpenter, you are Company 198," the Petty Officer said.
I thought that sounded pretty cool, even though I had no idea what it meant.

Before I could think any further, a bus pulled up, and lo and behold, I was politely told to stand up, join the others coming off the bus, and bring all my belongings with me. I used my coolest Chicago stroll and made my way toward the bus.

That is when all hell broke loose.

No more soft voices and polite directions. The yelling and screaming began, and the Navy Company Commander completely changed his tune.

They made us line up in formation.

That is when the fun began.

They flipped the script, and now it got real.

"Take all of your belongings out and dump them on the counter!" he shouted. "Welcome to week one, day one of processing week."

Processing week? What the hell does that mean? I wondered.

It looked like an assembly line for terrified young men. There was one line after another, each with a specific task.

Hair shaved completely off. Very humiliating.

Uniforms issued and put on.

Then the "shot line," where they used a pneumatic injection gun (A shot line consists of eight Navy corpsmen facing one another with injection guns that deliver a vaccine dosage into our arms).

I think I received six shots.

None of us had our shot records, so lo and behold, we probably received vaccines we had already gotten as kids. When I glanced at the other recruits and saw some of them faint from the shots, it was pretty eye-opening.

"Don't talk. Look straight ahead!" the officer shouted.

I knew I was in for another kind of whooping though without violence or bad intentions just the start of my long journey toward becoming the person I was always meant to be.

After all, I was in the U.S. Navy now.

After a few hours of this line dance, this phase was thankfully over. We transitioned into formation or at least what we thought was a formation.

Since they needed someone to call cadence, and me being the cocky city boy from Chicago, I stepped forward and started calling it.

(Cadence is the call-and-response work song sung by military members while marching or running.)

Little did I know my initiative would soon pay off. The company commander gave me my first professional moniker, "Recruit Petty Officer in Charge (RPOC)".

While I felt like a million bucks and was adjusting fairly well to military life, I still missed my family though certainly not Stan. Since we did not have cell phones back then, we wrote letters home to our families. At night, there were only two ways to make a call: either call collect or use an AT&T phone card if you were lucky enough to have one.

I always called my mom collect and stuck her with the bill, as if she had money which of course she did not.

For the first three weeks of boot camp processing week, confidence week, and academic week I was the person who answered directly to the company commander and passed the word to Company 198. It felt good to be recognized for something other than my hustling skills.

I began to observe the many different personalities in my company. What a melting pot of humanity. They came from all over the United States, with different nationalities, accents, and drawls. (Yep, I learned some new words, and I can even spell them now).

I developed a friendship with an Asian kid in my company. One day I told him, "You are one cool Chinese dude."

Oops.

The reason I said that was because, in the hood, we used to go to the Macvicker Movie Theater and watch Chinese karate movies. We pretty much referred to all Asians as "Chinese."

My attempt at kindness failed miserably.

It shocked me when he replied, "Call me Chinese again and I'll knock your chicklets out."

I said, "I'm sorry you're not Chinese?"

"Hell no, I'm Korean," he said.

Lesson learned.

There were many more lessons to come. Mainly because I had never really been exposed to the real world or to other parts of the country outside my hood.

Even getting over my craving for weed was an experience I did not soon forget.

After chow every evening, before lights out, we had what they called a "coke and smoke break," where the smokers among us were allowed to have a cigarette.

I would go to the coke-and-smoke area and ask one of the white guys smoking Lucky Strikes or Camels for a cigarette. I would pull off the filter and take a deep inhale. It always gave me a head rush.

Looking back, it is remarkable that I never became addicted to nicotine.

Our assistant company commander, a First Class Petty Officer who wore a boat pin on his chest (the precursor to SWCC), exposed us to a variety of music that everyone could groove to. His reasoning was that when we served aboard Navy ships, we would need to embrace diverse cultures and the music that came with them.

So, there we were, adjusting to boot camp and developing a routine.

Every morning at 5:30 a.m. we woke to the call:

"Reveille, Reveille! All hands heave out! Trice up! Uniform of the day is as follows wear dungarees, carry guide-on, carry competitive flags. The smoking lamp is lighted in all authorized spaces!"

We jumped up, got dressed in a flash, and made our beds with forty-five-degree corners tight enough to bounce a quarter.

We learned how to march, shine shoes, and shoot guns.

I also realized there were different levels of competence among the recruits. Some had already attended college. Some were in their thirties and knew how to keep their mouths shut and their heads down. Others had been preparing for military life for years and were already entering as E-3s and E-4s right after boot camp.

But they all had one thing in common.

They never hesitated to tell me who they were, where they came from, and what they were capable of.

One of those capabilities had to do with swimming.

I feared the confidence phase like nobody's business. I knew I could not swim very well and had to hold on to someone as they swam across the pool. To this day, I do not know whether the company commanders turned a blind eye or simply did not notice me in the crowd.

There were so many people in the water.

Nevertheless, I passed the floating and swimming tests literally on the back of someone else.

I am not proud of that. But I do know this: if Special Operations truly wanted more minorities in their ranks, they should invest in teaching at-risk kids how to float and swim. The payoff would be enormous.

Every American should know how to swim, and it should not be something people have to pay to learn.

After a few weeks, I was still the RPOC and apparently doing a great job, according to my company commanders.

Later I learned there was also an ulterior motive.

They wanted our company to win the coveted "Cheerio Flag" not the cereal and they needed every advantage they could get to make that happen.

The flag actually looked more like the symbol for the Olympic Games. Just a bunch of circles overlapping one another.

This also meant they needed an RPOC with a high ASVAB score. So going into week three, I was stripped of my RPOC position, and they gave it to a kid I had always had problems with because he scored something like a ninety-eight on the ASVAB.

Shockingly, I went from hero to zero on the very first day of week three.

That was my trigger.

That was when the pain body took over and I reverted to the old me. Having been the recruit leader of my company and now having to interact with the new RPOC who did not like me I started getting written up for every little infraction.

I assumed the company commanders knew what was going on, but they did nothing to address it. In fact, they frequently called me into the office and told me to assume the "position of learning," which was the push-up position. I would have to do a ton of pushups and could not stop until I was literally shaking with exhaustion.

I was pissed.

And as my attitude got worse, all I did was rinse and repeat the same cycle over and over again.

Eventually, my company commanders got tired of me too and started sending me to the IT (Intensive Training) division at the end of the day. I remember IT being filled with all the troublemakers from other boot camp companies guys just like me.

Think of it as a time-out for adults.

The punishment involved one-on-one interaction and "realignment" through extreme physical training.

And who were the instructors? None other than Navy SEALs.

And boy, did they kick our asses every evening.

As painful as it was, it was what I thought boot camp was going to be like anyway.

Luckily, there were only a few more weeks left before boot camp would be over.

Hallelujah.

All the recruits eventually made it to week six, and we were excited about choosing our jobs. We were allowed to choose three assignments and place them in order of preference.

Then we would be interviewed by a detailer who reviewed our ASVAB scores and told us what we were qualified for.

Long story short, I was assigned the role of Gunner's Mate Guns. They were responsible for maintaining small arms, gun mounts, weapons systems, and ammunition magazines, as well as serving on the ship's security force team.

At the time, that sounded pretty good.

At the beginning of week seven, we entered something called "Service Week." During this time, they placed us in different sections of the base to cook, clean, sort paperwork, and assist with medical services, among other tasks.

Looking back, it was simply a way to keep the Navy machine running on the base.

At any given time, there were more than 7,000 recruits training at Great Lakes, so you can imagine the amount of food needed, garbage generated, and paperwork required.

It truly took a village of recruits to keep that machine running smoothly.

So, they stuck me in the galley the Navy term for the dining facility.

Yes, gourmet Ron, the guy who could make a mean mayo sandwich.

But to my surprise, I was working with other recruits from Chicago. I was hanging out with Chicago homies again. It felt like home, talking trash while we worked.

The most senior recruit from the previous week was in charge, and the rest of us were his helpers.

Our job was to make 25,000 cinnamon rolls per day.

The first night we missed our quota by 5,000 rolls.

Shame on us.

The cook fired the leader and put me in charge.

The first night under my leadership we met our quota. We were ecstatic.

The second night we missed the quota and I was fired.
So much for success.

As a result, they placed me in the "deep sink," where all the fired leaders go.

In the Navy galley there are two areas: the deep sink and the scullery. Had I known the difference, I would have chosen the scullery, where you simply scrape food off plates, load the dishes into trays, and feed them into gigantic dishwashers.

Instead, I got the deep sink.

Damn, this was really messing with my head being fired twice in such a short time.

I was definitely competing for the bottom slot.

Growing up in the hood, I was used to struggling, but this time I had no one else to blame.

Reality sucks.

The mountain of pots was intimidating. There were several deep sinks with high-pressure nozzles hanging over them that you squeezed to release a jet stream of water. Every cleaning and scraping tool imaginable was scattered around the area.

And don't forget the black rubber boots and apron. It was a dirty and potentially dangerous job. Heck, with all the grease on the floor, you could practically ice skate across it.

My job was to scrub pots and pans for eight hours a night.

One night, one of the recruits from Chicago got so sick of the job and boot camp that he told me, "Man, I'm done with this shit. I'm getting on the Metra and going home."

He said he had pull in the streets and made a lot more money hustling than what the Navy paid us. Hell, I agreed with him.

At the time we were making a whopping $608.40 per month, which came out to about $7,300 per year.

With numbers like that, he convinced me to go with him. After all, who the hell could live on $304.20 every two weeks?

In my naïveté, I thought that was going to be my salary forever. So, I told him I was in.

The two of us threw off our black rubber gloves and aprons, walked to the back side of the galley, and followed the fence line where three more guys were waiting.

Please, don't imagine some kind of dramatic escape from Alcatraz.

This was just a few Chicago boys who were tired of taking the abuse and decided to leave the Navy because none of us understood the consequences.

When we got to the fence, there was already a hole cut into it. A few other guys were crawling through it toward what they thought was freedom.

I followed along.

But with each step I took, I started thinking about my mom and how I would be letting her down again.

We slipped past Navy security, probably because it would have been impossible to watch every corner of the base. I figured the Navy probably assumed that the recruits who wanted to leave would eventually get caught anyway. Maybe they thought the police would pick us up once we got home.

My homies and I made it all the way to the Metra station. That was when the fear finally kicked in. I thought the Navy police or local police would be waiting there for us. They weren't.

Then it hit me. What a stupid thing I was doing.

I was about to throw away the best opportunity I had ever been given. I wasn't escaping the Navy; I was escaping the hood.

I told the Chicago boys I was going back. And that is exactly what I did.

Naturally, they called me a few choice names for chickening out.

I retraced my steps. It took what seemed like an eternity to find the hole in the fence, but eventually I did. I knew I was in deep trouble not just because of the escape attempt, but because the pots and pans had been piling up while I was gone.

To catch up, I decided to scrape and rinse the pans thoroughly but only the outside, not the inside.

It cut my work in half, but some other poor soul would end up getting blamed for me half-assing the pots and pans. My little time-saving system was too big to trace back to any one person.

I was saved, and no one was the wiser.

Thankfully, Service Week finally ended, and we transitioned into week eight.

I often wondered what happened to the guys who actually went AWOL.

Despite my attempted escape and my questionable pot-cleaning strategy I was about to graduate boot camp. Looking back, I cannot believe what I was thinking. That I would leave the Navy, go back to the South Side for a day and look cool, then return to boot camp just to tell a wild story because I was a Chicago kid?

Who knows?

But I lived to fight another day inside the U.S. Navy.

Oddly enough, the company commanders became more cordial toward us during that final week. One day they even allowed us to ask questions, which was practically unheard of.

We were all sitting on the floor in front of our bunk beds, facing the aisle. The company commander was playing different types of music while answering our questions about the Navy.

As you rise in rank in the Navy and begin to understand the significance of ranks like E-6 and E-7, you realize that these company commanders were as influential in our lives as movie stars.

We respected them immensely and constantly sought their approval much like I had sought validation growing up with Stan.

Maybe it is simply human nature to look for validation from others. I know I was doing exactly that.

I asked the First Class company commander, "Sir, what does that pin on your chest mean?"

"Carpenter, it's a 9533 pin," he replied. "It signifies that I was a boat captain in the Special Boat Teams."

I was mesmerized.

He went on to explain that their job involved supporting Navy SEALs and ensuring they could get off the beach safely even under heavy enemy fire.

"These operators have to know each other's jobs," he added.

It was quite the capabilities briefing. He then started explaining survival training and asked if anyone wanted to serve in the Boat Teams.

Luckily, I kept my hand down.

One unfortunate recruit raised his hand, thinking it might be a fun opportunity. He quickly regretted it.

The company commander called him forward and ordered him to assume a squat position against the wall.

"This is the type of training you will go through," he said.

He began explaining survival, evasion, resistance, and escape.

After a few minutes, the recruit shifted slightly.

The company commander slapped him just like Stan used to hit me.

Tears streamed down the recruit's face. It was that intense.

The company commander finally ordered him to recover and return to his bunk.

"You see, men," he said, "Naval Special Warfare isn't for everyone." He got that right.

With most of the drama behind me for now I sometimes still cannot believe that I graduated from boot camp.

We actually had a very nice graduation ceremony.

What made it even better was that my mom and my sister Sheri showed up.

It was quite a day.

For once, I had earned a feather in my cap that was not stolen or hustled.

I had succeeded on my own legally for the first time in my life.

After graduation, all the belongings we had arrived with at boot camp were returned to us. Some recruits were sent on their way, while others waited for transportation to airports for further training around the country.

My rating as a Gunner's Mate Guns meant that my next step was actually just a short walk across the base to the A-School side.

Ironically, it was the same side of the base I had mistakenly walked into when I first arrived at boot camp.

Now I was legit. I had an ID card and full access to the base.

I was in.

There were several training buildings on that side. One was called "Snipe Castle," where the engineman, boiler technicians, and gas turbine specialists attended classes.

Then there was the "Greenhouse," Building 521, where the Gunner's Mate Guns and Gunner's Mate Missiles courses were taught.

A Gunner's Mate is responsible for operating and maintaining gun mounts, small arms, heavy weapons, ammunition magazines, and other ordnance equipment.

The official motto was:
"I bring not the rays of the sun, but the thunderbolts of Jupiter."

Later in my Navy career, I adopted my own unofficial motto, something from the Vietnam era that many Gunner's Mates embraced.

It went like this:
"Why are you so big? Because I'm a Gunner's Mate and the biggest guns are in the Navy."

It had a pretty good ring to it, I thought.

Starting A-School was actually pretty exciting for me. I was informed that my course would be a long one twenty-six weeks.

But before I could get to what I thought were the cool parts, I had to pass nineteen modules of Basic Electricity and Electronics.

I imagined this must be what college was like except we had to muster, meaning account for every member of the unit, two or three times a day.

And of course, we still had to wear our uniforms and keep our rooms spotless for inspections.

I remembered that one of my sister Angie's old boyfriends had gone through Gunner's Mate A-School and had done very well for himself. He was about to graduate and be sent to a ship. I asked if he would meet me at McDonald's so I could pick his brain and get a feel for what I was about to face.

He basically told me the course was pretty easy and that I should be able to pass the tests without too much trouble.

As you may recall, I was always in the top ten percent of the bottom one percent of my class, and summer school had been a constant in my life.

But it was during this time that I discovered something important about myself.

I was what some people call a concrete learner others call it tactile learning. I retain information through practical application. Put something in my hands and show me how it works, and I will remember it forever. But place me in a purely academic, knowledge-based environment and I quickly get lost.

I was nervous walking into that testing room.

After each master unit test, a computer system would grade the exam and immediately issue a pass-or-fail result. As the course material became more advanced, the tests became harder.

I started failing.

Then failing again, and again.

It was devastating.

All the old demons from my days in the hood came rushing back the feeling that I never quite fit in and that failure was the one constant in my life.

I did so poorly that I had to appear before three performance review boards.

After three months of struggling in Gunner's Mate A-School, they finally dropped me from the course and transferred me to a place called the Academic Training Division (ATD).

I called it the "Can't Cut It Academy."

It was essentially where academic washouts were fast-tracked to the fleet after about four weeks of basic indoctrination. The goal was to make sure the Navy could trust us not to accidentally kill ourselves or anyone else once we got to a ship.

The ASVAB test is no joke and should be taken very seriously. It is a strong indicator of your academic aptitude.

Looking back, I realized the detailer probably gave me the benefit of the doubt. My scores likely told him that the odds were stacked against me from the beginning.

The ASVAB is rarely wrong.

It was introduced in 1968, and nearly one million people take it every year. A score of fifty percent is considered average, while sixty percent or higher is above average.

ATD was a four-week program designed to prepare non-designated seamen like me for the fleet. Because we failed to complete our technical schools, we were now assigned wherever the Navy needed us most.

We received a crash course in shipboard life, firefighting procedures, and basic operational processes. After that, we were sent back to the detailer to receive our official orders.

My orders were to report to the USS Pyro (AE-24).

I was ecstatic.

I figured I could not be that dumb after all.

Pyro meant fire, right? So naturally I assumed I was headed to a ship packed with firepower. And since I had already been on the firebug list back in the hood, I figured this assignment would be right up my alley.

Man, was I wrong.

Still, I was excited. I learned that there was a program on the ship that allowed sailors to "strike" for a rating meaning I could still work toward becoming a Gunner's Mate even without completing A-School.

My dream was not completely dead.

During this time, I was granted two weeks of leave before reporting to my duty station, so I went home to celebrate with my family.

My mom was beaming.

"Ronnie, you made all of us so proud," she said. "You've always had the ability to pick yourself up from the worst situations and rise above them. God is watching out for you."

Oddly enough, even Stan seemed proud of me in his own strange way. Because I was now officially in the U.S. Navy, he appeared a little afraid of me.

The best part?

He even backed off my mom.

My secret dream one I never told her was that someday I would get her out of the hood and away from Frankenstan for good.

During my leave, I also went to visit Jackie.

When she saw me standing there in my uniform, she laughed.

It hurt.

Looking back, I realize I was too young to understand that her laughter probably came from immaturity . Maybe she simply did not know how to react to seeing a guy in a Navy uniform especially one wearing an "ice cream suit" with a shaved head that made me look like a cancer patient.

But at the time I took it personally.

I wrote her off.

To hell with anyone who cannot see what I am trying to become, I thought.

Sorry, Jackie.

It really was not your fault.

It was me, struggling with my own insecurities while trying to figure out who I was supposed to be after growing up around pimps, drug dealers, and gangbangers.

Wherever you are, I hope your life has been wonderful and blessed.

For the next week I paraded around the neighborhood like I had accomplished something far bigger than just surviving boot camp.

I hooked up with my old friends and Tommy to celebrate.

Naturally, Tommy and I got way too drunk and ended up hanging out with some girls from a local bar.

I do not remember much about that night.

I only remember going to bed around 2:00 a.m. with what I thought was a ten and waking up around 10:00 a.m. next to what looked more like a two.

I quietly snuck out of her house.

And then I discovered something even worse.

She had given me crabs.

For those who do not know, crab lice are parasites that live in pubic hair and feed on blood.

Okay, so technically I did practice safe sex.

Still… it was quite the experience.

One of the old guys in my neighborhood even offered some not-so-wise advice. He told me I should shave half my pubic hair, then light the other side on fire and use an ice pick to kill the crabs one by one as they ran out of the burning forest.

Kids, do not try this at home.

And like I said before never trust your homies with anything related to medicine, dentistry, accounting, politics, spelling, or math. Well… maybe math. Definitely not sexually transmitted diseases.

The hood is a lot like those crabs.

Both are hard to get rid of.

I kept listening to these street hustlers, and ninety percent of the time they did not know what they were talking about. What kind of idiot recommends fire or an ice pick as medical treatment?

Even though it was mostly joking around, those street homies had a way of steering us wrong. Thankfully, I had learned a little more since joining the Navy. I went to a pharmacist, who gave me some blue ointment that cleared the problem up in about a day.

Despite that little setback, I had a great time at home. But like all good things, it eventually came to an end.

I packed my bags, kissed my mom goodbye, hugged my brothers and sisters, and headed to the airport to begin the next chapter of my Navy adventure.

I could hardly wait to see the USS Pyro (AE-24) in person.

I was flying to San Francisco to meet my ship at Naval Air Station Alameda. When I arrived, I found my way to the base, only to learn that my ship would not be pulling into port for a few more days. They assigned me a temporary room in the barracks.

That is when reality hit me.

What reality, you might ask?

Loneliness.

A deep feeling of loneliness and depression washed over me as it sank in that I was truly on my own.

I walked outside and wandered into an open field behind the barracks. In the distance I could see the Oakland Bay Bridge and the bright lights of San Francisco.

It felt like I had landed on a different planet.

I had no idea what to do.

For the first time in a long while, I broke down and cried.

I thought about the mistakes I had made in my life and how many times I had let people down. Standing there alone in an unfamiliar place, stepping into the unknown, I felt scared and isolated.

Having no one to watch your back is a terrible feeling.

When you are in that state of mind, all you can imagine are worst-case scenarios. Doom and gloom seem like the only possible outcomes. I felt like I was destined to fail and eventually end up right back where I started. Finally, I decided the only thing I could do was go to sleep and see what tomorrow would bring. That night I tossed and turned in the open-bay barracks, lying in a narrow bunk bed. Eventually I drifted off to sleep.

It must have helped, because when I woke up the next morning the daylight shining through the window and I felt a surprising sense of calm. No one was yelling at me. No one was criticizing me.

For the moment, I was simply at peace.

I put on my uniform and walked to breakfast through the cool, foggy San Francisco Bay morning.

The fog was so thick I could barely see anything not even the bridges just the distant sounds of boats and foghorns echoing across the water.

A few days later, my ship finally pulled into port.

I walked down to the pier and checked in with the gate guards before being allowed to board.

Welcome to the USS Pyro (AE-24).

She was a large ship, but she looked more like a cargo vessel than the destroyers and battleships I had imagined. She was painted the standard Navy haze gray, and you could tell she had been around for a while.

Layers of paint covered the hull.

Rust streaked down from the superstructure.

The overboard discharge pipes made it look like the ship was crying rusty tears down her sides.

I stood there staring at the ship, trying to make sense of what I was seeing.

Wait a minute…

Those gun mounts on the bow did not look like five-inch-fifty-fours, and what were all those cranes and booms for?

What exactly did "AE" mean?

I was completely confused.

Then it hit me.

I had misunderstood everything back in Great Lakes.

AE stood for "Ammunition Ship."

That meant the Pyro did carry firepower but not for us.

Our job was to carry and transfer ammunition to other warships throughout the Pacific Fleet.

During my four years aboard that ship, I would have the privilege of helping replenish countless vessels throughout the Navy. The most memorable were the aircraft carriers and the old World War II–era battleships.

The USS Pyro (AE-24) was a Nitro-class ammunition ship. She measured about 487 feet long and 72 feet wide, carried a crew of roughly 331 sailors, and had two forward twin three-inch-fifty rapid-fire gun mounts. She could carry thousands of tons of ammunition, bombs, and missiles.

Commissioned in 1959, she was already twenty-nine years old when I reported aboard.

She was also part of the last generation of ships that still used boiler technicians to start combustion and steam systems using actual fire.

It was impressive in its own way.

When I reported to the quarterdeck with my orders, I informed them that I had been dropped from Gunner's Mate A-School.

Ironically, that turned out to be a lucky break.

They assigned me to the Weapons Division as an undesignated seaman which meant I did not yet have a Naval Enlisted Classification because I had failed A-School.

They also assigned me a sponsor who was supposed to help me adjust to life aboard the ship.

A sponsor is typically someone who sets a good example and helps guide new sailors.

Well…They missed the mark on that one.

The guy they assigned me was trouble from day one.

There is an old saying in the Navy:

"A sailor can become a rock star or a complete screw-up in seventy-two hours. It all depends on who is on your bus."

As I would soon discover, there would be plenty more characters like him throughout my Navy career.

And so, it began.

U.S. Navy.

Full speed ahead.

Chapter Five

The US Navy Rescued Me

"Even a rock, when exposed to excessive heat and pressure, becomes a diamond."

Author Unknown

It was late September, and I was finally aboard the ship. My first order of business was a quick meet-and-greet in the Weapons Office with Warrant Officer Anderson and GMG1 Otero; better known as Bossman. They welcomed me to the division and explained the reputation of the ordnance division: second to none, followed by a rundown of their expectations. Wow… no pressure there.

The meeting was brief, and "knock off ships work "sounded. This just meant most of the crew would disembark and go home to their families. Me? Like many other poor, lonely souls, I would be calling the ship "home."

I was escorted to the Weapons Division berthing. Spotless. The floor that we called the deck shined like polished boots from Boot Camp. I couldn't believe how cramped the space was. So many men had to call this place home and still maneuver around. The bunks referred to as racks, were only three feet wide. They're also called "coffin lockers" because under the mattress is a compartment running the length and width of the bed, meant for storing your belongings.

Being the FNG (fucking new guy), I got the top bunk. Lifting the mattress, I discovered the compartment was only six inches deep. I thought, How the hell am I going to fit all my stuff in this? My sponsor then showed me the assigned standing locker no more than three feet high and eight inches wide. It was a weird lesson in downsized living: my uniforms took up most of the space, and I literally felt like a sardine.

Just as I was figuring out my new cramped quarters, I heard: "Dinner for the Crew." That meant, head to the mess deck for supper. I grabbed a tray and got in line. The food presentation could have been better with servers just dumping it on our plates.

I sat with the other FNGs, introduced myself, and started eating. The food wasn't spectacular, but it did its job. No offense cooks, but the Navy has a habit of buying the worst-quality meat.

After dinner, I returned to my bunk, organized my locker, and even found the laundry. By now, I considered myself an expert at making beds, even though these were half the size of the Boot Camp ones. It was crazy trying to get comfortable, twisting my body around steam pipes hanging so low that I was a little intimidated. But after an hour, I settled in and decided to explore the ship.

Then came the call, "First call to colors," signaling sunset and retirement of the ensign.

No sooner had I left the bunk than the 1MC blared: "Security Alert! Security Alert! Away the Security Alert Team! Away the Backup Alert Force! Reason for security alert: Hold 2 Alarm!" Sailors ran past me at top speed with flak jackets donned and weapons in hand.

Message received. I scrambled back to my rack to avoid any trouble. It was around 1900, 7:00 p.m. for all you civilians.

I crawled into my rack and tried to figure out how I would manage sleeping under the awful pipes. Honestly, I had better sleeping arrangements in jail overnight. And the mattress? Only three inches thick. I'm sure I wasn't the first, nor the last, to complain. I thought: Suck it up, Ron, and figure it out.

I had to laugh though. For most of my life in the hood, I slept on the living room floor with couch cushions. I was already primed for this life.

Sleep, however, was impossible that first night with the ship creaking and lightly bumping against the pier. Strangely, though, the movement was calming.

At 0600, the 1MC rang: "Reveille! Reveille! All hands, heave out! Trice up! The smoking lamp is lighted in all authorized spaces!" Thirty minutes later came: "Sweepers, sweepers, man your brooms! Give the ship a clean sweep down both fore and aft, sweep all lower decks, ladderbacks, and passageways. Empty all trash into proper receptacles provided on the pier. Now Sweepers!"

Once you're a sailor, you never forget these routine announcements. I can still recite them as if it were yesterday.

Next up: navigating the showers. I had no clue how they worked and was embarrassed to ask. It's a process. You hold a button for water and release it to stop. It's the Navy's way of conserving its most precious resource: water.

Once I mastered that, I returned to my rack to get dressed standing inches from complete strangers. Weird and extremely uncomfortable at first, but I got used to it.

After chow, I headed to the Weapons Division muster location. Every day we took muster, received and got assigned our tasks. Bossman introduced me to the division, and my Navy life officially began.

Bossman was quite the character. A slightly overweight, career-first-class sailor for whom time seemed to have stood still. He joined the Navy in the 1970s, back when smoking weed and beards was legal. His mentors were Vietnam-era sailors who could drink anyone under the table, loved bars and hookers overseas, and did things their way. Bossman was no different. He was well respected, knew the job better than anyone, and was the 911 call whenever things went wrong in the Gunners Mate division.

Two things about Bossman always stuck out. First, he refused to embrace modern technology. Even when computers capable of tracking ammunition more accurately were installed, he wanted no part. Second, he did not give a damn about your feelings. He would even beat the crap out of you if you kept screwing up. Still, he was undeniably a father figure for most of us. Certainly, more than Ronald Senior or Stan. He was our Sea-Daddy.

After checking into the division, I was sent to numerous ammunition schools. There, I learned everything including driving all types of forklifts to blocking and bracing ordnance, bombs, and missiles. I also learned to shoot shot line across to other ships during underway replenishment. It was a lot to absorb, but I embraced every minute. The most profound lesson though, came from every instructor, regardless of the subject: US Navy ammunition ships were overdue for a catastrophic explosion. It was a story that left a lasting impression.

The story was rooted in the "Port Chicago Incident" during WWII. On July 17, 1944, during an ammunition onload of 4,606 tons of ordnance in the town of Port Chicago (now Concord, California), two ships; the USS E.A. Bryan and the SS Quinault Victory were involved in a disaster. Explosions caused a sympathetic detonation that completely destroyed the USS E.A. Bryan, severely damaged the town with falling debris, and scattered unexploded bombs. Even the ship's anchor landed 13 miles away. The blast instantly killed 320 sailors (most of them Black) and injured 390 others, including 100 Port Chicago residents.

The seismic shock wave was felt as far away as Boulder City, Nevada. This disaster accounted for 15% of the Black servicemembers killed during WWII. Its impact left instructors and later, us students with an indelible lesson: respect ordnance and prioritize safety.

Despite the Navy's investigation, immediate controls and training for ordnance handlers were not implemented. Less than a year later, predominantly Black ordnance handlers refused to load ammo and bombs onto ships, leading to major tensions. These sailors had been trained for combat but were instead relegated to loading ships. After threats, all but fifty returned to work.

Tragically, these sailors were court-martialed, found guilty of mutiny, and imprisoned. They became known as the Port Chicago Fifty. When the war ended, they were released, but their story was overshadowed by news of WWII's conclusion. Yet the event remained unforgettable for instructors and students alike.

During my tour on the Pyro, we would transit to Concord Naval Weapons Station to onload ammo. Driving off base, we passed through the abandoned town of Port Chicago, where stop signs stood in the middle of nowhere and remnants of destroyed or demolished homes remained. The entire area had become a Naval Weapons Station.

On July 15, 2022, the US House of Representatives officially exonerated the Port Chicago Fifty.

Finally, after completing all my training, I was ready to participate in ammo onloads, ordnance security watches, and the Personnel Reliability Program (PRP) a prestigious program in which very few shipmates participated.

PRP was a program overseeing special weapons, demanding tremendous oversight and attention to detail. I was a "B Keyholder," and it was fascinating to see how it all worked. It was quite a process. First, an officer with the combination to the main safe would open the drawer, pull out the key log, and step away. Then the A-Keyholder would open their safe, remove the key, and sign the book. I would follow suit, opening my safe, signing the book, and then walking to Number Two Magazine. There, a security guard would open the cage, and we would sign the entry log. A and B Keyholder would then open their locks on the hatch that led into the magazine.

Before entering the magazine, we strapped on our preassigned Thermal Luminescent Device (TLD), which measured the millirem ionizing radiation that our bodies was exposed to while inspecting special weapons. There were many types of bombs and missiles that mesmerized a young sailor like me. There were even backpacks designed for Navy SEALs to parachute behind enemy lines.

They say, "youth is wasted on the young," but not for me in the Navy. I wanted to stand out on in my division, so I volunteered for the Nuclear Weapons Emergency Destruct Team. Should an extreme situation occur, this team trained to place shaped charges on all weapons rendering them tactically useless and destroying all design information.

It should come as no surprise that I enthusiastically volunteered to go into a magazine and attach explosives to bombs, thinking I would survive the experience. Like I said, youth is wasted on the young!

By the way, "I can neither confirm nor deny the presence or absence of nuclear weapons onboard the USS Pyro or any other US Naval vessel." Despite all my training and qualifications, I soon realized that the Navy's initials, in reality, might as well have stood for "Never Again Volunteer Yourself."

Still, the training onboard the ship, though rigorous at times, was fascinating. After three months of attending schools including one for the PRP program, which featured replicas of the atomic bombs dropped on Hiroshima and Nagasaki "Fat Man" and "Little Boy," I was ready to get to work. And I realized the job was not that bad.

There were only a few bad apples in leadership positions who abused their authority. For example, they would give me extra duty, making me paint the deck and then the ceiling. Even a single spec of paint on the deck meant I had to repaint it. Though the Navy invested heavily in my training, I despised how some Petty Officers treated me, but I endured as long as I could. My mother was my refuge. I always called her collect to complain and also to ask for money because I didn't have a pot to piss in or a window to throw it out.

December sailed by quickly, and I was authorized to take my final week of leave, having already spent time at home before checking into my ship. I spent my last $175 on a plane ticket home, with no intention of returning to the Navy. Though I had learned a great deal, I was sick and tired of people abusing their power and dictating what I could eat, wear, or even think.

I arrived home but didn't let my mom know I was there. I didn't want to disappoint her again, especially since she was so proud of me being a sailor.

I literally stayed on my grandmother's porch, making it my temporary home. The week flew by. I was supposed to be back on my ship, but I decided to take "Weather Leave" Weather They Liked It Or Not! Yes, folks, I was officially AWOL (Absent Without Leave). There I was, AWOL from the Navy with no money, relying on my grandma to feed me and take care of my needs. Then my big-mouthed sister, Sheri, snitched and told my mom I was living on the back porch. Clearly, Sheri didn't get the memo that snitches get stitches.

My mom was furious. My excuse? That the Navy was prejudiced, and I could make more money on the streets of Chicago than in the military. But the truth was simpler: I felt I had no real power or say in anything that went on with shipboard life.

"Ronnie, you're insane," Mom said. "There is nothing on the streets for you, and you better get your butt back there now."

Mom borrowed money from Sear at Asia Chop Suey to get me on a plane back to the Navy. She knew the bigger picture: if I stayed on the South Side, I would have no future and would most likely end up dead, in prison, or in a gang. She was not having it.

She also knew that the punishment I would face for being AWOL was the lesser of two evils compared to the streets. So, I took Mom's advice, returned to my ship, and accepted my punishment possibly even going to the brig, the Navy's version of prison.

Warrant Officer Anderson and Bossman found me, ordered me to the quarterdeck, and sent me to the office immediately. These old, salty sailors, with decades of experience between them, already knew I was AWOL.

"Get your shit together, sailor," Anderson said. "I'm not looking at your current situation. I'm looking at your future potential. We will overlook your bad judgment. After all, very few people can be on the PRP program," he added.

I was stunned but thrilled that they expressed such confidence in me, especially because I really screwed up. They told me a huge inspection was coming up. Anderson and Bossman chewed me out a little more and finished by telling me I was on "Special Liberty" due to the snowstorm in Chicago. I gave them one of my well-honed Chicago South Side looks.

"Sir, there wasn't a snowstorm in Chicago," I said.

They didn't miss a beat.

"That's your damn problem, Carpenter! You talk too damn much! Now get the hell out of here!"

"Aye-aye, sir!" I said.

Little did I realize that these old wise guys had given me my first opportunity to return to honor after doing something as stupid as going AWOL. I wish I could tell you it would be my last, but remember, the return-to-honor concept.

They say that in moments of clarity, we achieve clarity of consciousness. What I learned was not to let a few bad apples ruin the bunch. There were only a few people I thought abused their power. It was time to change my attitude and become more productive than I ever had before. I wanted to do good once again in my life but needed guidance on how to achieve that.

So, I asked another Petty Officer for advice on getting promoted in the Navy. Luckily, I found one piece of advice that stuck with me for the rest of my career.

The advice came from a Boatswain's Mate. He told me: "I look at all the shitty Petty Officers who only had time in rate and still got promoted. Every dog has its day in the Navy. There was always an opportunity to study while you wait for time in rate. Then you'd be ready to pass the test, get promoted, and tell the shitty leaders to fuck off legally because you were the same rank."

That was some damn good advice. From that day forward, I always looked at the long-term potential in people. My leadership style became more like Anderson's and Bossman's giving people opportunities to return to honor.

All it takes is a willingness to change your attitude to reach your goals. I learned that if I wanted power and respect, I had to earn it and start being a team player. As a result of this epiphany, things started to change for me. Dodging a bullet was exactly what I needed. Going AWOL, was the kick in the butt I needed to grow up and start molding my life into something I could finally accept and be proud of.

About a month after returning from my escapade, our ship was headed for my first six-month deployment, which we called WESTPAC (Western Pacific). It wasn't like I was leaving much behind. Everything I owned fit into two small lockers. I was ready for the adventure of my young life,

Low and behold, we were back at Concord Naval Weapons Station for our ammo onload. This was my first time experiencing the full magnitude of my new job. The onload lasted a week, with onboard cranes and pier cranes systematically transferring bombs, missiles, and ammunition onto the ship. Bossman was a great teacher and treated us like his kids. More like a father, who had enough confidence and trust in us to drive fork trucks, and block and brace ammo in the magazines. This was to prevent them from shifting while underway. Being a Gunners Mate on this ship required teamwork, precision, and extreme attention to detail. Some of the ordnance we handled was incredibly sensitive and could cause a serious incident at any moment.

The potential for accidents increased dramatically during underway replenishment, so we had to be careful and precise. Underway replenishment, or UNREP, involved ships coming alongside in close proximity. A Gunners Mate would use an M-14 rifle with a Mk-87 line-throwing gun to shoot a shot line over to the visiting ship. Boatswain's mates would then send cables across to connect the two ships. A winch operator would feed out and take in cable while both ships maintained course and speed. Gunners Mates stood by with an explosive pole cutter in case the wires locked up. It was a frightening job; we all feared injury during these evolutions.

But we persevered.

Our job was to run up to the tensioned cable connecting the ships. Wearing Kevlar helmets and flak jackets, we would hook the pole cutter to the cable. The pole cutter used an explosive cartridge that propelled an iron chisel at extraordinary pressure to cut the wire. The technique was precise: hook the cable, get a running start, pull the cable to actuate the cartridge, and avoid the shrapnel. Walking down the corridor to the UNREP station with all eyes on you felt like stepping onto the moon. Again, I still didn't get the message that Navy stood for "Never Again Volunteer Yourself."

Day in and day out, we moved ammo. We became experts at operating fork trucks and ammunition elevators. Even repairing fork truck guards that prevented the vehicles from falling into the elevator shaft. This was especially important while underway.

Sometimes we were yelled at for not being as fast as the old hands, who occasionally threw caution to the wind and removed all blocking, bracing, and stanchions from the magazine. That left the ammo unsecure and ready to topple at any moment. Not us. We were the newly trained 3rd Division members doing everything by the book. We placed ammo on the elevator, brought it to the main deck, and let a fork truck transport it to the UNREP station. I was the young buck who was just AWOL, and now I was on my way to becoming a responsible sailor handling serious shit.

And then there was one incident I will never forget.

The USS Enterprise and the USS New Jersey were both alongside, and we had to conduct a dual UNREP sending ordnance from the port and starboard sides, as well as the flight deck. Senior Gunners Mates ordered us to remove all bracing and stanchions.

Todd Holtzclaw and I were hesitant. We even spoke to Bossman, who was running a fork truck feeding pallets of ordnance to the UNREP stations. He yelled, "Get the fucking ammo on the main deck faster!"

We went down into hold three and pulled all the bracing and stanchions. The USS Enterprise was already alongside, and things were going smoothly until the USS New Jersey, a WWII dreadnought battleship with massive sixteen-inch guns, came into position. Its bow wake bounced our ship like a cork, rolling it dramatically to port and starboard.

Todd and I knew we had a serious problem, so we started re-bracing the ammo and replacing the stanchions. No sooner had we completed two rows than a stack of 1,000-pound bombs toppled off the pallets. Holy shit! They were rolling across the deck, dangerously close to the broken fork truck guards, and could have fallen thirty feet into the elevator shaft

Todd and I worked frantically, trying to stop the bombs from rolling. We grabbed wooden wedges normally used to brace the ammo and threw them under the bombs to stop them. The bombs rolled right over the wedges until we adjusted our approach.

I tried to slow the bombs while Todd slid the wedges underneath them. Thankfully, we stopped one and felt like we had just won the Super Bowl. But our celebration didn't last long. Five more bombs were still rolling around and crashing into everything in sight. It was terrifying, to say the least. After a few frantic minutes, we finally managed to stop them all. We were completely exhausted.

"You idiots are too slow! You didn't feed Station 3!" Bossman yelled. "And who told you to pull all those damn stanchions?"

Lesson number one: never listen to senior guys who bypass and compromise safety.

Even though we got yelled at, we still learned something valuable from Bossman that day. He showed us how to use a fork truck adaptor to reset the bombs back onto pallets and band them together again.

News flash UNREPing an aircraft carrier at sea is an all-day affair. Add a battleship into the mix, and you are looking at twenty hours of work. Catching a few minutes of sleep on the main deck or down in the magazines before the next ship came alongside was just part of the routine.

As the day wound down, we took turns grabbing sleep wherever we could on the main deck or inside the magazines. When night fell, we had our life vests on and our green chem lights activated. The USS New Jersey eventually completed its onload and sounded five blasts for an emergency breakaway drill to starboard. We all stood on the main deck watching this national icon sail away, knowing there was probably nothing on the planet that could kick her ass.

"These colors don't run," as we liked to say back then.

Just as I was hoping to catch some sleep after that long day, they pulled me back in. We thought we were finished when suddenly a fast frigate came alongside and began offloading its five-inch fifty-four shells because it was heading into the shipyard for repairs.

There were nearly a thousand artillery shells.

Bossman was working in the hold with us and had a copy of OP-4, the procedural book that served as the bible of rules and regulations for handling ammunition afloat. He wanted to check the guidelines for creating a magazine within a magazine. So, we also learned how to do it.

This time it was me, Todd, Blackburn, and Swanson helping.

Bossman threw caution to the wind. That became obvious when he started handling seventy-pound explosive shells and tossing them into the ready-made magazine we had built using plywood and steel stanchions.

The more he tossed, the more nervous we became.

We all tried to find places to hide behind waiting for the explosion as if there were any real protection that close to someone tossing explosive shells like they were empty boxes. We voiced our concerns, but we also feared Bossman's wrath and just wanted to finish the job.

So, we joined in and started tossing shells like he was.

It was a classic case of damned if you do and damned if you don't.

Despite the tension, we finished the job without any explosions or major incidents.

Still, many of us had four-hour ordnance security watches to stand afterward. These watches rotated twenty-four hours a day, seven days a week. Our job was to monitor the ammunition and report anything unusual. We inspected every magazine for fire hazards, loose ordnance, or anything out of the ordinary.

Every hour we checked in with the Officer of the Deck in the pilothouse and reported:

"Officer of the Deck, Ordnance Security reports all conditions normal!"

The quartermaster would then log the entry.

Each month we also submitted the hourly sign-in sheets located in every magazine throughout the ship.

We survived and lived to fight another day.

Just when I felt like I had finally accomplished something meaningful, I was summoned to the office after morning muster. Bossman had a surprise waiting for me.

I had to complete my mess-cooking tour. He said he had held it off as long as he could.

You've got to be kidding me.

Apparently, every enlisted sailor checking onto a ship had to complete a mandatory ninety days of mess cooking.

Meaning, I had to relive the service week of boot camp for ninety days.

At least this time I worked in the scullery and set up the tables for breakfast, lunch, and dinner. It wasn't that bad.

Fortunately, the time passed quickly.

Unlike boot camp, though, I had to answer to two chains of command: my own division and the supply division.

Many of these Petty Officers had positional authority but terrible bedside manners. You know the drill, yelling at us, assigning menial tasks and treating us like dirt.

In retrospect, I can't entirely blame em. I blame the people who were supposed to mentor them into becoming the leaders of tomorrow.

I think they looked down on us because we weren't "mess specialists." We were outsiders working in their field. To them, we were nothing more than manual labor.

You would think they would have appreciated the help.

But that just wasn't in the cards.

But the good news was that I befriended a few of the cooks. I won't mention their names to protect the innocent.

Even though I made a new friend, I couldn't wait to check back into my weapons division and escape this messy cooking job. My new partner in crime, Steven Sass. We couldn't have been more different. Steven came from a pretty affluent and close-knit family, and he joined the Navy to make his own mark. I had no one to lean on, which is why Steven became my closest confidant.

We did a lot together on the ship, and his charisma was contagious. Our claim to fame was making lemonade by boiling lemons in huge pots and adding sugar until it tasted like old-fashioned lemonade. It was always a hit with the crew until we got chewed out from north to south for using all the ship's lemons.

During my mess-cooking stint, our ship departed the San Francisco Bay Area, heading for the Persian Gulf by way of Hawaii and the Philippine Islands. The mission: to onload more ordnance. We left Concord Naval Weapons Station and transited through the bay.

I couldn't believe how much my life had changed in just eight months. I left the South Side of Chicago with no future and was now departing my country for the first time in my life, embarking on a new adventure. Talk about leaving your old life behind. Unlike some sailors on the ship, I had nothing and no one to leave behind. No wife. No children. Only the emotional baggage I carried from Chitown. Everything I owned fit on the ship, and I was okay with that. The good news: my mom still accepted collect calls, sent me money occasionally, and exchanged letters since the internet wasn't yet a thing.

After about fourteen days, we arrived in Hawaii at the ammunition depot for onload. I couldn't shake the label of mess cook or "Boot Crank," as we were often called. Those old salty dogs on the ship made sure you never forgot it. But I persevered.

The ammo onload lasted two days, giving us enough time for liberty in Maui. This was my first experience in a place so far from the U.S., yet still part of our country. Once we arrived, after dinner and cleaning duties, we were allowed into town. The only rule: be back on the ship by 0530 to set up tables and make coffee for breakfast. My buddy, MS3 Coleman, and I went to explore.

Being underage, we had to get creative to grab some "forties" of Olde English 800, sold only in forty-ounce bottles. It was malt liquor that tasted terrible but did the job. We followed it up with a second course of E&J brandy, better known as "Irk and Jerk." That combination gave me classic "whisky goggles" on any girl I met.

As we walked down a major street, we noticed two beautiful women heading in our direction. Looking like starving animals, we pounced.

Coleman decided to back off, leaving me alone with the two women. He tagged along but stayed quiet. I had my arms around both their waists, feeling like I was in one of those movies depicting sailors on liberty.

We walked up a building with a lot of stairs. The women asked to take a photo with me, and Coleman became the photographer. He couldn't stop laughing as he snapped their Polaroid.

Then something spooked the girls. They moved ahead, and I asked Coleman why he was laughing so hard.

"Dude, didn't you realize those two girls were men?"

I refocused my whisky-goggled eyes and it hit me. Their Adam's apples were as big as mine. I was pissed. So, I tracked them down.

"I want that photo back!" I said.

They bolted like bullets from a gun, their sky-high heels making them far from graceful. One tripped, and I couldn't let anyone get hurt male or female. I helped them up and asked for the photo back.

"You know, you should be more honest about being men, not women," I said, peppering my words with a healthy dose of South Side cussing.

And just like that, at eighteen, I had my first encounter with cross-dressers and came out unscathed. Coleman couldn't wait to get back to the ship to report Chitown Ron was hanging out with homies dressed as women. Only in America!

After the adventure, I returned to the ship around 3 a.m. and had to be up by 0530 to set tables and make coffee. It was my first, but not my last night of going to bed late, waking up early, nursing a hangover, and having some wild stories to tell.

We left Hawaii after the onload and headed for the Republic of the Philippine Islands "The P.I." Subic Bay was the largest naval base I had ever seen. It was massive, and it would be my first visit to a foreign country in my life. We all had "channel fever," and I had already endured eight weeks of mess cooking. Thank goodness.

Upon arrival, we were briefed on the do's and don'ts of Subic Bay Naval Base and local culture. One simple rule: never bring food or produce off the ship or into the country.

I was excited watching my ordnance division working late hours to finish onloading ammo before liberty. I had a feeling this was going to be awesome. Since I had liberty so early, I joined the other green mess cooks to limit the amount of trouble I could get into.

Fortunately, now we could drink and do what we wanted. It only took American greenbacks. We were part of the loose morals of the time: free love, all-hands-on-deck, and a party culture inherited from mentors who had been in the Philippines since Vietnam and WWII.

Stepping off the ship, the heat was stifling. It took nearly thirty minutes to exit the front gate and reach Olongapo City. We walked over a river called "Shit River" biologically dead, pitch black, and smelling like sewage. Yet kids swam in it, calling us names and begging us to toss pesos so they could dive for them. We obliged, laughing as they surfaced with coins. I wondered if they were immune to the river's bacteria. I know us gringos would have been hospitalized immediately.

Crossing the bridge, we entered town. Bars lined the streets, colorful buses called "Jeepneys" passed by, and motorcycles with cabs "called Trikes" zoomed around. I felt an incredible sense of belonging in this new country.

I wandered from bar to bar, drinking Redhorse Beer and a local concoction only Vietnam vets could craft: MOJO Punch. And it packed a punch.

Rum, vodka, Amaretto, brandy, beer, Coke, 7-Up, orange juice, and pineapple juice combined to create a sneaky, mind-altering cocktail that could make even the toughest sailor forget the night before.

On my first night, after sampling everything under the sun, I found myself at the Blue Haven Massage Parlor with a few sailors who had been to the P.I. before. They explained how it worked. Feeling adventurous, I approached the counter and scanned the menu. The VIP massage cost six dollars. I went for it.

Escorted to a dark room, I experienced a beautiful woman and a great hour-long massage. Other options on the menu were too intimidating. After my Hawaii debacle, I didn't know what could jump out of the closet at me. I declined and somehow staggered back to the ship drunk as hell with a few other guys.

It was 5:00 a.m., and I had to be up at 0530 to set tables. Despite fatigue and inebriation, I decided to stay dressed in my civilian clothes from the night before and set up early. The hangover was brutal. I swore I would never drink again. That statement, I repeated numerous times throughout my career.

Luckily, we survived the day. And then came the sound that reenergized every hungover sailor on the USS Pyro (AE-24): "Knock off ship's work!" Sweepers were sounded, and liberty was granted.

We were briefed on watch section duty that night. The rest of us headed back to our lockers, quickly changed, and returned to town for another night of debauchery.

That evening, I went out with the big guns. The old guys who knew the P.I. like the back of their hands. They called it "popping my cherry," meaning they would show me the ropes.

Our adventure began on side streets. Ones I would never dare navigate alone without this posse of misfits. I couldn't believe the bars stocked fifty-five gallons of MOJO Punch sold by the pitcher. Fifty-five gallons!

We hit bar after bar that I lost count. I remember one bar with about thirty women on stage. It was crazy, like a cattle call. I was stunned when the old guys pointed to a woman or two, took their hands, and walked up stairs. I could only assume this led to an unwholesome encounter.

Sitting at the bar, drinking my MOJO and Redhorse Beer, an old sailor walked up, slapped me on the back, and said, "Carp, you little asshole." He grabbed my beer, chugged it, and walked back upstairs. Something tasted off like metal in my drink. Wiping my mouth, I realized there was blood on my hand. The old timer had gone down on a hooker who was on her period, and by proxy, I had earned my "red wings."

Disgusted, the only solution my drunken mind could devise was more alcohol. That unfortunate lesson followed me for the rest of my life.

That was it: no one drinks after me or grabs my drink at a bar. None of these salty dogs we call "sailors" would ever do that to me again!

My time in the Philippines settled into a routine: work, drink, rinse and repeat.

I met an older woman called Mamasan at the airport disco. All American sailors knew her by that moniker. She was always nice to me, and I returned the favor by sneaking her fruit off the ship. Soon, I realized that she was essentially a madam, doing what Stan did back in the States: arranging girls for American sailors when they arrived at port.

One night on liberty, Mamasan introduced me to one of her "girls," Jennie.

She had long dark hair, and her skin glowed like an evening sunset. No surprise we started having an affair. I would bring Mamasan fruits, vegetables, or even a spaghetti dinner, and she would release Jennie from her duties. Hanging out with Jennie kept me out of trouble and gave me a sense of normalcy.

Jennie knew exactly what to do. I wasn't the first sailor she'd entertained, and I wouldn't be the last unless some innocent guy struck gold and married her. In the Navy, that happened more often than you think. Many sailors fell for their girls and wanted to take them back to the U.S. Some even got into trouble marrying them without permission, which was a strict no-no that could affect your security clearance.

Me? I got the message. I helped Jennie as much as I could, knowing our time together was short-lived. Normally, I'd spend a night at her tiny house, using a bucket for a shower. We had a "thing" for about four days before moving on. We promised to write each other.

Funny thing about the P.I., the bar girls knew more about ships movement than anyone. They were like a massive intel network. Not to sabotage our mission, but to inform each other when ships were returning. Loose lips sink ships, indeed. The enemy could have paid off a Filipino bar girl for a treasure trove of intel.

We should have known better. Leaders on the ship constantly reminded us to abstain from risky behavior and to use protection. Ironically, some of those same leaders were the first in medical line, likely having contracted STDs themselves. This wasn't entirely our fault. We perpetuated alcohol abuse and drinking to fit in and gain favor with the old guys. They learned it from their mentors. And, so, the cycle of debauchery continued.

But the fun had to end eventually. Our ship was finally pulling out of the Philippines, headed for the Persian Gulf to support "Operation Earnest Will," escorting Kuwaiti oil tankers.

The Iranians, in all their infinite wisdom, thought they could lock up the Strait of Hormuz with mines and attack Kuwaiti-flagged oil tankers. Our role, as part of "Battlegroup Foxtrot" better known as the Enterprise Battle Group was to support the effort by supplying the warships with every type of ordnance in the U.S. arsenal.

My mess cooking tour was finally over, and I returned to weapons division. It felt incredible. Being a Gunners Mate on an ammunition ship was like being part of a professional NFL team: every task had to be perfect and safe, lest we experience another Port Chicago.

We stayed mostly in the Gulf of Oman for safety but routinely moved towards the Strait of Hormuz. Throughout the night, while we rotated the watch on machine guns and gun mounts, we could hear Iranians calling us "infidels" and other bad words over shortwave radio. "Infidels…Tonight you die!!"

Battle Group Foxtrot had an insatiable appetite for fuel and ammo. Watching combined replenishment and vertical replenishment with helos was incredible. Our ship resupplied fuel, ammo, and food seamlessly.

The teamwork between Gunners Mates and Boatswains Mates was astonishing. Sailors from all over the U.S. consistently rose to the challenge.

Once resupply was complete, the ships broke away, saluting one another while playing breakaway songs. Ours was by Hank Williams: "We got a long way to go but such a short time to get there."

Things heated up toward the end of March 1988. We had just completed forty-five days at sea, known as "hump day." The ship hosted a steel beach picnic, and every sailor was authorized two beers while eating BBQ and playing sports. It was a great time.

The Commanding Officer was proud of the ship's accomplishments and authorized liberty port to decompress. We would move off station and transit to Mombasa, Africa. It felt like hitting the lottery. Man, this was it!

We once again suffered from channel fever and couldn't wait to get off the boat and party in Kenya. During the transit, we still had work and watches to stand, but it seemed easier knowing we were headed to a liberty port. The day before we pulled in, I paid $250 through the ship's Welfare and Recreation services for a helo safari over the Serengeti and Mount Kilimanjaro. Heck, all I did was save my cash every two weeks. Back then, the Navy paid us in cash. When my watch was over, I ate chow and went to bed, planning to wake up in Mombasa the next morning. Oh, by the way, let's not forget the card game on the ship called Tonk. I lost my share of money playing damn game.

Reveille sounded, and we climbed out of our racks, buzzing about our adventures. When we hit the main deck, we realized we weren't near land. What the hell…?

Before we could figure it out, the commanding officer came on the 1MC. The Samuel B. Roberts had hit a mine in the Persian Gulf, and the battle group was ordered to reconstitute in the Persian Gulf best speed possible. Major bummer!

Our mission changed. We were no longer part of Operation Earnest Will, but now "Operation Praying Mantis," ready to exact revenge on the Iranians. Ships came off station to rendezvous with us, restocking missiles, five-inch projectiles, and ammo.

We were replenishing ships left and right. Out on gun mount watch, you could hear battlegroup communications on the radio:

"Iranian Oil Platform, this is US Navy Warship. You are authorized to retrieve survivors from the water; however, should you attempt to extinguish the flames, you will be destroyed."

Those were fighting words, and I wanted in. We were now officially in a conflict with Iran.

Our commanding officer, Commander Macpheeters, had a flair for the dramatic. Once, he set up speakers at the ship's exhaust vents so that during breakaways, the 1MC made our ship sound like the gas turbines of every ship in the battle group, even though we had boilers.

One time, Boatswain Voshall, the warrant officer in charge of deck operations called me into his office. "Want to be a California Raisin during UNREP?" he asked. The CO wanted the entire battle group to hear through the grapevine that the USS Pyro had dancing raisins. I asked what's in it for me? He replied, "Your fucking paycheck,". I didn't volunteer; I was voluntold.

So, me and three other sailors became dancing raisins on the flight deck during UNREP. Humiliating, to say the least.

After that, we had too much ordnance and too much time on my hands. To ease my boredom, I calculated the amount of ammo on board: $1.6 billion, with two more holds to count. This old ship was worth a lot. Not just in dollars.

We also had regular mail calls. Helo drops delivered letters to the postal clerks, who distributed them by division. Out of the blue, I received a letter from Jennie in the Philippines. She and many other beautiful Filipino women cast a wide net. Her letter was nicely written, and I was impressed.

The same day, one of the Boatswain mates a white guy was grinning from ear to ear while reading his letter. "Hey man, is that from your boyfriend?" I asked.

"No, you asshole. It's from my girl in the P.I. I'm going to marry her when we get back," he said.

"What's her name?" I asked. "Jennie," he said.

I pulled out my letter and compared the pictures. They were identical. Jennie's wide net had landed on the Pyro.

I could have been more sensitive, but instead I said, "Man, it's just that one of us got played and it wasn't me." Surprise. He never spoke to me again but didn't marry her. Ungrateful bastard!

With that behind me, day two of Operation Praying Mantis began. Our mission: replenish warships coming out of the Persian

Gulf. First up was the USS Bagley (FF-1069), a fast frigate with a grey superstructure blackened by firing so many five-inch projectiles.

The CO meant business. Pallets of projectiles and powder were standing by on the main deck, ready to transfer as soon as UNREP began. It was one of the most incredible scenes of my Navy career. After transferring more than 700 projectiles, the USS Bagley called for an emergency breakaway.

The Boatswain mates handled it like pros. The Bagley almost took our highline wire, but our crew reacted quickly. As it sped back into the Persian Gulf, it flew the largest U.S. flag I'd ever seen: the Battle Ensign. It was massive, at least ten by twenty feet. Any enemy seeing that Battle Ensign approaching knew trouble was coming. THESE COLORS DON'T RUN! Hell Yeah!!

In the end, Iran pushed too far and paid the price. Battlegroup Foxtrot sank or destroyed: one frigate (forty-five killed), one gunboat (eleven killed), three speedboats, two oil platforms, and damaged one fighter jet.

One thing is certain: it kept Iran in line for most of my thirty-two-year Navy career. My, my… how history repeats itself. Iran has returned to its old ways and is now acting much like it did in 1988. They are harassing ships through proxies, attempting to interfere with trade and disrupt the flow of oil through the world's most important chokepoint, the Straits of Hormuz. Fast forward 38 years and in March 2026, Operation Epic Fury has crippled Iranian military infrastructure that supports its military operations and set Iran's conventional capabilities back decades. This significantly limits its ability to threaten regional stability. Hooyah U.S. Military!

Another part of the battlegroup was a destroyer tender the USS Gompers with female sailors onboard. It could repair anything on any ship. If a part was missing, they could fabricate it. Having been at sea for so long and hearing all the off-color stories I dare not mention, my curiosity peaked. I even faked a raging toothache just to visit the ship and see some of the female sailors sunbathing for myself. It was quite the experience.

Just the scent of women was refreshing after being around smelly men 24/7.

After I left the dentist, I ran into one of my homies from the South Side of Chicago, who had joined the Navy at the same time I did. I had only met him at MEPs during processing, but he remembered me. He transitioned smoothly on his ship and even brought some of his Chicago hustle along. Unlike my hustle which was breaking my generational curse, his was downright devious.

What did he do? Well, he convinced about ten female sailors to essentially become "nautical prostitutes." Can you believe it? He had them selling their bodies for $25 a pop, then split the money with them. He was quite the entrepreneur.

So, now I knew for certain that you could pay for sex on the USS Gompers. The ship was nicknamed "The Gompers Stompers." Of course, I was offered the opportunity to take one of his girls to the bow of the ship, but I had no idea how the system worked. He explained that the girls would wear blue coveralls with slits in the middle, but nothing underneath. Then he added the details: they would walk in front of me, bend over the capstan winch, and it was a one-and-done situation do your deed, then leave.

By the way, the scuttlebutt (that's Navy speak for gossip) in the battlegroup was that the USS Gompers busted a sex ring on the boat. One girl couldn't open her coffin locker and needed the master-at-arms to cut her lock. When they opened it, she had more than $20,000 in cash! Unheard of. There are no ATMs at sea, and pay was cash-only. This meant she should have had no more than five thousand dollars in her locker.

The master-at-arms probably already suspected something and was waiting for proof. The girl had no credible excuse for her behavior, so to save herself, she turned everyone else in.

When I heard this, I realized that if she earned $25 per act, she must have averaged five or more encounters a day, totaling around 600 to hit $15,000. (I gave her the benefit of the doubt and subtracted her Navy pay of $5,000.) Gotta admit she was committed!

Wait how did the pimp get paid? And why are you listening to me, someone who skipped high school math just to graduate? You know those were the best fifteen years of my life.

I was impressed by how thoroughly he and his girls strategized. In addition to prostitution, he and many others was tied to a drug ring. If I didn't know better, I'd have thought he was one of Stan's boys!

But I turned him down. I actually wished him well, though the truth was I was too chicken and needed to get back to my ship. I was transforming from a kid from the hood into a sailor with a purpose, and I loved 3rd Division.

After that crazy encounter, I walked to the stern of the ship and noticed an Iranian gunboat tied up astern. I asked the lookout about it, and he said the Navy SEALs had boarded an Iranian vessel called a "Bog Hammer." The SEALs took the boat, but what happened to the Iranian sailors? Your guess is as good as mine, because the boat returned empty. Hooyah, Navy SEALs!

When Operation Praying Mantis ended, so did our deployment. We were relieved by another ammunition ship, and Battlegroup Foxtrot transited out of the Persian Gulf. We set a new record for ammunition ships: 117 days straight at sea and safely transferring thousands of tons of ordnance with zero incidents. We even had 2 "hump days," and the beer stayed in 3rd Division magazine. Don't think we didn't enjoy more Budweiser than the crew!

Now it was time for liberty. Hallelujah! The battlegroup was on a victory lap, visiting several countries on the way home.

First stop: Pusan, Korea. Modest and culturally rich but what do you do when you unleash more than 7,000 sailors and Marines on the city? You'll see!

We were there for five to seven days and were even invited to attend the 1988 Seoul Olympic Games. Day one went off without a hitch. Minor incidents popped up from pent-up testosterone, but day two had a different outcome.

Early evening found Texas Street in Pusan alive with parties and drinking. Just another Navy adventure no harm done.

But around 7:00 p.m., the old rivalry between Marines and sailors flared. A fight erupted, started by a USS Pyro sailor. The sailors and Marines battled in the first club, spilling into the streets. Looting followed. Guys who had just completed serious, dangerous missions were now smashing windows, grabbing knockoff shoes, bags, and whatever else they could find. Clearly, this was not professional behavior.

Long story short, Battlegroup Foxtrot was kicked out of Korea three days early. I was most irritated that I missed the Olympics. By the way, I did not participate in the looting. CANI (Constant and Never-Ending Improvement). In hindsight, maybe I should have nabbed a bomber jacket. Just kidding.

With our tails between our legs, we headed back to the Philippines for more debauchery and drinking. No longer cherry boys, we knew the ropes. But this time, my friends were more mature, reserved, and just wanted to go home. Could you blame them? After all, we set the record for the longest underway for ammunition ships, and yes, they made me dress like a California Raisin.

Finally, we arrived back in California at Concord Naval Weapons Station. Of course, they made me and a few others wear the raisin costume and dance while we were pulling in. The California Raisins sponsored the USS Pyro, which probably emboldened more skippers to think up more crazy ideas.

A Few of us Blackburn, Holtzclaw, Swanson, and I had no one waiting on the pier. Many others did, and I felt a pang of sadness. For us single guys, ordnance watch was assigned. We took more watches and duty days for $60 since we had no one. I didn't mind, as long as it didn't involve selling my body like the USS Gompers!

My twenty-four months onboard USS Pyro AE-24 taught me that I couldn't escape my past. I was a product of my environment, unsure I would measure up, and the Navy forced me to confront a culture clash. The old Vietnam-era mentality was fading, replaced by a Navy with a strict moral code. We were all changing and that was good.

For those of us from tough backgrounds, structure and discipline were the only way to change self-destructive patterns. I had to adapt or be left behind. By the way, some of the old guys rotated out and I moved to a bottom bunk. I was now a salty dawg.

Looking back at my early years, it was all about who was on the bus. I got mixed up with the wrong people in bootcamp, almost walking away from the Navy. I went AWOL within the first six months and even ran into a Chicago homie who ran a drug and prostitution ring on his ship.

Sometimes I thought I'd never survive this new reality. I learned to say "no" and avoid trouble at least temporarily. Stan used to listen to Motown, and when I secretly listened, I wondered: how could someone express such love so openly? Would I ever feel that way and find that type of love?

This strategy worked for a while, until the fading Vietnam-era sailors taught us how to drink like fish. Mix alcohol with underage, immature sailors carrying emotional baggage, and chaos was inevitable. We were adults overseas, but that privilege vanished when we returned stateside. I was angry for a thousand reasons, and the Navy and alcohol brought all my demons back. Frakenron was always lurking in the shadows.

Chapter Six

The Blame Game

"Neither heredity nor environment determines character. But whether we give in to or overcome the negative messages we are exposed to as we wind our way through life."

Michael Josephson

It's easy to blame our parents, teachers, bosses, the world for your problems. My transition into the U.S. Navy from a harsh environment certainly presented challenges. But I was determined to overcome them, even though I'd face a few more chances to revert to my old self. The Navy could rescue me, but first, I had to rescue myself. After all, the military is a machine designed to chew you up and spit you back out every time you mess up. They take your time, your money, and then push you back into the same system.

When I returned stateside, things moved quickly. I was trying to integrate into a life where my apartment literally was the ship. Many of my shipmates were looking for girls and getting married a couple of months later just to have a place to stay. My path, however, was more convoluted. While I had some girlfriends, none of the relationships worked out. And, surprise, surprise, a few of the women were a little crazy. One girl from San Francisco even stalked me after our breakup. She caught up with me in a parking lot one day and told me she should have "cut my face up" when she had the chance. Imagine that a girl capable of something like that. Just another bullet dodged. Still, I was determined to meet someone, though it turned out to be harder than I thought.

One Saturday night, the single guys and I went to "City Nights Disco" in San Francisco. Drinks were flowing, and I had a particularly bad experience with Brass Monkey, That Funky Monkey. After having way too much to drink, I was vomiting in the parking lot. Not exactly a romantic introduction.

I managed to stand up, and as I stumbled from behind the car, I noticed two girls walking towards me. I put on my best Chitown swagger and mumbled, "Where you two ladies headed? You look really good. By the way especially you." I pointed at the girl on the left. She seemed to like me and said her name was Jenifer Smith. Lucky me, even drunk out of my mind, my ship was docked in Vallejo, California, exactly where they lived. I asked Jenifer for her number, and within a week, we were dating. Over the next six months, Jenifer and I became inseparable. She let me stay with her off-base and even rushed me to the ship for muster in her Volkswagen Bug.

Jenifer had long blonde hair, was incredibly sweet, and came from a modest background like mine. Neither of us had role models to teach us how to be responsible adults. We soon lived together sharing chores and bills. We were both a little irresponsible, often missing payments, which led to creditors threatening us sometimes with bodily harm! Jenifer, however, was far more mature than me and knew how to handle things I had no clue about, like writing a check or balancing a bank account. Why I never learned these essential life skills in high school is still a mystery. I wish every kid were taught basic financial literacy. It would make life so much easier. Those six months with Jenifer were some of the best in my young life. I knew she was "the one."

Soon, our ship had to report to Long Beach Naval Shipyard for a quick repair and then return to Mare Island. Steven Sass, who had become a radioman on the ship, was leaving to attend college and pursue a naval officer career. I would truly miss him and all the memories we shared from crashing my first car to college parties. He was genuinely a good dude.

Before departing, Steven and I decided to spend a night on the town. It would be our last excursion before the ship left, and having a girlfriend didn't stop me. Naturally, Steve and I caused a ruckus. It was destiny. We crashed a prom, jumped over the marina fence, and took a dinghy to shorten the trip back to the ship. Stupid? Definitely. Sure enough, the police arrived, questioned us, but thankfully let us go.

You'd think another law enforcement encounter would deter us. Not a chance. Steve decided he wanted the flag flying in front of a hotel on a fifty-foot pole as a souvenir. Being the good guy, I was, I wanted to give him something to remember the night. I pulled the flagpole from the ground, and it slammed onto the road blocking traffic, but neglected to grab the flag.

We ran to the beach, laughing all the way. "Ron, I really wanted that flag," Steve said, his expression priceless. I told him to stay put and promised I'd get it. Always up for a challenge, I ran back, retrieved the flag, rolled it carefully under my arm aware of flag protocol and handed it to him. "Thanks, man, you're the best," he said. We headed back to base, Steve proudly carrying the flag as if he'd scored big.

When we returned to the pier, I decided to get some snacks from the vending machine. Potato chips, to be exact. I put my money in the slot, punched the right number, and waited for the chips to slide off the little belt to the bottom of the machine. But the damn thing got stuck! I shook it a few times, hoping the bag would come loose. The Master-at-Arms of Latin descent and a few other Latin guys who hung out like a gang on the ship saw me shaking the machine and were not happy.

"Vato, stop breaking the machine," the Master-at-Arms told me.

"I'm not breaking it, my damn potato chips got stuck," I said, giving it a few more shakes.

"You're full of shit. All you gringos are the same," he said, clearly pissed. I told him that if he didn't like our Navy, he could join the Mexican Navy.

Those were fighting words. The next thing I knew, he punched me in the gut, and I instinctively hit back. A fight broke out on the pier. Okay, maybe I was a bit inebriated. With my inhibitions down, I was determined to kick his ass until he relented.

Just in the nick of time, some of the officers from our ship heard the commotion and broke up the fight. They had me wait until the Latin guys boarded first. Little did I know, they were lying in ambush in the deck department berthing, ready to jump me.

It was actually exhilarating. My street-fighting experience gave me the adrenaline I needed to defend myself. Still, I sprained my ankle in one of the crane tracks on the pier when Steve tried to pull me away from the fight and my foot got caught.

After the melee, with my ankle killing me, Steve helped me back onto the ship. We passed through the quarterdeck and made our way up to the berthing. No sooner had I hobbled through the door than I was jumped again by about three testosterone-fueled Chicanos. I think I did alright for an intoxicated Chitown boy punching and kicking in a small, dimly lit berthing. I even punched one of them so hard that he slid across the deck.

This incident forced our ship to go on security alert, which caused a chain reaction, making the rest of the ships in Long Beach Shipyard follow suit. That was not good; I would soon find out why.

The next day, there was an investigation, and guess who knew how to write statements perfectly because it was his specialty. The Master-at-Arms. Just my luck. He submitted a perfectly penned statement and had his boys follow suit. I filled out my statement as if I were defending America and its way of life from a Mexican Master-at-Arms who hated our country.

Apparently, my strategy didn't work. I was written up for disrespecting a Senior Petty Officer, assault, and racial prejudice. Go figure, me, being a racist? I was a newly frocked E4, meaning I had the rank but not the commensurate pay. I was demoted from frocked

E4 to E2 and given forty-five days restriction, forty-five days extra duty, and fined half a month's pay for two months.

I was devastated. I hadn't started the fight, nor thrown the first punch. All I did was tell the truth, and I got slammed for it, while nothing happened to the Master-at-Arms or his posse.

It was another setback; one I hoped would never haunt me again. My actions that day represented one of the lowest points in my life.

I couldn't remain on the ship with a sprained ankle, so I was sent to Concord Naval Weapons Station to work in the gym for two months while my foot healed. This allowed my extra duty and restriction to be served on base. The petty officer in charge of me, named "Blue" didn't care what I did, and always gave me something benign for extra duty. Interestingly, he was being kicked out of the Navy for drug use.

Jenifer would visit me to hang out since I was stuck on base. She even snuck me off base in the trunk of her car a few times (though, as you know, I was accustomed to small, cramped spaces). She told me that her roommate had moved out and that it would be hard to keep up with rent. My immaturity and desire not to be alone motivated me to suggest to Jenifer that maybe we should get married to defray the apartment costs. She hesitated, so I let it drop.

But the next time she visited, she brought up marriage. I was shocked the idea had become serious. I told her I would have to get permission from my mom, expecting her to say no. Of course, my mom immediately said yes. My plan went south. But Jenifer, this feisty, blonde-haired, blue-eyed girl, didn't stop; there would be no more excuses.

I tried another tactic. I told her I couldn't get married because I was on restriction and doubted my commanding officer would grant special liberty for three days. Surprisingly, and much to my disdain, Commander Smith approved my extended liberty.

Long story short, I was sunk. I agreed to the wedding. We drove a few miles to Jen's house, where I sat in the bathtub and cut off my cast with a butcher knife. We decided to drive to South Lake Tahoe to get married, which was fairly easy back then. We had dinner with Jen's mother, a very nice lady with a heart of gold. I even asked Steve Sass to be my best man. I was resigned to the fact that I would soon be a married man and join the ranks of many of my Navy buddies.

The night before the wedding, Jen had her sister Beth's boyfriend watch me like a hawk. His mission: make sure I didn't run away and actually followed through with the wedding. Jenifer was not going to have a runaway husband!

The next day, we bought two wedding bands from a bubble-gum machine, because neither of us had any money. Heck, we didn't even pay for the wedding. Jen's family did. That's how broke we were.

Jen and I were married on June 3, 1989. We stayed married for twenty-eight years, through highs and lows, through everything the Navy and life threw at her. She remained committed and tough, like many Navy wives whose husbands were always away for long deployments or emotionally unavailable. More on that later.

Now, as a married man, I returned to the ship wearing my dungarees but where my E4 chevron once proudly sat, there was nothing. It was humiliating. At least some people were still talking to me. Generally, when you get into trouble, most sailors treat you like a walking contagion, they want no part of the stigma. By the way, as an E3, they sent me back mess cooking for 90 more days.

Enter Chief Louis Singleton. He was an amazing leader who, to my astonishment, became my mentor.

A short, thin Mississippi man, he was as professional as they come. What he lacked in size, he made up for in stature and presence. His quiet demeanor and expertise earned my immediate trust I wanted to follow him.

Over the next few years, he gave me advice drawn from years of Navy leadership and experience. One lesson stands out:

"Carpenter, you're a slave. Every time you get into trouble and are sent to Captain's Mast, you're just a slave. Why? Because all they do is take your money, take your time, give you extra duty, and take your freedom."

He reminded me that slaves worked for free, and I would always remain one unless I changed my attitude. Boy, did that hit me hard.

Chief Singleton was also a Golden Gloves boxer. Thanks to him, I learned how to box and carry myself with dignity, confidence, and strength. He was one of the coolest Chiefs I've ever known, and his life lessons changed me. I had to stop blaming everyone and everything for my problems. My Chitown ego far from saving me was getting me into trouble. Wearing the South Side of Chicago like a badge of honor was old news. Too often, someone on the ship would remark, "It don't surprise me. He's from the Southside of Chicago." Oddly, I thought it was a compliment. Once again, I was wrong.

I found in Chief Singleton a mentor worth emulating. He lit a fire under me, helping me let go of old habits and learn from my mistakes and from others'. You could say he was the father I wished I had.

Trust me, these "Old Gs" in the Navy had made their share of mistakes, and they weren't shy about sharing them.

Thanks to the Chief and my own realization that I could change for the better, I began moving back up the ranks. My alcohol issues and "FrankenRon" moments were fewer and far between. I realized that if I kept waking up drunk, apologizing for my previous night's antics, things had to change. If this was all I knew, ingrained in my DNA, shedding the past and embracing a new path would take time.

But slowly, things started to look up. I was doing so well that I was Command Advanced to E4, back in line with my peer group. I had enough time in rate to take the E5 test and passed on my first try. But the Navy pushed back: I wasn't supposed to be an E4 yet, nor eligible to take the E5 test.

The ship immediately demoted me to E3 to align with my time in rate, due to my Captain's Mast. Another setback. I was demoralized, but with newfound confidence and good behavior, I decided to fight. I was grateful that JAG on our ship helped me.

I submitted a chit requesting mitigation instead of remission. Mitigation means eliminating everything; remission means wiping out only part. The Commanding Officer signed it. By the way, we call it a "chit," from the Hindu word "Citthi," a slip of paper used for money so sailors wouldn't carry heavy bags of silver or gold.

I immediately requested a Captain's Mast to explain my case. Commander Smith was intimidating, and no officer dared question him, so I wasn't confident my request would be approved.

But after the Navy integrated women into ships, our executive officer was now female. I presented my case, and Commander Smith said, "Well, Seaman Carpenter, the reason I remitted your sentence is because your performance has been stellar." Crazy! Only a week ago, this same man called me "Petty Officer." Now, all of a sudden, I was a Seaman.

"With all due respect, sir, you did not remit my sentence you mitigated it, and mitigation means doing away with it entirely," I said defiantly.

"Are you calling me a damn liar?" he snapped.

"No, sir. Here's the chit you signed," I replied.

He looked at it, smiled, and said he'd take a knock on the cheek for that. Then he asked the panel how many Command Advancements he had left. They said, "One." That did the trick.

"We are command advancing Carpenter to E4."

"You can't do that, sir," the executive officer said.

He was really pissed now. "This is my damn ship, and I can do what the hell I please! Get all necessary paperwork to commence a package for the Board of Correction for Naval Records!"

My persistence paid off. A few months later, the board approved my appeal, reimbursing me for all the money I lost over the previous two years from E2 to E4, and erroneously promoting me to E5 because I had passed the earlier test. It felt like hitting the lottery! After so much turmoil, after wondering if I could ever change and become the man I wanted to be, I knew I could. Here I was finally, this Chitown troublemaker had turned the corner.

From this experience, I learned that if you aren't willing to stand up for something, you're liable to fall for anything. Boy, did I fight and win. When I was promoted to E5 at a command muster, the commanding officer said,

"Congratulations, Petty Officer Carpenter. You're like one of those country songs: if you play it backwards, you get your car back, your wife back, your dog back, and many more things. You've done a phenomenal job pulling yourself up by your bootstraps."

Those were words I will never forget. Words I had rarely heard about me. I saluted and said, "By your leave, sir!" He responded, "Carry on, sailor!"

With my rank restored and my behavior under control, life on the ship was finally coming together. I still got into minor trouble occasionally, but Chief Singleton kept an eye on me, as long as I wasn't hiding secrets or tarnishing the reputation of Third Division.

The older sailors, especially the brothers on the ship, called themselves the "Pyro Dawgs," and us younger sailors, the "Pyro Pups." Like many ships, our identity was tied to our vessel. For instance, the USS O'Bannon crew wore Boston Celtics caps because of their ship's Irish name. It was the Navy's version of Chicago gang life minus the drugs and violence.

With women officers onboard, a lot had to change. During a yard period, we created enlisted women's berthing and went through sensitivity training. Hunters Point Naval Shipyard, forty-five minutes from Vallejo, was where all repairs were done. The shipyard was in a rough neighborhood. During our first briefing, the police advised us not to stop at any lights or stop signs. Even a kid whose Mustang broke down had been killed calling for a tow truck.

Female officers adapted quickly because they had their own staterooms. But enlisted women took longer to integrate. With a female executive officer and more women onboard, we all had to adjust. Honestly, it was like high school all over again. At first, forgetting that women were present, we accidentally walked into the lounge in our underwear. Fortunately, we had tough senior female petty officers who didn't tolerate slacking or bogus sexual harassment reports. They were the rockstars of female integration onboard navy ships.

Initially, there were challenges. Some male sailors tried sneaking into female berthing with their onboard sweethearts, only to be caught and sent to Captain's Mast for restriction and extra duty. Ironically, the couple would be placed on restriction together. Did it stop them? No way.

After the yard period, in preparation for deployment, we transited to San Diego for Refresher Training (REFTRA). Our weapons division excelled; machine guns, gun mounts, and magazine sprinklers we nailed it. While transiting San Diego Harbor, I was on the bow manning an M60 machine gun with the forward lookout, calling out contacts. We spotted a red channel buoy and warned the bridge repeatedly, but it was too late we ran over it. The buoy, chained to a concrete block, tore up the propeller and wrapped the chain around the shaft. We had to pull into Naval Air Station North Island for assessment. The propeller was unsalvageable.

The replacement propeller was in Hawaii and shipping it would take thirty days. We informed our families and made the best of it: nightly liberty, flying home on weekends, or having our wives visit. Divers tried replacing the propeller in the water using detonation cord. It worked, but the new propeller wasn't properly installed. We had to be towed to 32nd Street Naval Shipyard for repairs. In the meantime, we maintained the ship by painting, scraping, and prepping for the next yard period.

Remaining in San Diego wasn't bad. I was a short timer on the boat, hoping to complete another deployment before leaving. San Diego, home to one of the largest naval fleets in the world, was a wild mix of ships, crews, and colors. Thirty-Second Street Naval Station even had a sports bar with a boxing ring for a dance floor. The Pyro Dawgs and Pyro Pups went to check it out. I was dancing with our ship's yeoman when I accidentally bumped into a sailor from the USS O'Bannon. He slapped me on the back of the head. I instinctively punched him, knocking his hat off. My buddy pulled me away, but all hell broke loose.

A massive fight erupted inside and outside the club. Some women, dressed to the nines, ended up unconscious in the street. BM1 Taylor, a burly country boy from our deck division, separated everyone. We ran back to the ship, went straight to our bunks, and passed out.

The next morning, I was summoned to the Master-at-Arms shack. I gave a truthful account. The USS O'Bannon singled me out as the instigator, charging me with breach of the peace, destruction of government property, and assault. I asked to see witness statements, but they weren't provided. My division wasn't informed either. Every Pyro Dawg corroborated my story: I only defended myself.

After the investigation, I was called back to sign a Page Thirteen, which was a permanent mark on my service record. But Chief Singleton intervened. He walked into the shack and tore the document in half. "Either take him to mast with evidence, or this stops here!"

Chief Singleton and Warrant Officer Ford always had my back, perhaps seeing a bit of themselves in me. I stayed on the ship a few more months and, surprisingly, earned "Sailor of the Month."

In July 1991, I received orders to Special Boat Unit Twenty-Six in Panama. I was about to become one of the guys with the Black

Berets who drove riverine boats and was an elite group with egos as big as the jungle and never responded to me when I said hello to them. Now, I would tryout to become one of them.

The blame game was over.

From here on, it was all up to me.

PART THREE

SPECIAL OPERATIONS TRAINING

Chapter Seven

Very Special Boat Teams: My New Tribe, Special Boat Unit Twenty-Six

"When you pray for rain, you gotta deal with the mud too"

– Robert McCall

The book Hero with a Thousand Faces, written by Joseph Campbell in 1949, outlines the hero's journey as consisting of three essential stages: The Call, The Quest, and The Return. In essence, if we do not pursue a purpose, we risk becoming lost, unfulfilled, or even depressed. Below are the three stages that Campbell identifies as shaping a hero, along with my personal adaptation to my own life's transformation.

The Call: To fully transform into the hero, you are meant to be, you must answer the call. When this calling tugs at your soul, you know you are exactly where you need to be.

The Quest: This stage is defined by hardships and challenges that forge you in fire. Through these trials, you discover who you truly are and refine your character. The Quest encompasses our highs and lows, failures and triumphs. It is simultaneously unsettling, demanding, and deeply rewarding. There is a saying that fits perfectly here: "Today's nightmares become tomorrow's memories." Another, equally apt, is: "Get comfortable with being uncomfortable."

The Return: This stage represents the fulfillment of your purpose and the complete transformation into a stronger, more confident self. For me, it was returning to Chicago as an honorable, self-assured person with a renewed sense of accomplishment and direction.

My journey to Panama mirrored this pattern. When my wife learned I had orders to Panama less than two years after "Operation Just Cause" she decided not to accompany me. I wish I had a choice, but I did not. I even went to Special Boat Unit 11 (SBU-11) to see if anyone would swap orders so I could stay in Vallejo, California with my wife. The operations officer promised to check for volunteers after morning muster. Almost the entire command stayed behind.

I wasn't naïve. I sensed there was something extraordinary about Special Boat Unit Twenty-Six. Their motto, "Somos Pocos, Pero Somos Locos" translated as "We are few, but we are crazy" spoke to their unique spirit. So, I kept my orders and boarded the plane, hoping my wife would join me later.

When I arrived in Panama, the tropical heat hit me like a slap from a hot oven. The duty watch picked me up at the airport and drove me to Rodman Naval Station. The base was sprawling, with two entrance gates; the back gate led to the main road connecting to Howard Air Force Base.

Sweating all the way, I checked in and was assigned to barracks on Radio Farfan, the Navy section of Howard AFB. By then, I was used to taking the base shuttle bus to work and navigated easily.

Once checked in, I was immediately assigned to the weapons department to learn every weapon system in our arsenal. That was when I realized this unit was different. The mindset and leadership style of my old ship didn't fit into Naval Special Warfare. I got the message loud and clear when a subordinate refused to follow my order as a second-class sailor. Like a fleeter, I tried to bring him up on charges but go figure, an FNG trying to write up someone who had been there longer and was about to transfer to the riverine detachments. Even the SEAL officers refused to hear my complaint, simply saying, "Work it out."

This Boat Unit was unlike anything I had ever experienced. Naval Special Warfare was the great equalizer. Predominantly white, with a smattering of Latinos and Black sailors, everyone got along effortlessly. Each member was determined to succeed. You could see it in their eyes, a mix of extreme confidence and a "Don't fuck with me" attitude. They carried themselves like a tribe, about 140 strong in SBU-26. Race, gender, religion, and social class didn't matter. They truly embodied, "Somos Pocos, Pero Somos Locos."

Navy SEALs from SEAL Team 4 were assigned to Unit 8, just blocks away from our compound. Our compound featured a massive, fenced section called the "Boat Barn," where riverine boats were kept, along with pier space on the Panama Canal for larger patrol boats. Many of the boat operators had served in combat during Operation Just Cause. Vietnam-era SEALs and Boat Guys, respected and feared simultaneously, were also present. Though over twenty years removed from Vietnam, they were still masters of the jungle environment, ensuring we were ready for anything.

I had to spend six months in the Armory before attempting Jungle School, which was necessary to become an operator rather than remaining in a support role. The unit's hierarchy, operator versus support gave me something to strive for and became motivation for my new beginning in Naval Special Warfare.

When I expressed my intention to try out for the three-week Jungle School, the leadership asked if I could swim. I admitted I could, but only a little. They took me to the pool to test my skills, including an exercise in which I had to walk across the pool bottom carrying a heavy sandbag, taking no more than two breaths along the way.

I knew I could sink at any moment, so I grabbed the sandbag, but I wasn't much of a floater. I went under, clutching the sandbag for dear life. Somehow, I made it to one end of the pool, but I had no idea how to surface. I kept struggling across the pool until I realized I was at the side.

"Are you stupid, Carpenter?" they yelled.

"Why?" I gasped, breathless from holding my breath so long.

"Because you blacked out in the water." I got the message.

Though humiliated, I refused to give up. I told them I just wanted a chance and didn't want to be a loser. It felt like a lightning bolt striking me. Like a positive message from the universe. To my surprise, like my experience on the ship, these SEALs and SWCC embraced me and began teaching me how to float and swim. Senior Chief Mann was a beast with a heart. He never asked us to do anything he wasn't willing to do himself. He would PT us mercilessly, and his claim to fame in Naval Special Warfare (NSW) was that he had once been hospitalized for exercising too much. Think about that, getting hospitalized for working out too much! Priceless.

I got invited to my first country bar at Clayton Army Base. Being a city kid from Chicago, I had no clue about country bar etiquette—I showed up in a GQ shirt with the top button done. I was there with Boatguys, SEALs, and Bullfrog Hershel Davis—the most senior SEAL at the time.

I was making rounds, saying hello, when out of nowhere an older guy lit into me about talking to women in cowboy hats and having my shirt buttoned up. I told him to fuck off… and instantly got surrounded by a bunch of Army SF. One of them yelled, "You just disrespected the most senior Green Beret." I'm thinking, here we go—Captain's Mast, rank gone again.

Then Bullfrog stepped in. "Carpenter, what's the problem?" I told him. That I just told the most senior Green Beret to fuck off. He walked straight into the middle of the group, asked who it was, and when I pointed him out, Bullfrog started jabbing fingers and handing out a very direct "fuck you, fuck you, fuck and fuck you too" to each of them.

By then the SEALs and Boatguys had surrounded the group. That was all it took—they knew they were outnumbered and backed off.

That's when it hit me—I was part of the biggest gang in the world. You mess with me; you mess with all my boys. This was where I wanted to belong my entire life.

After about four months, nearing the end of my Armory tour, I was ready to try out for Jungle School. I passed the screening and attended the three-week course. The physical training was brutal: run swim runs, San Juan Hill times two, Seven- mile run from Pedro Miguel Locks back to base, capped with a 500 or 1000 meter pool swim, and then run back to the unit. It got to the point where we would literally be sweating while swimming in the pool.

The grueling training hardened our bodies and sharpened our minds. We learned communications, weapons, explosives, land navigation, ambush and counter-ambush tactics, and a wide array of jungle techniques dating back to the Vietnam War. Technology may change, but jungle warfare remains timeless.

Week three brought us to Fort Sherman Base on the Caribbean side for Jungle Operations Training Battalion (JOTB), the culmination of everything we had learned. There was an obstacle course called the "Green Hell" that tested us relentlessly. We were divided into five teams and tasked with setting up camp in the jungle. Marine Force Recon acted as our opposing force, attempting to infiltrate our camps at night. If we detected them, we were instructed to flash our flashlight and shout "halt."

Our chief cleverly placed our camp on a hill so water would drain away. Our jungle hammocks had waterproof roofs and mosquito netting on the sides keeping us dry and bite-free. But when the instructors visited, they forced us to relocate to the bottom of the hill during Panama's monsoon season. Being a city boy, I was terrified.

No sooner had I taken the watch than it began to rain as if someone had turned on a firehose. Our basecamp turned into a swimming pool, with water ankle-deep in the darkness. My imagination ran wild; I remembered that there were supposedly thousands of snakes per square mile of jungle. I flashed my light frantically and shouted "halt," turning our camp into a disco of flashing lights until my chief told me to "shut the hell up." Thank goodness my two-hour watch ended, and I survived without a single snake bite.

I crawled back into my hammock, with my boots dangling upside down from sticks I planted in the mud to keep critters out. I should have wrapped a stick around each hammock line to deflect water, but I skipped the step and paid the price. Within an hour, I awoke freezing, lying in fifty gallons of water that had pooled in my hammock. Exhausted, I used my MK3 ("we called Mark Three Mod Shitty") dive knife to puncture holes to drain the water. Big mistake. The water's force split the hammock, dumping me onto the ground. With nowhere else to sleep, I took the remainder of the night watch. By the way, our knives couldn't even open a coconut without the tips breaking off.

Jungle School continued relentlessly: more running, more swimming in rivers and open water, more physical fitness, and more land navigation in triple-canopy jungle. We learned how to tie parachute cord correctly so it wouldn't slip as our team forded rivers holding the line. And why did I, weighing barely a 150lbs, volunteer as the M60 machine gunner?

Carrying ammo belts and my machine gun, I clung to the line as we crossed a river. In the military, there's a "ten percent rule," meaning some people will fail or need remediation. I saw this firsthand when someone tied their knot incorrectly; the line slipped, and I sank. My feet hit the river bottom. I decided to walk along it to the other side only to realize later that I had become disoriented and was walking in the wrong direction.

The line broke, and I sank, rotating as I went. I walked along the river bottom for what felt like an eternity, but my breath ran out in less than a minute. Struggling to reach the surface with all my gear, ammo and weapons I swallowed my pride and called out to my team for help. Note to self: if you are drowning in life and about to black out, ask for help and take the lifeline.

It was humiliating and it wouldn't be the last time I needed a swim buddy in my career. Our egos often get the best of us, and we tend to hold everything in our bucket until it overflows. I learned early, that I couldn't function in the boat teams without my team, and I needed them to help empty my bucket when it got too full. This lesson requires having two or three close friends with whom you can share your burdens, so your bucket doesn't get too full. More on this later.

During this phase of my early career, we continued learning a wide range of tactics and techniques. I especially loved mastering ambushes, counter-ambushes, and immediate action drills designed to survive a firefight. The Vietnam-era SEALs were incredible teachers; many looked as if they had been teleported straight back to Vietnam. Their senses were almost supernatural. They could hear a snake slithering in the underbrush where none could be seen. They could identify trip wires instantly and taught us the proper use of lights in the jungle. Red lenses were essential; green lenses were prohibited because maps could not be read under green light.

Next, we learned how to construct a poncho raft. Imagine using a Vietnam-era poncho as a raft: lay it on the ground, place all your gear on top, and wrap it to float. Your rifle remained on top as you pushed and pulled the raft across water. This would have saved me a few days earlier when I nearly drowned. Jungle training with the Vietnam SEALs forced me to take every lesson seriously, especially if I wanted to act like a macho man carrying the heaviest weapon on the team.

Our teams were regularly sent on missions rescuing downed pilots, conducting extractions, or performing reconnaissance. Once a plan was made, we executed it. "Plan your op and op your plan," we were always reminded.

Sleep was scarce between missions, and we learned to depend on each other. I became so exhausted that I was no longer afraid of the jungle, and I would lay my head anywhere under my poncho to avoid vampire bats. These bats don't land on you they creep near you. They lick the spot they plan to bite to numb it. Stories circulated of soldiers losing chunks of flesh because they failed to cover themselves properly while sleeping. This was a world I had never encountered in Chicago.

Training became more frequent and intense. We learned fire-and-movement tactics, including center peels, peel-left, and peel-right maneuvers during ambushes. Peels involved laying down heavy fire while retreating without hitting one another. We studied booby traps and explosives under SEAL instructors, then learned the Green Berets' more precise methods. SEAL techniques, often tracing back to World War II Underwater Demolition Teams, favored raw power: "That looks big. Place a satchel bag on it." One satchel contained twelve one-pound blocks of C4, obliterating not only the target but everything nearby.

Green Berets, however, insisted on calculation. They chastised us for using a satchel without thought, measured the object, and determined the precise number of C4 blocks needed. Their approach minimized collateral damage while cutting the target cleanly. We appreciated the correctness but secretly preferred the louder, more satisfying explosions of the SEAL method.

Jungle missions were deceptive in distance. A target might be thirty minutes away "as the crow flies," but a new boat guy could take ten hours, crawling over hills, hacking through sawgrass, or disentangling from "catch-me-fuck-me" vines. Then there were Black Palm thorns that pierced leather gloves, deadly snakes, killer bees, tiny but lethal Golden Frogs, and howler monkeys that sounded like King Kong and chased us into rivers. Fun times indeed.

Night operations were equally treacherous. Lacking night vision, it was pitch black. Point men frequently fell into unseen holes, followed by the rest of the team. At times, we reached extraction points and successfully signaled boats with flashlights, but sometimes the bow of the boat slammed into our point man, sending us rolling down steep riverbanks. We would laugh and struggle back up the muddy bank.

Despite all this, I began to grow confident in my skills. If I could survive in the hood with limited resources, I knew I could handle the jungle.

We were rolling along, getting up checks for our missions, feeling pretty good about ourselves exhausted, but always ready to go. We were ordered to execute a Combat Search and Rescue mission. Quickly, we jumped into the helos that were waiting.

At one site, the helo simulated taking enemy fire and suffered a hard landing. We disembarked immediately and set a perimeter. We were taught how to establish a landing zone and worked on helo insert and extract procedures. Then we were given coordinates to rendezvous with PBR Street Gang, a Vietnam-era riverine patrol boat, at the extraction point. After about an hour, we met up with the boat. Riding on that boat, listening to the diesel engines and watching the gunners man their weapons, made us stay vigilant. It was incredible.

No sooner had we settled, we were tasked with another CSAR. The PBR would insert us at a point, and we would move inland to extract two downed pilots. As we prepared to disembark, the PBR got stuck in soft mud. When we hit the shore, a loud explosion lifted the boat out of the water, wedging it deeper into the muck.

The firefight that followed was deafening, amplified by the twin .50 caliber machine guns on the bow affectionately called "Ma-Deuces." Simulated grenades exploded in close proximity, blinding and deafening us. The enemy boarded the boat, pulling people off and beating them. I slid into the water, hugging the riverbank. A large figure leaned over the bank. I pointed my rifle, fitted with a blank-firing adaptor, and emptied half my magazine at him. He was so big he lifted me out of the water with one arm, threw me to the ground, and demanded I drop my gear.

"I'm talking to a dead man," I said.

He walked a few steps away, and I picked up my weapon and fired again. He turned and executed a karate kick that flipped me ass over teakettle. That was it, I complied. Soon we were stripped nearly naked, left in our UDT swim trunks with boonie hats duct-taped to our faces.

Then the "torture" began. Cages, gadgets, and simulations designed to extract information. One guy caved, asking for a cigarette and an MRE and he would talk. That was the unacceptable "wimp factor," and he was barred from any deployable boat detachments.

As for me, I ended up hanging ten feet off the ground, arms tied behind my back. So much tension caused my hand to slip, and I fell to the ground. Hours passed, and bugs feasted on our exposed flesh, and let's not forget the water torture devices and cage at the river.

Eventually, we got into a routine. Around five in the morning, they untied us and went to Training Time Out (TTO) to debrief and reinforce key points of performance. New coordinates were given, and we had until 1400 to reach the rendezvous point for helo extraction or face a brutal ride back to Rodman in the back of deuce-and-a-half trucks.

Our team arrived with twenty minutes to spare and heloed back to Rodman Naval Station. How they crammed so much jungle training into such a short period was beyond me. I just knew I needed medical attention. My one-eyed Willie Worm had been burned by Vietnam-era insect repellent ("called bug juice") I'd foolishly kept in my pocket. Another fun day in the jungle.

I survived Jungle School by shedding more of my Chicago fears and learning to trust people with my well-being, as they trusted me with theirs. These men became my family. I realized there was nothing I couldn't do because my new Dirty Boatguy (DBG) tribe had my back. If I failed, they'd pick me up, brush me off, and tell me to keep pushing. A great man once said, "If you are going to fall, fall on your back, because if you can look up, you can get up." Surrounded by Boat Guys and SEALs who embodied this daily, I was on my way.

I was transferred from the Armory to the sixty-eight-foot patrol boats. I was assigned to PB 841. My quest to become a Special Warfare Combat Crewman (SWCC) had begun. I couldn't believe I had made it through this intensive training and was now part of a tribe I could be proud of. My old "bad boy" self, was transforming. My new family had my back. We were a team destined for some of the most difficult coastal missions. I was ready.

Go Hard or Go Home!

Chapter Eight

Qualifying as a Combatant Craft Crewman and Boat Captain

"Boats of Glass, Balls of Brass, Boatguys forever."

Vietnam Boatguys

I finally made it through SBU-26 Jungle School and six months working in the Armory. I mastered every weapon inside and out to keep them operational. What a journey but I learned survival techniques and the discipline necessary to survive any life-threatening situation in combat or during counter-drug operations throughout Central and South America.

After training, I was assigned to a MK IV Sea Spectre Patrol Boat, an oxidized grey aluminum gunboat loaded to the teeth with weapons. And I mean weapons! Forward and aft 25mm chain guns, an 81mm mortar with a .50 caliber machine gun mounted on top, a 60mm mortar, a Mk-19 grenade launcher, a .50 caliber machine gun, 4–7.62mm machine guns, plus various small arms and rifles. The boat had three 12V71TI Detroit diesel engines, capable of propelling it close to thirty knots. We had a saying for our boat: "You may run, but you will die tired."

We were a seven-man crew, able to live aboard for extended periods. Six bunks and a three-in-one kitchen unit allowed us to store food and cook while underway. The boat could sustain us for at least five days with water and supplies and could transit continuously for twenty-four hours. That was enough to get from Panama to Cartagena, Colombia, before needing to refuel.

Becoming a qualified NEC 9533 crewman was daunting. I nearly passed out when handed the stack of qualification manuals.

They were more than a foot thick. Thousands of line items required signatures for tasks performed. We had to master weapons, engineering, navigation, communications, coxswain training and the list never ended. The qualified boat captains at SBU-26 were a breed apart. Brutal taskmasters, but necessary for the complex, dangerous missions ahead.

Signatures were earned, never handed out. Their mantra: "Earn it! If you want it, go get it!" I had assumed qualifications would be quick but not at SBU-26. It took about a year to qualify as a Crewman. Another year to qualify as a Boat Captain. Then you had to pass the Crewman and Boat Captain Boards, which tested whether you "knew your shit" and could represent the team.

Thus far in my nascent Navy career, I had survived Boot Camp and a tour on a Navy ship, but nothing compared to the satisfaction and sense of accomplishment of serving in Naval Special Warfare SBU-26 on Patrol Boat 841.

At the time, SBU-26 was the Navy's only hybrid coastal and riverine boat unit. The unit prided itself on its reputation and professionalism. Boats were always combat-ready and maintained meticulously. Weapon systems were lubricated, tested, and prepared for war.

Our missions supported SOUTHCOM across Central and South America, and the Caribbean. Most missions were Building Partner Capacity for US Counter Drug Initiatives, but some felt straight out of a movie.

For example, three-man teams consisting of a boat guy, a SEAL, and a communications expert would integrate with partner forces. Secret tactical satellite messages were downloaded, decrypted, read, and then burned. Once we knew the content, we passed it to our partner force to execute direct-action missions on drug labs, or narco planes about to land in the jungle, or on the roads. Being assigned to SBU-26 was like hitting the lottery. Mastering the skills needed to take out bad guys and defend the US was exhilarating.

Our patrol boat frequently transited the Panama Canal between the Pacific and the Caribbean. We had to pass the Panama Canal Commission test for a license to transit the canal, so we developed an acronym: "Miles Per Gallon 213" MPG-213.

The canal has three locks, powered by eight-horsepower motors that open and close massive doors. Water levels differ between the Pacific and Atlantic, so moving through the canal is like walking upstairs, crossing a passageway, and walking downstairs. MPG-213 stood for: Miraflores locks have two, Pedro Miguel has one, Gatun has three. After Miraflores and Pedro Miguel, we enter Gatun Lake, one of the world's largest man-made lakes, which took five years to fill and eight hours to cross before reaching Gatun Locks on the Caribbean side.

Transiting was intense. Larger cargo ships often loomed behind us, and we smelled diesel exhaust as we tightened or slacked lines securing the boat to the wall. We embraced the challenge, summed up simply: "We hate this fucking canal."

But we pushed through, as good boat guys are trained to do.

Looking back, my early years in Naval Special Warfare were an experience of a lifetime. Transiting this engineering marvel was awe-inspiring, a tribute to President Teddy Roosevelt, who ensured the canal's construction during Panama's fight for independence. Traversing this historic waterway repeatedly was part of defending the southern approaches of the United States.

NSW patrol boats were literally deployed around the world. These frequent deployments were hard on us and even harder on our families.

Like other Special Operations communities, Naval Special Warfare had a very high divorce rate. Balancing work and home life was a daily battle, and the guilt of not being there for our families weighed heavily. Emotional availability was scarce. How could we be present when we were in foreign countries on high-pressure missions? There was no time to dwell on the baseball game you missed or the kid's dance recital you couldn't attend. Those moments were gone forever. You get the picture.

In the early 1990s, our culture around marriage was very different than it is today. I cannot tell you how many times I heard commanders say, "Your wife didn't come in your fucking seabag! So, do your fucking job!" I "Charlie Miked" continued the mission because I had no choice, and I loved my job.

Being married for just three years, with my wife living in Panama, presented its own challenges. Departing for one to three month deployments and leaving Jenifer, a California girl, alone in a country recently at war, was tough. To make things worse, she lived in Obarrio, spoke no Spanish, and had to navigate riots, student protests, and criminals who removed manhole covers to rob unsuspecting drivers. Jenifer and I fought constantly. She felt my absence and lack of communication meant I didn't care, but in truth, I had to hyper-focus on missions and training. Dividing attention could have deadly consequences for my team and me.

Things improved once we moved on base after a year of living in town. The lack of housing and leaving families without support, had caused many marriages to fail. On base, NSW families were all we had, and we leaned on each other.

The best part of the Special Boat Teams, unlike my experience on the ship, was the camaraderie among the Naval Special Warfare members. We always had each other's backs, protecting one another tirelessly on land and at sea.

On PB 841, our watch sections rotated every four to six hours, with three-person teams: one man drove, one navigated, and one checked engines and took readings. As a South Side Chicago native, I could hardly believe I was entrusted as a watch section leader, responsible for safely transiting to other countries. Often, I had to pinch myself to remind me that I was actually succeeding at something far greater than my youthful expectations.

Being part of an exclusive team and training together in some of the most difficult environments in the world made me love the boat teams even more. We did everything together; the bond we shared was unshakable. EN1 Carol, BM2 Ball, GMG2 Macgregor, RM2 Wainscott, BM1 Edmondson and Chief Prystop, and me formed a gang devoid of drugs and violence. We truly became a band of brothers.

My expertise was weapon. The quartermaster handled navigation, the engineer oversaw engines, the radioman managed communications, and the boatswain mate taught boat handling, preservation, painting, line splicing, and knot tying. Over time, we all became versatile, knowing each other's roles intimately as if we collectively embodied every NEC on the team.

My first journey to Cartagena, Colombia, was amazing. A sixty-eight-foot patrol boat, and a team that became my family with each having a different expertise that they were unafraid to share. We created redundancy in our capabilities by knowing each other's roles.

With this stellar team, we transitioned in the open ocean, utterly alone, save for the occasional military or Coast Guard overflights to confirm our status. After twenty-four hours, we arrived in Colombia and stayed thirty to forty-five days training their boat team and Coast Guard.

These missions became increasingly complex. Our skill level grew, and the missions became longer. PB 841 and our sister boat PB-842 could operate anywhere, and there was no task too difficult.

One mission to Maracaibo, Venezuela, stood out. The five-day transit included refueling stops in Cartagena, San Andres, and Aruba. In Cartagena, we stayed overnight, but not at a hotel. The good thing was, we visited Cartagena so much that we would go back to the same hotel that we just stayed at to jump in the pool to wash off our twenty-four-hour stench before breakfast.

San Andres offered brief luxuries, though modest. The hotels were far from upscale, with brackish water showers that never left you feeling clean. Still, it didn't stop us from exploring town and drinking. A local strip club even kicked us out after we unleashed stink bombs from Cartagena.

Aruba, by contrast, was highly Americanized. English was widely spoken, and many American expats lived there. That was comforting.

During temporary assignments, the Navy issued cash advances for travel. Each of us often had $8,000–$10,000 to cover hotels and meals. Early on, many of us mismanaged these funds, leaving families financially strained. I became more responsible after my Aruba experience.

My South Side nature emerged. I tried my luck as a high roller, losing eighty percent of my per diem at the local casino. Four days remained, and I barely had money to sustain myself. I survived by eating at Wendy's and sticking with officers who covered drinks in Venezuela or invited me to VIP functions. Despite the chaos, I maintained professional behavior in-country, completing missions and learning from experience.

Macgregor was an exceptional operator. He was an unassuming blond-haired southern boy who weighed a buckle-five soak and wet, he excelled at everything he did. His personality made people love and want to protect him. Pleasant, knowledgeable, but never a show-off. Underway, he was in his element, demonstrating unmatched skill in survival, weapons, and fishing.

Our transit to Bocas Del Toro in Panama's San Blas Island chain exemplified Macgregor's expertise. The U.S. government was required to conduct medical, dental, and veterinary assistance to remote communities, and our team provided force protection for Army Landing Craft transporting supplies and personnel.

When we arrived, Macgregor and Lipps, our electronics technician, drove a Zodiac ashore to make first contact. It seemed straightforward until a Kuna Indian ran toward them, pointing a rusty revolver at their faces. I reacted immediately, grabbed an M60 machine gun with one hundred rounds of ammo, and covered them from the patrol boat's deck. Macgregor recognized the situation, backed off, and returned to the boat.

Hours later, we learned the village chief second-in-command had unnecessarily escalated the incident. The village chief was furious, chastising him and hanging him upside down by his feet. The Army medics described the scene as chaotic, unsure whether to intervene.

Deployments often required careful judgment regarding partner force intentions and adherence to human rights. On multiple occasions, we had to halt training because partner force leadership overstepped, engaging in outright violations. These experiences were a valuable lesson in respecting human life and cultural differences while maintaining operational effectiveness. Special Operations forces, in my experience, excel at understanding culture and local dynamics. Our lives depended on it, when embedding with partner forces under the "By, With and Through" concept.

This period of my Naval career was filled with unique, memorable experiences. From walking among topless Kuna Indian women that were certainly not familiar with Americans providing medical care, assisting in dental procedures, calling in medevac helicopters, and administering rabies vaccines to animals ranging from dogs and chickens to cows and goats, it was a culture shock and a once-in-a-lifetime experience.

During this time, I was constantly amazed at the talent within Naval Special Warfare. Macgregor, for instance, called to animals in Kuna language to administer vaccines "Cope, Cope, Cope" demonstrating extraordinary skill. Individually, we may not have seemed impressive, but together, combining all our Naval Enlisted Classification (NEC) skills, we were unstoppable.

Occasionally, veteran engineers provided lessons on Detroit diesel engines. Though older, they brought decades of experience and a calm confidence that I admired. Their guidance was invaluable, tempered with humor and a rough-and-tumble style cursing freely.

One day, while working on the engines, the starboard turbo blanket unexpectedly caught fire. Of all people to be the hero, EN1 Carol the first-class engineer, though unassuming and slightly nerdy in appearance, he was incredibly knowledgeable. Shorter than most of us, with thick glasses and a slightly awkward demeanor, he was nonetheless the heart of our engineering capability on PB 841.

Of course, he had been trained by the cranky old engineers. He knew his job inside and out and carried the same confidence as the veterans. It didn't take long for him to earn our respect.

One day, BM1 Ball and I were in the engine room replacing the starboard engine head, when EN1 Carol suspected he had put the Halon system in test mode. (Routine checks like this were done periodically.) But he hadn't. So, he brought the flame from his lighter to the heat sensor, activating the Halon system. Ball and I were stuck on the side of the engine and couldn't get out fast enough. So much for "test mode."

White dust billowed everywhere. Ball and I struggled to escape. We could barely breathe and were completely covered. Our first instinct was to throttle Carol but instead, we jumped into the water, rinsed off, and went back to work. After all, we were a team.

Carol redeemed himself later that week when a runaway engine on the starboard side caused the turbo blanket to catch fire again. Everyone panicked except Carol. Had he not been there, we would have triggered the Halon system and pulled the emergency flappers, potentially destroying the engine. Like the old engineers who likely taught him under similar circumstances, he called us "idiots" and shoved us aside as the engine screamed out of control. He made sure he had an audience. Leaning over the roaring engine that sounded ready to explode, Carol lit his cigarette from the flames. It was pure Humphrey Bogart.

He covered the turbo blanket with a rag, cutting off the air supply, shut off the fuel, and let the engine starve itself. Then he looked at us with disdain: "If you idiots had pulled the flappers, we'd be rebuilding the engine because the O-rings would have been sucked in." His scolding became a critical learning moment, delivered with respect.

Carol and others were heroes that taught us to think before we acted and to understand every detail of our patrol boat and complex systems.

Over time, our patrol boat became the prototype for all types of exercises and training. We would fire 60mm and 81mm illumination rounds for Army SF on one side of the canal, then support SEALs in Gatun Lake within the same week. We transported the SEALs' rubber boats and outboard motors called Z-Birds along with all their ammo and explosives.

One training session tested our resolve like never before. We moved so much RDX explosive that it covered a large area of McFall Base Camp pier. It was located in Gatun Lake after the Pedro Miguel Locks. As I dusted off a box, I noticed the date: 1944. When the exercise ended, we were ready to relax but orders prohibited returning the explosives to base. The SEALs decided to place the remaining boxes on an out-of-service navigation buoy, only about 400 yards from camp.

Four SEALs got their Zodiac underway, attached the explosives, and pulled the time fuse. They made it roughly 100 yards from the pier before their engine stalled. Furiously rowing back to the pier, they were a sight to behold. We laughed so hard it felt like watching a comedy show. But once they reached the pier and ran into the jungle, our laughter stopped. We jumped up a ran behind em.

My teammates and I sprinted after them almost 200 yards into the jungle when the biggest explosion I had ever heard detonated in the canal. The training area limit was twenty-five pounds of explosives. Clearly, we had exceeded it.

We hunkered down as water from the blast rained down. No one knew how high the buoy had flown, but the explosion was deafening. My first thought: Did our boats survive? The nearby Army base reported shattered windows. The SEALs insisted they had only used twenty-five pounds, conveniently omitting a zero. But "shit" happens during training and actual missions. Fortunately, we treated every incident as a learning experience, guided by our mantra: "Admit nothing, deny everything, and make counteraccusations." Accountability? Optional.

After countless grueling exercises, I completed my tour on PB 841 and earned my 9533 Boat Crewman designation. I became a seasoned boat professional except in the riverine environment. The best was still to come.

Having patiently awaited my turn, I was transferred to Riverine Det Alpha under Chief Martin. He was the detachment commander of a two-boat riverine detachment. Chief Martin, an Alabama native, judged us solely on performance, not race or background. He treated everyone harshly until we mastered our jobs. His confidence was contagious, and he instilled leadership in every aspect of our work. His Navy rating was Boatswain's Mate. A rate that forces sailors to become leaders at lower ranks. Chief Martin brought that leadership to the table every single day.

This was the pinnacle of my tour and a place every boat guy dreams of being assigned. I soon discovered why SBU-26 was the best boat unit in NSW. I retired my ocean charts, picked up maps and compasses, learned riverine tactics, mastered light and noise discipline, and loved talking to Vietnam SEALs about their experiences during the war.

Unlike PB-841, which was loaded to the hilt with weapons and would have made any enemy a fool to challenge us, this boat was less complex, but the mission was far more serious. Engagements were up close and personal, where the enemy could grab you by the belt and you would have to fight it out in close quarters. This reality was true in Vietnam, during my Panama tour, and again in Iraq, where my Riverine Troop participated in the largest waterborne firefight since Vietnam. I will tell that story later.

The boat was a twenty-five-foot Boston Whaler Guardian with twin 300-horsepower engines, navigation and communication systems, radar and GPS, one forward gun mount, and two aft gun mounts. Unlike the open ocean, the rivers were so narrow that our boats could barely fit. We had to learn the terrain and understand the bends and shifting shoals and natural formations like ridges or bars that rise to the surface of the water. We also had to master board and search, waterborne guard posts, and ambush/counter-ambush tactics from the water. Night vision goggles were rare; we were lucky to receive a single pair per detachment back then. We had to learn the old ways of riverine warfare.

We had to become experts at the art of insertion and extraction of Navy SEALs a task that was anything but easy. To complicate matters, there was precision fire, among the most challenging tactics in Naval Special Warfare. Essentially, we had to maneuver close to land and SEAL teams, laying down suppressive fire while extracting them under fire. This is called a "Hot Extract."

The SEALs would mark their left and right flanks, which they called UDT left and right, using smoke, flashlights, or chemlights tied to a rope and spun to create a unique light pattern. We conducted dry runs over and over, switched to blank ammo, and finally moved to live ammo. Over the radio, we would hear, "Blackjack, Blackjack, this is Kilo One, Kilo One, over." We replied, "Kilo One, this is Blackjack, over."

They would respond, "Roger, request immediate hot extract, primary extract point. We are taking fire from our nine o clock," troops in the open. We would repeat their message, give an estimated time of arrival, and confirm, "You mark, I identify?" (Watch the movie Act of Valor to see it in action.)

During the hot extract, we drove at high speed. Once we identified the method the SEALs used to mark their flanks, they would confirm, and one boat would scream toward the bank, going neutral about twenty feet from the beach so the stern wake would push the boat onto land ,all while firing at the enemy. Boat 1 would beach the boat, pick up the SEALs, then shift to take overwatch. Boat 2 would transition to extract the remaining SEALs.

We practiced fire suppression with no lulls to maintain fire superiority and get the SEALs off the beach. To this day, apart from our senior NSW leaders, many high-ranking officials outside NSW considered this training too dangerous because of the precision required firing miniguns and heavy machine guns near friendly forces while boats maneuvered within three feet of one another. A well-known SEAL Master Chief once said, "It's not that we're that good; it's just that everyone else sucks." I will always embrace that saying, because Special Operations relies on volunteers who execute basic skills extraordinarily well. It is how we separate the rock stars from the groupies.

The bottom line: we trained for war the way Vietnam-era boat guys did. Chief Martin was an Operation Just Cause veteran. This offensive was launched against Manuel Noriega in December 1989, when the US Air Force transported more than 27,000 troops using 300 aircraft.

Chief Martin, as you can imagine, was a tough son of a bitch. Over time, we realized he was an "asshole" strict. Demanding nothing less than precision from our team. We were too young to fully grasp why he trained us the way he did, but he sure made his point clear. His abrasive style became his signature, and it made us better boat guys.

After all, Chief Martin focused on one goal: the mission. Success. No excuses.

We also had to deal with Vietnam-era SEALs, such as George Anger and his cohorts Ted, Scott, and many others whom George skillfully trained as his personal little "Mini-Me's." Looking back, it was clear they wanted us to fear them more than any other enemy we would face on real-world missions. Even during the fiercest firefights in Iraq, no enemy scared me more than Senior Chief Anger and the ambushes he would set up. (And yes, there is some irony in the fact that his last name was "Anger.")

For example, many times he and the rest of the OPFOR (Opposing Force) set up gasoline cannons on the riverbanks. As our boats passed, these cannons ignited, sending walls of fire onto the boats. Detachments would return from training missing eyebrows and with half their hair singed. All we had to ask was, "Senior Chief

Anger?" They would respond with a hound-dog look and a simple nod. Even if your detachment hadn't experienced it directly, the thought alone had a psychological impact, sharpening our focus during every training scenario. We learned to avoid soap or any unnatural chemicals that might betray our presence. We understood that peeling an orange could send the scent for a mile. In the jungle, sound travels up to 2,000 yards during the day, and up to 5,000 yards at night. Over and over, we practiced our tradecraft against a formidable enemy. One of the deadliest on the planet if his full potential were unleashed: a Vietnam-era Navy SEAL.

Occasionally, some detachment leaders would complain to Commanding Officer (CO) about Senior Chief Anger's heavy hand. This is after suffering an ambush that set the boat and passengers on fire and forced everyone to jump into the river. Here's how the conversation typically went: as the detachment stood before the CO, George Anger would walk in. The CO would ask why the detachment had singed hair and why a boat had been damaged going down the river. Senior Chief Anger would reply emphatically, "Sir, Train Like You Fight, Fight Like You Train!" The CO would nod and say, "Carry on, Senior Chief." Justice or reprieve was nonexistent.

And don't forget his training cadre. He taught to be as mean as he was. In retrospect, lord knows we needed Vietnam Navy SEALs and SWCCs in our lives. In reality, they brought us as close to the real thing as training could allow. Eventually, we all realized their experience was invaluable.

Senior Chief Anger was also an incredible instructor for partner forces in Central and South America. I had the privilege of being part of his four-man mobile training team to Bolivia, consisting of SEALs and SWCC. Every aspect of training demanded precision and was extremely dangerous. He would insert us boat guys onto the shore and order us to hunker down. Then the Bolivian version of SWCC called Blue Devils would conduct a hot extraction using live ammo. Talk about terrifying.

I didn't mind our boat guys conducting hot extractions with me on the beach, but the partner force experience was unforgettable.

I learned what the sound of rounds whizzing past your head feels like and believe me, it was terrifying. Oh, and Senior Chief Anger spoke fluent Spanish, giving him near rock star status in Trinidad, Bolivia.

During our deployment, Senior Chief Anger wanted to help celebrate Bolivia's Independence Day, so we prepped the opposite side of the river with explosives. This included two fifty-five-gallon drums of fuel with explosive sheets called "data sheets" underneath, plus twelve-pound satchels of C4 on top. We dug ditches and laid detonation cord (Det Cord) in them. We then extracted illumination parachutes from white pop flares, stuffed C4 inside the tubes, and placed them in the ditches with about sixteen flares alternating white, red and green, followed by a C4 tube. The goal: shoot these tubes into the air with different colored flares, then launch a ball of C4 that would explode in the air.

My responsibility, along with the SEAL medic (we called him Doc), was to ignite the flares using a clacker connected to the detonation cord, then run back to our ditch for cover before the large fifty-five-gallon drums exploded.

Doc and I were hiding when something strange jumped out of the water. Holy shit! It looked like a mix between a gigantic rat and a beaver but was as big as a large dog. We stayed in position, knives ready, throwing clumps of mud to startle it. Turns out it was a "Capybara," a giant rodent native to South America, weighing up to 108 pounds. Luckily, it eats grass not humans. After an hour of wading in the mud, and just after dark, the giant rodent finally wandered off.

Once our unwanted visitor was gone, we noticed hundreds of Trinidad locals watching from the opposite bank. Suddenly, the Bolivian Blue Devils started shooting their 7.62 machine guns in our direction using blanks. Doc and I ran along the ditches, igniting the pop flares with the clackers.

All that remained was to run back to our ditch and hunker down for the explosion. Senior Chief Anger must have thought we were in position, because all hell broke loose. Before we could reach

cover, the fifty-five-gallon drums were ignited by the C4 and data sheets. All we felt was unbearable heat; we dove for safety.
You could say it was just another day learning the ropes from Senior Chief Anger. Among the many lessons he taught, one of the most important was that it takes about three weeks for human eyebrows to regrow! Now that is something to remember.

Overall, despite the danger and complexity, the training we received was second to none. They pushed us to the limits we were accustomed to. Without that preparation, the survival of our SWCC and SEAL teammates could have been on the line. Some simulated combat scenarios mirrored real-world threats in riverine environments anywhere in the world.

For example, they would drop trees in front of our boats and behind us, leaving no escape and placing us in a kill zone. Of course, they always used blanks and mild explosives. It was so stressful that sometimes I would retreat into the jungle to let off steam. I needed a few minutes alone because, when I failed to master a tactic, I felt I had let my team down by not seeing the ambush. I knew I was capable of more. Being a boat captain under instruction meant that continued failure could jeopardize my position and that was not an option.

The beauty of these scenarios was that the training cadre pushed us against insurmountable odds. After each exercise, they dissected the entire scenario and walked us through how to perfect our response. We learned that if there were no other options and we were pinned in place, we had to charge the ambush and fight to survive. The probability of survival increased by attacking the ambush head-on, but the reputation of the cadre instilled both fear and respect and we certainly experienced both.

Panama was an incredible training ground for the Boat Units, for both coastal and riverine environments. Riverine detachments trained hard, often spending weeks in the jungle to hone our skills. The SEALs were based at Snake Pit Base Camp, and we were at McFall Base Camp. Both were close to each other and provided direct access to live-fire waterborne ranges.

The training cadre and our chief perfected our nighttime navigation skills, essential for many of our missions. We were taught to operate effectively even when all modern advantages are stripped away.

Back then, our detachments didn't have night vision. We learned to function in complete darkness by reading the river—using the shadows cast from each bank and steering toward the point where the shadows converged.

We also trained in operational deception, shaping how others perceived us—making the boat seem larger or smaller, nearer or farther, while using camouflage to break up our outline and blend into the background.

The learning curve was steep, but repetition made it instinctive. In time, these skills became second nature—something that stayed with us long after the training ended.

We learned to shoot blanks and live fire from the boat while running "point man" courses of fire where a cove was filled with cardboard targets as we drove past. Many times, .50 cal ball ammo hit trees and ricocheted back toward our boats. On one occasion, I watched Scott jump on the gunwale, with a .50 cal round missing him by inches. Needless to say, we abandoned ball ammo and moved to the "good stuff" Armor Piercing Incendiary Tracers (APIT) that went through anything. No more ricochets. No more mistakes.

During this time, I gained enough confidence to test for my Boat Captain qualification. After learning more from failures than successes, I had become an expert in coastal and riverine warfare, trained by the best the US Navy had to offer. I checked the board to see my scores, and to my surprise, the person I thought disliked me had actually been rooting for me all along. It was Chief Martin.

I saw him approaching the room where the board was located. He walked over and, in his gruff voice, said, "Welcome to the brotherhood, Carp." Shocked but thrilled, I watched as he took a boat pin from his pocket, removed the back tabs, and pounded it onto my chest. "Congratulations, Carp. I am making sure this doesn't come out." He then pinned the other new Boat Captains, pounding each pin onto their chests just like mine. It was a rite of passage that finally gave me a home. A home I had never truly had in the hood. I finally knew this was my family: a family with purpose, the biggest, baddest gang in the world, where if you mess with one, you mess with all of us. SOMOS POCOS, PERO SOMOS LOCOS.

Like many serving in Panama, our tour lasted a little over three years. After that, the Navy would pull us back to our original rates and return us to the fleet. NSW had invested heavily in our training, but the big Navy viewed the boat units as a "diversity tour." If we stayed too long, we risked falling behind in our ratings because we would have limited sea time. We lost many fine operators who could have perpetuated precision and lethality. The Navy is great at creating leaders but struggles at retaining them. After all, we were precision-trained, and now we had to accept orders back to the large ships.

During this time, Senior Chief Kelly Webb better known as BOHICA started an effort to create a schoolhouse for the boat teams. He was frustrated that so much investment in training would be lost. He and the Chiefs' mess pulled it off and established the SWCC Schoolhouse. Young operators who were not yet Boat Captain-qualified went through this training. The training mirrored the SBU-26 jungle school. Of course, I missed the window because I was already a qualified boat captain, but it marked the beginning of a formal system to maintain precision-trained boat guys.

Finally, it was my turn to receive orders. I had two options: Norfolk, Virginia, or Washington State neither aligned with the promise I made to my wife to return to California. I discussed my options with many trusted advisors, but nothing seemed to make sense.

That was until I was told to try out for BUD/S (Basic Underwater Demolition/SEAL), one of the most grueling training pipelines on the planet to become a Navy SEAL. Though I loved my SEAL brothers and had the utmost respect for what they do, I did not want to be a SEAL. I truly loved the boats and being a boat captain. I loved everything about the boat teams, but I would have to bite the bullet to try out for BUD/S to get back to California. Damn it, now my ASVAB score came back to haunt me. Go figure. SEALs have to be smart as hell and at least intelligent enough to handle arithmetic reasoning, and verbal expression at the highest level.

To compete, I had to complete additional courses, retake the ASVAB, and obtain a high score. I studied like no one's business, passed, and also passed the screening test. I received orders to BUD/S and went through the initial screening followed by the first phase in class 199.

BUD/S training was amazing yet, as you've likely heard, extremely demanding. The only problem was that my heart wasn't in it. I viewed it as another kick in the nuts like Panama. I did have a few failures, including diving down into a fifty-foot tower to tie knots underwater and failing to pass drown-proofing on the first attempt. That was a big no-no! City dwellers, take note: learn how to swim and be confident in the water, lest it comes back to haunt you. I was a great swimmer, but I never mastered surf zones or freediving 20–50 feet to tie knots.

A week before Hell Week the cadre took us to the mudflats on the bayside and had everyone rolling around in the mud. After playing around in the mud flats by the bay, I became seriously ill and couldn't shake it. It was serious and I couldn't hold anything down or in.

During the last PT session before Hell Week, I vomited uncontrollably on the grinder but continued to PT. The instructor warned that if I vomited again, I'd be pulled and sent to medical. Somehow, I finished the session. I then went to medical, where they could not figure out what I had. A few classmates had also contracted a flesh-eating virus, likely contracted from the mud flats.

The medical team recommended rolling me back to improve, but with so many students gaming the medical system, those actually sick sometimes couldn't roll. Plus, I had a few performance issues.

On Sunday, I got through breakout which is the start of Hell Week and was doing well despite still feeling sick. I pushed through Monday, but my body was out of sync. That night, we were instructed to flip our boats and push through high surf. I looked at the instructors like they were crazy and said, "I'm done." I walked away, went to the tent, and fell asleep.

The next morning, still not feeling well, I went to medical and received antibiotics for Hepatitis A. My BUD/S training was officially over.

I was actually happy in a sense, because my heart yearned to be a boat captain, the job I loved most. But how would that even be an option if I was going back to the fleet? At least I'd be in California, where my wife could visit her family and friends.

I was assigned to a holding division until I received new orders to a ship. While doing some manual labor, I ran into Navy SEAL Master Chief Frank Walters and Senior Chief Jose Trevino both from SBU-26. They couldn't believe they ran into me. Master Chief Walters asked, "What the fuck happened to you?" I replied, "I let BUD/S kick my ass." They gave me that look of disappointment. But I knew I hadn't wimped out. I was simply not aligned with becoming a SEAL. Being a boat guy was my passion.

In every sense, I respected the SEAL training and loved every minute of it. But when your heart tugs in another direction, you follow your heart and purpose. While trying out allowed me to get back to California, I likely took the slot from a more deserving sailor. Sometimes, career decisions must support the promises you make to your family. And anyone who completes BUD/S and becomes a SEAL? You are a bad MOFO.

Looking back, I was destined to be a Boatguy. I never regretted voluntarily dropping out. Everyone has their story for not finishing BUD/S; mine is simple: I went with an ulterior motive. My heart was not in it. The thing you do with the least effort is often your God-given gift. Being a boat guy was mine, and supporting SEAL Teams for nearly my entire adult life has been the greatest honor of my life. Enough said.

As I awaited my next orders, they came: SBU-12. I knew Frank and Jose had a hand in it. On one hand, I was happy; on the other, nervous. Rumor had it that SBU-12 boat guys were out of shape and that SEAL teams had little respect for them, because their boats frequently broke down and SEALs had even been injured during extractions. The stories were endless.

The good news: I kept my promise to my wife. We would live in San Diego, an hour by plane from her family in the San Francisco Bay Area. Boy, did I get lucky. God had answered a prayer. Special Boat Unit Twelve, here I come.

No regrets. Just focus on my passion

"God, Country, and Fast Boats!".

Chapter Nine

Mess up; Make up; Never Give up. Learning to Lead

"Do not follow where the path may lead. Go instead where there is no path and leave a trail."

Ralph Waldo Emerson

The 1990s was a decade generally associated with peace, prosperity, cool music and innovation. The Internet was thriving, the Soviet Union had fallen, and the Cold War was over. Yet the decade was also marked by violence with the LA riots and the Oklahoma City bombing, to name a few examples. You could say my experiences in Naval Special Warfare up to this point mirrored the 1990s in many ways. I messed up more times than I care to remember, but with each mistake, I tried to improve. I was determined never to give up and never revert back to my roots of hopelessness and despair.

In January 1995, transitioning from my janitorial job as a "BUD/S Dud" (the label given when you quit training) to Special Boat Unit Twelve (SBU-12) was relatively easy. All I did was officially check out of BUD/S and walk across the street to check into SBU-12. SBU-12 was a coastal-centric unit, meaning all its capabilities focused on coastal warfare and open-ocean tactics.

Contrary to the horror stories I had heard, I quickly found the unit was well-organized. Most of the old problems had become relics of the past. These operators at SBU-12 were beasts! They exercised daily, ran long distances, and swam constantly. The detachments ranged from High-Speed Assault Craft (HSACs), to Rigid Inflatable Boats (RIBs). These dedicated operators worked every single day in the open ocean. It was extremely taxing, especially on their bodies. Imagine carrying heavy gear while standing on a high-speed boat for hours. While necessary, it was brutal. To this day, I'll never understand why they allowed this for so many years. But these warriors were tough and knew their jobs better than anyone.

A number of us riverine experts came from SBU-11 in Mare Island, SBU-22 in Louisiana, and a few from SBU-26. We had different mindsets than the coastal warriors we were about to join. There was Carl, Jay, and Stacey, all just as cocky and confident as I was. I know it's hard to believe, but it's true. The training cadre knew we would hold them accountable and call out any inaccuracies. That was our responsibility. There was no room for error in Naval Special Warfare.

We were ready. Riverine tactics transitioned well into coastal operations, but coastal tactics didn't translate smoothly into riverine operations. This dichotomy would become somewhat of an issue later.

After checking in, all new boat guys had to undergo a three-month indoctrination course, testing and retesting every qualification from our previous commands. We even had to sit a "refresher" boat captain board aligned with the SBU-12 boat inventory.

Jay was a boat guy from SBU-11 and a former shipmate from the USS Pyro AE-24. Like typical boatswain mates, he ordered me around and made me do sweepers on the ship. "Bro, I can't believe you made me do that shit. You were such an asshole on the ship, so no surprise," I said jokingly. We laughed and ended up in the same detachment. Jay was an amazing boat driver, boatswain mate, and gifted mechanic. You would assume from his skill that he was an engineman rather than a boatswain mate. He could keep an engine running with duct tape and pantyhose. Where he got the pantyhose? Your guess is as good as mine.

Our training continued with land navigation and shooting in the mountains of San Diego, followed by heavy weapons training at Camp Pendleton first aid, navigation, and many other competencies. I enjoyed learning and refining my skills. Soon, we completed our indoctrination course and were assigned to our first coastal detachment.

NSW had major issues with boat designs at the time and relied heavily on Combatant Craft Division (CCD) to build them. The first iterations of boats from CCD was ten-meter and thirty-foot RIBs that didn't align with our missions. The Navy's big-picture thinking produced heavy boats with shipboard equipment, like battle lanterns and Halon systems, that only added weight and reduced our Iron Triangle (Speed, range, and payload). Historically, CCD stymied innovation and neglected operator safety. They should be held accountable for injuries aboard boats. For God's sake, operators need seats that mitigated lateral and vertical impacts, active ride control and ergonomic consoles to reduce stress on the human body. Why operators continue to stand on boats is gross negligence, period!

We always needed more fuel and more speed. Literally more of everything, but all the unnecessary equipment reduced capability. So, there we were, highly trained yet limited by suboptimal boats. Fortunately, a new boat was being designed by SOCOM's Maritime Office specifically for NSW. In the meantime, we operated twenty-four-foot RIBs with a single Volvo Penta engine and a stern drive, producing a maximum of 215 horsepower with very limited range and payload. Four boats were required to transport an eighteen-man SEAL platoon. Go figure, we violated our own rule of "Two is one, One is none".

Talk about cramped quarters. None of us had a place to stand comfortably. Even worse, we had to ride with our feet angled forward so we could bend our legs. Current boat guys reading this: you should know that we went through hell on these early boats, paving the way for your rides today. Oh, and why are you all still standing on boats? As if the boats hadn't already destroyed our bodies enough, and now destroying yours? Your guess is as good as mine. Fight this and fight for your safety. Submit your ODRs.

Our first deployment was to Guam to preposition for redeployment to the Philippines, Thailand, Korea, Japan, and a few other countries. Upon landing and checking into Naval Special Warfare Unit One, The Commanding Officer made it abundantly clear that he did not like boat guys. Nor was he interested in a capabilities brief on boats he deemed to have little to no capability. Initially, he refused to let us drive around the island on our own and insisted the Coast Guard escort us. It was humiliating being a boat detachment whose task unit commander had zero confidence in our skills. It quickly became obvious that we would have to prove ourselves worthy of his trust.

To show him our "mojo," we drove around the island in one direction, then turned around and drove it in the opposite direction, setting records in both attempts. It was all for nothing the man wouldn't budge.

Around this time, our commanding officer and command master chief from SBU-12 visited and asked how things were going. Our chief gave a diplomatic answer to keep the peace with the chiefs' mess. We, on the other hand, spilled the beans and complained loudly. Soon after the commanding officer departed, the unit master chief entered our space and lined us out from north to south for talking crap about his unit. Lesson learned but there was more drama to come.

Eventually, we earned more operational freedom, which was empowering. One day, returning from an underway, the commanding officer met us on the pier and asked, "I hear you all want to hold heavy weapons training." "Yes, sir," I responded. We assumed he would allow us to use the Mobile Prepositioning Ship as our support vessel to transit to the island 171 nautical miles from Guam. He had other plans. "Since you want to operate your boats so much, we expect you to drive there. It's approved. But no per diem or hotels, men," he said.

We took it in stride. Being treated like a "redheaded stepchild" was nothing new. The Navy culture thrives on acronyms, sayings, and colorful terminology.

Our detachment was a band of PT beasts. We swam like fish and held our own in any scenario both in town and on missions. Me, Chuck, Jeff, Carl, Ryan, Jay, Mark, and Matt were brothers on the smallest boats imaginable.

Our Gun shoot trip was an island hop: Guam to Rota, Rota to Tinian, Tinian to Saipan, and finally to a deserted island forty-five nautical miles north of Saipan, called Farallon De Medinilla. That's where we shot our weapons. The seas were unforgiving, with swells ranging from ten to twenty-five feet. Off the northeast coast, the Mariana Trench is the deepest trench on the planet. Why the waves were consistently massive? Who knows. Our small boats strained to crest each wave. Progress was measured in inches.

Even the fuel caused problems. Suppliers often watered it down to make extra money. Clear at first glance, it still fouled our fuel filters. Bad fuel meant injector tips blowing off mid-transit, shutting down the engine, and forcing us to raise the console in massive seas to change injectors and reprime the system. Jay had the last injector and tossed it to my boat but missed. That could mean fifteen hours of towing versus three hours of progress.

When the injector hit the water, I dove in without thinking. The seas were fifteen-to-twenty-foot rollers. Little did I know a whale shark had surfaced by me. Jay and the rest of the guys yelled, but I had no idea of the danger. All I knew was, I had the injector and was swimming back to the boat. Luckily, the whale wasn't interested in me. I was spared once again.

Reflecting on those times, I am reminded of the caliber of men willing to take tiny, underpowered boats into such seas. Definitely modern-day Vikings.

After another incident, we reached Saipan, where we stayed overnight on the pier under tarps because the commander refused us hotel rooms. The next day, we completed the gun shoot and transited back to Guam with only a few minor hiccups in seas that were as tall as a house.

Back at the pier, we began offloading gear. The unit executive officer happened to be at the bar on the water. He walked down the pier with two cases of beer and two women in tow. "You boys did good. Great job," he said. He dropped the beer at our feet and added, "I not only brought beer, but broads as well." We laughed. He smirked and clarified, "Just kidding, boys that's my wife and her friend."

Before leaving, he added one final note: "Don't worry about the per diem; we'll handle that next week. Enjoy your weekend you boys did great."

Officers like the unit XO and many others in Naval Special Warfare set a standard second to none. These were the leaders we would fight to the death for: servant leaders who earned respect. In this small community, reputation is everything. Underachievers and assholes are remembered, even in civilian life. The standard is high for a reason.

Fortunately, I completed this deployment with only one major incident, affectionately dubbed the "Cool World Incident." Back then, many frogs and boat guys on deployment moonlighted as dive instructors or bouncers in local bars. Grunge music was booming, and the incident took place in one of those bars.

My brothers and I went to the grunge bar Cool World and saw some… unusual dancing. People were jumping up and down erratically to the music and not anything like Chicago house music. I just stood on the sidelines, nursing a few beers.

Then I noticed a heavy-set guy on the dance floor wearing a Metallica T-shirt. He was pushing people around, but this time, he pushed the wrong guy. It was the biggest SEAL in one of the deployed platoons. I knew something bad was about to happen.

The massive SEAL shoved the man back, and as he stumbled, he reached for his gun. Jeff yelled, "He's got a gun!"

Suddenly, my buzz evaporated. I ran over, smacked the guy on the back of the head with my bottle, and fell on top of him.

Chaos erupted. The guy was being punched and kicked by multiple people, and his gun skidded across the floor I have no idea who grabbed it.

The SEAL bouncers intervened, and the man shouted, "Get the fuck off me! I'm a cop! You're all going to jail." The irony wasn't lost on me.

Like a true Chicagoan, I ran, climbed two fences, and found refuge in a hotel bathroom. I cleaned my cuts and pulled glass shards from my arms. Once presentable, I returned to the club, climbed onto the roof, and watched two SEALs being arrested. Though we were all involved, they bore the brunt of the consequences. The man we fought was moonlighting as a bouncer and shouldn't have been armed or on the dance floor. This happened December 23, 1996, two days before Christmas.

We bypassed an executive officer inquiry and went straight to captain's mast on Christmas Eve. All the boat guys, SEALs, and the police officer were summoned. I feared being identified, especially since I was only frocked to E6. Official pay and rank could take almost a year. If I got busted, I'd be reduced to E4. Not an option.

The commanding officer asked the police officer if he could identify who hit him with the bottle. He could not. Our Explosive Ordnance Disposal team, who were deployed with us, testified that the fight was started by Construction Battalion sailors who often pushed us around. Yeah, right if you'd seen our EOD guys, you'd have laughed.

The two frogmen were convicted: forty-five days extra duty and forty-five days restriction. The rest of the punishment was suspended, activated only if they got in trouble within six months. We gave them grief during extra duty, honking horns as they pressure-washed buildings, and they returned the middle finger. Lucky for them, their extra duty lasted only two weeks before rotating back to San Diego. The commanding officer banned the command from returning to Cool World.

That singular event taught me that even when you're in the right, the system will hold someone accountable. I was just glad it wasn't me because the unit CO would have thrown the book at a Boatguy!

Upon returning to San Diego, Carl (from SBU-26) and I were assigned to the Training Cadre. We took issue with some of the training senior leadership. I wasn't impressed. For example, I'd ask the Training Master Chief a question, and he'd respond irritably: "What do you want, Carpenter?" I replied, "Master Chief, you're taking the Hooyah out of our job." Bold? Yes. Necessary? Absolutely.

The reason: leadership wanted us to insert SEALs five miles off the coast which was a strategy none of us agreed with. We signed up to be their insertion/extraction platform, ensuring they arrived safely and were picked up.

He did not like me, and I did not like him as an operator.
I became the training point of contact for a detachment led by SEAL Chief Fitzhenry, a great mentor who helped break through bureaucracy to ensure NSW paid per diem for long-distance training. He once told me, "Don't let the last thing you do be the only thing they remember you by."

I never micromanaged his detachment. They planned operations while I observed. During a recon mission off Santa Catalina Island, evading US Customs aircraft, everything that could go wrong did. Comms failed, and one boat sustained an engine casualty.

The chief made the decision; the detachment stuck with it. We were under tow for twelve hours back to San Diego Harbor. Everyone returned safely. Me? I returned to find the Training Master Chief had removed me as training point of contact, citing, "Carp failed to check in." I could have called a timeout and motored into Catalina Harbor, but doing so would have broken the detachment's operational focus. Some lessons are learned the hard way.

My training master chief called me in and told me I was being relieved. What the hell? I was furious, especially since the det had successfully executed its mission and overcome numerous challenges. Plus, Chief Fitzhenry was an outstanding SEAL Chief and mentor. His det loved him and knew he always had their backs. Tragically, he died in a Humvee rollover on June 16, 2004. Doc will never be forgotten by us.

Even though I was relieved, I remained in the training cadre. The leadership created a new position for me called "Asset Coordinator." Little did they know, they had given me more power than I had as a training point of contact.

Oh, happy day. Don't give me a job that has a title but no guidelines. I now had the freedom to write Navy administrative messages, attend planning conferences, coordinate with other commands, and essentially do anything I wanted. As the saying goes, "When life gives you lemons, make lemonade."

I had C-130 Spectres come in for our close air support training, and I could barter sections of fixed-wing air support from the Anglico Marines. They were experts at calling in fire support. You name it, they could call it. Artillery, Naval gunfire, mortars, bombs and missiles. These boys were legit.

They were bad-ass Devil Dawgs. For them, a section of air equaled two fighter jets. They would give me eighteen sections of air, naval gunfire, and artillery just to make calls with the C-130 Spectre. They had so much air and artillery that it was effortless for them to provide it, since fighter pilots needed flight hours. For me, pulling a C-130 Spectre was a piece of cake.

I worked my butt off in my new role and nailed the asset coordinator job. I earned "Sailor of the Quarter." During this time, I also witnessed many of the old guard in the boat teams fade away. There were good ones, of course, and far too many bad ones, but the bad ones made the good ones look bad. Sometimes people simply stay in their positions too long for various reasons. Since the boat teams were now close looping in 1998, meaning we could remain in the boat teams for our entire careers we had to maintain our own standards and continue competing for leadership positions.

As I neared the end of my tour in the training department, I was astonished to be selected as "Sailor of the Year for Special Boat Unit Twelve" as well as "Sailor of the Year" for headquarters. Being a CSBR-1 Headquarters Sailor of the Year was a major accomplishment. It practically guaranteed me a promotion to chief the following year. I could not have been happier.

My next move was transferring out of the training department. I took over as assistant officer in charge for RIB Det Bravo, which was set to deploy in support of Amphibious Readiness Group Bravo out of Okinawa, Japan. These large amphibious ships carry Marines ready for war at a moment's notice. We would ride the ships. The SEALs rode on the Landing Helicopter Assault Ship (LHA). We rode the Amphibious Transport Dock Ship (LPD). This was an incredible opportunity, especially since I was practically guaranteed a promotion to chief or so I thought.

The det consisted of eight members, Senior, Ronnie, Mike, Jerrod, Chad, and three of us whom had riverine experience. Me, Jay and Stacey were all qualified to take the assistant det commander position, but I had slightly more seniority. We got along superbly and even watched our chief become a senior chief. After his promotion, we noticed a change in him. He became different, reminding us of a chief with a traditional shipboard mentality. We all wondered what they put in his coffee to change him so quickly.

By this point, I had ideas of my own. I wanted to use this work-up and deployment as a way to grow into a better leader. I would soon be tested.

We completed our long work-up, and believe me, Stacey, Jay, and I made it harder than any other det we had experienced. We honed our skills and took our boats out into the open ocean, even when other dets refused to go out during small craft advisories. We were determined to be the det of choice.

We had another interesting experience when our detachment was stationed at White Beach Naval Base in Okinawa. When the ships were out, we had the run of the entire base. It was a beautiful place, with white sandy beaches and cliffs overlooking the water. Though our senior chief tried his best to play us against one another, and the threat of getting fired was constant, we handled it.

Ironically, his divisive leadership only brought us closer. Even though one day he fired me and the next day he fired Stacey. We said, "To hell with it" and decided to handle this as a detachment. Luckily, when the senior chief's wife visited, he departed for Tokyo. This was the opportunity we had been waiting for to bond as a detachment and re-establish cohesion that his leadership style had been undermining.

Of course, everyone had their own ideas about what we should do. Some were reasonable, others… not so much. For example, a few guys read the uniform instruction manual and determined that we could all dye our hair as long as it remained a natural color. Smitty, one of my teammates, had no hair at all, so to align with the decision, he dyed the only hair he had his eyebrows! Every detachment member except me, paid to get their hair dyed, and they all looked pretty cool with blond hair. Me, however, reverted to my South Side roots. I went to the base exchange and purchased dark and lovely blond teal hair dye. I walked back to the room and worked on getting my hair just right.

I do not know what happened, but apparently, I left the dye in too long. No joke, when I rinsed it out, my hair was literally a rusty orange color. I looked like a walking carrot!

With my crazy orange hair, and after all the drinking that ensued, to include losing Ronnie twice in one night. Once to a row of bushes and then him being wedged behind the seat in our little haji van. We became a cohesive detachment once again. We resembled some sort of satanic cult.

When our senior chief returned, he was clearly not amused. He did not like our look, nor did he appreciate that we had used the instruction manual to our advantage. Despite his admonishment, we kept our hair color until it faded, then dyed it back to the original colors. As for me, I simply shaved my hair off.

With our detachment unified, we were enroute to Thailand for a "Cobra Gold Exercise." During a noncombatant evacuation operation, we were nearly killed by the deck department while they lowered our boat into the water. As the crane boomed out, it force the ship to roll to the starboard more. The line handlers took no action unless they received a verbal order from the Boatswain's Mate. This meant that even when slack in the lines needed to be taken in immediately, they waited for the order. Needless to say, we started slamming against the side of the ship about thirty-five feet above the water with 6-8ft waves. After the last slam, the boat swung out, and its bow hit the ship. There is an unwritten rule: if the boat does a 180, you jump into the water before it slingshots back.

This time, the bow slammed first into the ship, then twisted back to the port side. The hook tripped, and we fell more than thirty feet, with the boat hitting first and pancaking us. Mike hit the gun mount, and Jay hit the steering wheel. I landed on the deck and destroyed my lower back, shoulder, left knee, and neck. But the mission still had to be done, So we got back on the ship and had the medic give me a cortisone shot to get back to work. Eventually, my macho-man decision would come back to haunt me.

It was now time to return to Okinawa. Our senior chief decided to fly back to Okinawa, bypassing the Amphibious ship transit. That left me in charge. Though it was a successful deployment, one of my detachment members, was having performance problems. I had no choice but to write a counsel chit documenting his shortcomings. If he received two more, it would result in an Executive Officer Inquiry (XOI) or kicked out of the det and sent home.

No sooner had I started counseling him than a Marine officer walked into our berthing space, asking for his identification. The Marine had been disrespected by Jerrod the night before in town. Though I was in the middle of counseling him, he was still my teammate, and loyalty is paramount in NSW, but lying is not.

So, I told the Marine officer to leave our berthing area and follow proper protocol through the ship's chain of command. Well, it escalated. He was brought up on charges. In my infinite wisdom, I ordered another member from my detachment to stand as a witness at Captain's Mast. I was Sailor of the Year for two commands, and this is what I thought I was supposed to do: protect your teammate, even when he was not fully worthy. Boy, was I wrong and I paid dearly for it.

I attempted to help an underperforming boat guy by having someone else lie for him at Captain's Mast. In my ignorance or perhaps blind arrogance, I was counseling him because he failed to meet my standards, yet I felt he deserved me putting everything on the line. My reputation and the quality of life I had earned for my family were now at risk for someone who was not measuring up. Needless to say, the case was initially dismissed but later picked up by our Commanding Officer at SBT-12.

He was called back to the command for Captain's Mast. He explained what happened in town and my role in helping him. Had I not been Sailor of the Year, I would have likely suffered the same fate. He was discharged from the Navy. Though discharging him seemed extreme, I realized I had made a serious leadership mistake when factoring in his previous history.

I, on the other hand, did not make chief that year, and my transfer orders were held up. But this experience taught me a crucial lesson: I needed to up my game, be honest in all my dealings, and learn as much as possible to be an effective leader.

I finally saw a path toward that goal. Here is what I learned about leadership:

1. Do your job and be accountable. Don't allow anyone to shrink the mission.
2. Do not do anything that discredits our reputation, command, or the Navy.
3. Do not place me in a position where I must lie for you.
4. Do not compromise the quality of life I have earned for my family.

5. If you cannot stand in front of the commanding officer and explain your actions, don't do it.
6. There is no plausible deniability. Bad news does not improve with time. Loyalty is not demonstrated by withholding information from the leadership.
7. Let your work ethic and actions speak to your character.
8. If you are part of a team and make a mistake, own it and accept the consequences.
9. Failure to meet command and detachment standards is a form of disloyalty.
10. Respect is earned every day; loyalty is constant; team integrity depends on honesty and transparency.
11. Give everyone a voice on your team and stand up for one another with honor.
12. Develop your detachment and team so everyone wants to be part of your group.
13. Kick people out of your team and off your bus when they refuse to measure up.
14. Document when you have to, this will save you headaches when it gets really bad.
15. Train Motivate and Empower those around you, until you can't. If you can't. refer to rule #13.

With these insights and a solid blueprint, I was excited to transfer to the Naval Small Craft Instruction and Technical Training School (NAVSCIATTS) at Stennis Space Center, Mississippi. NAVSCIATTS trains foreign military personnel in maritime operations, maintenance, and sustainment of craft. This became one of the most rewarding experiences of my career. I realized how powerful this command was, training the leaders of tomorrow who may influence their countries.

I was promoted to Chief Petty Officer at this command and had some amazing mentors, including Commander Mike Lumpkin, Senior Chief Mark Presson, and Master Chief Danny Carol. While they were all SEALs, each brought a different personality and expertise to the table. Mark was a former operator and was also a boat driving expert with a natural knack for leadership and accountability. He consistently brought out the best in everyone he led. Danny cut his teeth in multiple SEAL Teams and is credited with saying, "It's not that we're that good. It's just that everyone else sucks." Mike had been my operations officer back in Panama and later served as XO at SBU-12. Now a commanding officer, he had an ease about him that allowed us to take risks and lean forward in our jobs.

NAVSCIATTS was a great command, but it offered very few creature comforts. We worked out of double-wide trailers and had to create everything from scratch since NAVSCIATTS had been shut down in Panama and was just resurrected. This command placed me on a trajectory toward success in building partner capacity and becoming a warrior diplomat.

Senator Trent Lott (R-MS) ensured that SBT-22 and NAVSCIATTS landed at Stennis Space Center, right in his backyard. While there, we all drove the boats. Mark Presson was an exceptional SEAL and boat operator, having learned driving at a previous command. The weird thing was, he was not in the training cadre at the time. It was routine for me to be in the thick of things, running training on the boats, but the training leadership was not functioning efficiently. Accountability was lacking, deadlines were missed, and there was little sense of urgency. Things needed to change.

Commander Lumpkin called me into his office one day and asked how things were going. I was honest. I said, "Do you really want to know, sir?" He walked from behind his desk, sat down in a chair, and motioned for me to sit at his desk. "Sir, am I you and you are me?" He nodded, so I proceeded to tell him exactly what was wrong with my command and the training department. "Carpenter, get the hell from behind my desk," he said abruptly. I knew change would come quickly.

I toured multiple commands with Mike Lumpkin, and wherever he went, he brought out the best in us. He gave us the latitude to do our jobs and take calculated risks. When we failed, it was still aligned with responsibility and pushing the envelope. He would tell us to get back out there and get it right. He was the type of leader you never wanted to let down, because of the confidence he instilled in you.

The next day, Mark Presson was installed as training officer, and together we created a high-performing team that consistently exceeded expectations.

I remained at NAVSCIATTS for three years and thoroughly enjoyed the tour. During every two-month class, we took our foreign students on trips designed to educate them about our democracy and show how we interact with law enforcement and other agencies in society. We visited museums, malls, and other cultural sites to ensure they had an experience they would not soon forget. These interactions were designed to demonstrate how a democratic society functions.

All these experiences showed me that I was worthy of having a seat at every table. Yet I still had to face the reality that I needed to continue reprogramming myself from my past. Failure was always lurking, and my impulsive poor decisions remained a potential stumbling block.

After being promoted to Chief, I committed to doing things the right way and remaining accountable to my leadership and my community. Senior Presson was a breath of fresh air, with a style that made me want to emulate him as a chief. He was clear and concise, demanded precision, ensured everyone pulled their weight, and assisted others on the team. He was one of the very few Navy SEALs who earned his SWCC pin. I learned a lot from him including how to drive a boat with precision alongside four other boats across a narrow river. He made all of us better by expecting us to do what he did. He would never ask anyone to do something he wouldn't do himself.

Up to this point in my life, I thought I knew a lot, but humbling myself and being open to new ideas allowed me to learn from everyone. Mark also held me accountable in subtle ways. If I had an issue with the command master chief and informed Mark of my frustration, he would wait until the master chief walked in and then casually say, "Ron's got a problem with you." That was leadership. Every day, he forced me to face challenges head-on. As a young chief, I was providing guidance to a SWCC senior chief and a SWCC chief in the training department, a responsibility I had never imagined.

Why did he do this? For one, he knew they would struggle taking orders from a junior chief. More importantly, he knew it would force them to get their act together. Our commanding officer could not have been happier witnessing the progress the training department made. To this day, NAVSCIATTS remains one of the Navy commands with the highest return on investment. For a command constantly on the chopping block, it continues to have positive and strategic impact worldwide. I even leveraged my experience at NAVSCIATTS to stand up the Manda Bay, Kenya Naval School of Maritime Excellence.

In good faith, and following Mark's example. I started holding monthly "emergency recalls" for the training cadre. It was on Bourbon Street, calling it team building while we bar-hopped our way through the night. One night was going great—I even ended up dancing on stage. When it was time to leave, a server grabbed my arm and said we owed sixty dollars for a two-drink minimum. I told her we'd cleared that three hours ago. What I didn't know was that a new frogman had already told her the same thing—but with a lot more attitude.

Moments later, a bouncer came back, grabbed me, and said I was going to jail. That's when instinct—and a little liquid courage—kicked in. I put my training to use, took him down, and suddenly found myself getting hit from all sides. I was dragged outside, fighting off a rear naked choke while taking punches and kicks. My cadre saw it and jumped in. Doc Soto—our Puerto Rican Hulk—launched one of the guys so hard he knocked down a balcony column, which unfortunately hit a woman passing by. Within minutes, police arrived, and we were all arrested.
At the station, we were a mess—Doc's clothes shredded, Cesar's glasses hanging crooked, and I was convinced my eye socket was broken. The duty sergeant knew the bar's reputation for scams and released us with a court date.

The next day, Mark greeted me with, "I heard you got beat up by a bunch of old people." We laughed, and he gave the team time to recover.

In court, dressed in our tropical whites, we watched charges being handed out—guilty meant a small fine, not guilty meant serious time or serious money. I told my guys we'd plead guilty and I'd cover it. Before we could, the prosecutor walked up and asked, "What happened to you, Chief?" After hearing our story, he states, you assholes follow me. He brought us into his office where a *Semper Fi* sign hung behind his desk. Tearing up the reports, as he sat down, he informed us that he was a Vietnam Vet and said the Iraq war was bringing back bad memories. Tears rolled down his face. I placed my hand on his should and told him he had answered the call in his time. Now it was our time. He said that we had a case and could sue the bar. I told him it wasn't necessary. It had been a good fight, and my guys showed up. That was enough.

I only asked for one thing: a letter clearing us and he obliged. Looking back, it's more than just a wild story. It was a moment of growth in how I handled chaos, responsibility, and leadership on my path toward self-actualization.

During this period, Jenifer and I faced significant marital problems, most stemming from my selfish desire to be part of a team. Our arguments worsened, and the potential for divorce loomed over us. Neither of us dared bring it up, so in my infinite wisdom and inexperience, I tried to force the issue by getting involved with another woman intending to be caught and thereby forcing a separation. That was classic old Chicago thinking, or rather, a lack thereof. Just a cowardly way of handling things.

Many of us come from backgrounds that haven't prepared us to take responsibility, so the only way we know how to act is a scorched-earth approach, leaving a path of destruction and collateral damage. Of course, Jen found out. Thankfully, cooler heads prevailed, and we decided to work through our issues and find our center. How she put up with my nonsense all those years is a testament to her character, clearly not mine.

During this tumultuous period, we still found our center. Soon after, Jenifer became pregnant, and we had a baby boy. We named him Jackson Apollo Carpenter (JAC). The Italian side of the family called him Jackie, the Black side called him Jackson, and the White side called him Jack. Being a father for the first time was transformative. I could not believe that having a son would immediately make me a more focused professional and someone who valued character more than ever. Jackson was a crème-skinned, curly-haired boy who brought a joy to my heart unlike anything I had ever experienced. He made life more important as if I had an additional mission to complete. I could not fail.

Since Jackson was our first child, I made sure we had child locks on everything. Yet somehow, he could pick the locks and was later found smiling inside a large cooking pot we used for pasta. I realized quickly that I had a lot to learn about being a father!

With my new baby and my tour ending, I followed Mike Lumpkin to the newly rebranded SBT-12 to take a detachment out the door. Jenifer, Jackson, and our cat Lucky (from Panama) all packed up for the move back to San Diego. Damn, it seemed like Naval Special Warfare was easier than the fleet. I loved this community!

After all these years, and after wrestling with the negative impulses from my past, I was finally becoming more self-actualized, reflective, and definitively less impulsive. I realized there would always be setbacks and opportunities for comebacks.

There would always be chances to return to honor.

I was getting better at this game of life, and my return to honor was no longer taking as long as it once did.

Constant and never-ending improvement became my new motto.

Mess up. Make up. But never give up.

Hooyah!

PART FOUR

MISSION COMPLETE

RINSE AND REPEAT

Chapter Ten

Kenya: Fighting Terrorists and Baboons

"What are you gonna do for a face when the baboon wants his ass back?"

Abraham Lincoln

I was back in San Diego at an operational unit! I checked into SBT-12 with the title of Chief Petty Officer, and I was pumped. Even more exciting was seeing the SWCC schoolhouse was gaining momentum and creating a standard of excellence. Our boat teams were becoming hard pipe-hitting, professional operators. These kids, and they were kids in my eyes, were in shape, smart, teachable, and all volunteers. They were the best of the best, the tip of the spear. Together, we would support counterterrorism operations worldwide and occasionally deal with other bad actors including, of all things, baboons.

What amazed me the most was that our community was about to close the loop with its new SWCC Warrant Officer Program just starting. This meant fleet officers would no longer have the opportunity to serve as detachment commanders. SEAL officers would still tour the boat teams and act as detachment commanders, but Navy fleet officers would no longer fill that role. It was bittersweet to see fleet officers depart. Some were exceptional, some less so, but we were now cut from a different cloth. SWCC had to operate at a high level of proficiency, and senior enlisted leaders could lead just as effectively as a fleet officer. They would often require training to reach even a basic level of competency within the team.

Ultimately, the creation of our own officer corps professionalized the community. Fleet officers would not carry their SWCC experience back to the broader Navy, and a clear pipeline from enlisted to officer ranks was established. SWCC

Warrant Officers became the only officer pipeline for the community. If a regular line officer pipeline had been created, it could have affected the SEAL officer professional pipeline. Their billets as operations officers, executive officers, and commanding officers of the boat teams would have vanished. NSW also benefited from young SEAL officers completing diversity tours at the boat teams; these tours helped them become well-rounded officers. Many would later say that their best tour was with the boat teams. This is where everything rested on their shoulders from maintaining boats, trucks, and gear to managing the SWCC mission. It is truly a never-ending job.

As a result, the Special Boat Teams were becoming a legitimate capability, supported by an officer pipeline that allowed us to grow our own leaders from the enlisted ranks. I faced a tough choice: remain enlisted and pursue Master Chief or submit my papers to apply for the SWCC Warrant Officer program.

Mike Lumpkin, our commanding officer and a close confidant of mine, with this being my fourth tour with him, told me, "Ron, I would want nothing more for you than to one day be my Command Master Chief, but you have to consider the politics of the Goat Locker. They may never allow you to promote to Master Chief. There aren't enough billets for everyone to be a SWCC Master Chief, and you ruffle a lot of feathers. My recommendation is that you become a SWCC Warrant Officer, where the community would benefit more from your drive, energy, and expertise."

Enough said. I withdrew my consideration for promotion to SWCC Senior Chief, completed my officer package, and was selected as Mike's top recommendation to the board. It was a gamble. If I did not pick up the commission, it would have set me back one year for Senior Chief.

I was initially assigned to a detachment deploying to Okinawa, Japan. This detachment was remarkably intact. My LPO, Tom Sonnier (Rest in Peace Brother), was a breath of fresh air a solid leader and performer who made taking over the detachment that much easier.

With the exception of mentoring and sharing my experience, work up and deploying with this detachment would have been a piece of cake. There was a SEAL officer serving as the detachment commander, which meant I would be assistant detachment commander alongside Tom as my LPO. I had definitely hit the lottery!

No sooner had I started shaping this detachment into a precision fighting force that I was pulled into the Command Master Chief's office. "Now what?" I thought. He informed me that they needed me to fix another detachment that was struggling with leadership and underperforming. While this was a vote of confidence in my abilities, a vote I was getting used to, I refused. I told him that after nearly four months with my detachment, I knew my guys were ready. I didn't volunteer; I was "volun-told."

I was pretty pissed off, but I checked into RIB Det Bravo. I had no choice but was determined to give it my all. The detachment commander was a Navy lieutenant named Sean, and a SWCC I had served with in Panama named Brian.

Brian was an exceptional boat operator, but he was short-tempered and, like many of us, struggled with anger. The detachment was not meeting the training cadre's expectations, and Brian was getting most of the blame. Sean, as a fleet officer, needed a strong number two to guide him into the role, and that fell onto Brian.

In retrospect, knowing what I know now, our deployments had broken Brian. We never realized the toll of repeated workups and deployments. Many of us believed our reputation and success were measured by the number of workups and deployments we completed. Brian had completed six or more deployments by that point. None of us fully understood how the boats and operational tempo were destroying bodies and deteriorating minds. I constantly clashed with Brian to elevate his performance as an LPO, when all he needed was a break from the relentless deployment cycle. This is the paradigm we needed to break in the Boat Teams.

Fortunately, the detachment was filled with stellar performers like Gabe. He had been in my training cadre at NAVSCIATTS and was one of the only SWCC in history to attend SWCC school while on TDY orders from NAVSCIATTS. He was that good a teammate and engineman that we had gamed the system to get him admitted to SWCC school. When he returned, his engineman detailer was unhappy. We had to send whiskey, cigars, and challenge coins to convince him to shift Gabe's billet to NSW.

It worked. I leveraged my "pissed-off" persona with the master chief to pull Gabe into RIB Det Bravo. Our growing team now included Sean the Lieutenant, me, the Chief, Brian, Gabe, Chris, Shawn, and two guys named Mark. With the exception of Brian and me, all enlisted personnel had graduated from the SWCC schoolhouse.

Off we went into a workup cycle. The training cadre gave me the latitude to design our own pre-deployment template, as long as we met all prerequisites. Boy, did I make it hard on us. Our boats were always ready, and with few exceptions, we operated like a fine-tuned machine. We always competed against other detachments for the Golden Wrench award. Both our sister det and us treated it as a no-fail mission. Gary Luna would win and rub it in our faces, then we would win and return the favor. The concept, created by our C.O. Mike Lumpkin, built better boat operators with impeccable attention to detail and boats that were always 100% operational.

Shawn, our creative teammate, carried a "Jack in the Box" filled with shot glasses and bottles of alcohol, including Jack Daniels. He was our go-to party guy.

It was Christmas time, and we went to the mountains for land navigation and small arms proficiency training. We completed the training, but Brian struggled to engage. Of course, the Jack in the Box was open and we started letting loose. Brian said a few things I didn't agree with, so I kicked everyone out of the room except for the two of us. I reminded Brian that we came from the same cloth in SBU-26 and told him there was no reason we couldn't build the greatest RIB Det SBT-12 had ever produced. He agreed and asked me to lay off him for a while so he could get things done. He made me promise.

I went on leave for two weeks and left a detailed tasking list for Brian to complete. When I returned, only a couple of items were done. I was shocked. I discussed the list with Brian, who had promised to complete everything. Even with the Christmas stand-down, I expected at least fifty percent completion as a sign of commitment. That would have been enough. Despite my frustration, we all had to pull together to prepare for the final battle problem. The training cadre would force us to isolate and transit over the road from San Diego to San Francisco to simulate operating in another country.

The training cadre ordered me to pull their weapons, blank ammunition, and ordnance, and transport them to San Francisco. Since I wasn't part of their cadre, I decided not to transport the items they would use to ambush us. Boy, was that a mistake! The training senior chief TJ took note and made us pay dearly.

As part of the same exercise, I had to check in with the Coast Guard Base. I was admiring their situation map on the wall, covered in thousands of tiny colored pins. I asked what the colors meant, and they explained each one. The black pins stuck with me the most. They represented the number of "jumpers" who had committed or attempted suicide from the Golden Gate Bridge. They were on the 999th pin, and the next jumper would be the thousandth. This was a sobering statistic to me.

It was winter in San Francisco, and it was extremely cold. The water was a chilly sixty degrees. We worked through the scenarios and were getting "up checks" on all required tactics, techniques, and procedures, including board and search, immediate action drills, insertion/extraction, and station keeping.

Finally, it was time to enter the river system where I had been stationed on my first ship at Mare Island Naval Shipyard. It had had long since shut down. That's when the training cadre got their payback. They simulated an ambush, kicked us off the boats with only what was on our person, and didn't allow us to take any third-line gear. That sucked, because third-line gear had extra food, water, and dry clothes.

Oh, and it was pitch black outside. The tide was rushing into the salt flats, and we had to cross the river to begin our escape and evasion plan to rendezvous at an abandoned Navy base about five miles away.

We consolidated. Unsurprisingly, Brian complained first but took point. Shawn and Chris, our young SWCC, were wide-eyed but tough. Mark had survived Hell Week twice but had blown out his eardrums. He was always a team player. Sean stayed behind at the base to manage comms and logistics. With Brian leading, all the training we had done in Panama made the scenario manageable, but the environment made execution brutal.

We tried to cross the river at an angle to let the current push us across, but the surge threw us into the salt flats. It felt like someone opened a dam and we were being flushed down a toilet. We slammed into the salt mounds repeatedly, stumbling over one, missing the next, for about an hour. All the while, we tried to keep our silhouettes low under a seventy-percent moon.

Finally, we reached the other side and started hiking through varied terrain: walking, swimming, crawling. Out of nowhere, we came to a complete stop and quietly backed away. We had stumbled across a crystal meth lab or marijuana grow. This happened multiple times, and none of us had a single round of live ammo, just blanks.

We found a place to lay up around 0400. Shawn awoke, claiming he had been bitten by a spider. We checked him thoroughly and found a dead brown recluse. Brown recluse spiders have necrotic venom toxic to humans. We immediately called for casualty evacuation, and Shawn was transported to the hospital for observation.

Game on again. More hiking, hiding, and observing. Night two was commenced. We made communications with Shawn back at base camp, asking him to drive to our rendezvous point and hide some food and beer. We thought we were close. When he arrived, he asked us to mark our position. I shot up a flare. His response? "Holy fuck, you guys are far!" Talk about a kick in the gut. Nonetheless, we kept moving. He gave us coordinates for the supplies and returned to base camp.

About five hours later, around 0100, we reached an open area with a nasty-smelling creek. Beyond it, was what appeared to be land, but the area seemed be flooded. We had two options: swim a mile or hike another three miles around the water. Brian was adamantly against swimming.

I gave the order. We began Crawling and wading through the nastiest-smelling water I've ever experienced. We finally made it across and walked about 200 meters, expecting more water. But what we thought was water turned out to be low-hanging fog. It was land. Thank goodness. We walked one mile (or two clicks) to the extraction point and located the food, and beer Sean hid. The boy did good. He had purchased twenty, one-dollar cheeseburgers. They were some of the best cold burgers I've ever eaten!

After gorging ourselves, we were picked up and returned to base camp. No rest for the weary. We reset our boats and gear.

Rinse and repeat.

Upon our return from the final mission, we moored our boats. Immediately after, a Coast Guard patrol boat pulled in and dumped a body bag on the pier. I wondered if this was the one-thousandth jumper. I asked the Coastguardsman on duty, "Hey, are you just going to leave the body here?" He responded, "Once it hits the pier, it's no longer our responsibility; it's the Police Department's." I replied, "Copy all," and asked him what the body bag number was. He told me rather unemotionally, "He's the thousandth."

Hearing those words hit me hard. That someone could feel so distraught that they would jump off the Golden Gate Bridge and die by suicide. It brought it all home for me. Later, we learned that the thousandth jumper had actually jumped once before and survived. To die this way, not from impact but from drowning, is a horrifying end. For anyone contemplating suicide, know that circumstances can improve. Have hope and don't give up. There is help available. Though the pain feels unbearable, the consequences of suicide are devastating to those left behind. You are loved. You are needed. Charlie Mike, Warrior.

We finally completed our final battle problem. I discussed with my lieutenant that I had tried to work with Brian but believed he needed a break from this boat shit. I didn't want to go on deployment with him carrying all of his issues. The LT agreed, and we pulled Brian from the det. He was sent to a Training Command to decompress and reset. The sad truth is that many operators, like Brian, endure back-to-back deployments without a break. We unknowingly were breaking the force and had our blinders on.

Back in the day, we didn't have the situational awareness we do now to recognize the impact of continuous deployments. Our culture teaches operators that their value is tied solely to their operational output during workups and deployments. The Navy promotion system perpetuates this mindset. We constantly push ourselves often at the expense of marriages, relationships, and personal well-being. Sooner or later, the bill come due. Something gives and the collateral damage appears on deployments, liberty, or at home. Though I was negatively perceived for pulling a superb operator from the det, I knew in my heart it was the right decision. I would hope Brian would have done the same for me if our roles were reversed. He earned a break.

Naval Special Warfare has come a long way in addressing these issues with the "Pressure on the Force and Families" (POTFF) Program. New protocols, called ITEMPO, tracked individual operators' time away from home. Operators are required to spend an equal amount of time at home as they do on deployment. When I was active, this sometimes caused frustration because ITEMPO restrictions could delay deployments or block training to align with a 180-day cycle. Nevertheless, POTFF has preserved marriages and retained skilled operators.

Though I felt conflicted back then, I now understand the importance of watching for warning signs and ensuring we don't push operators to the brink, then blame performance, alcohol, or behavior. Operators must remain self-aware, manage stress, and self-regulate. The key to doing this effectively is being emotionally aware and present - qualities that ensure longevity and resilience in both life and combat.

It's go time!

"Habari Za Leo, Rafiki. Nina Itwah Fundi Wambaho." (Hello, my friend. I am Carpenter.) Welcome to Manda Bay, Kenya.

We made it through our work-up and were now enroute to the African continent. Our detachment Sean, Shawn, Shawn, Mark, Mark, Gabe, Chris, and I commenced the turnover of gear and boats with the team already in country. We flew commercially and, if you can believe it, managed to drink ourselves sober on the plane. Boys will be boys, after all. The flight felt like an eternity. No surprise there.

We finally landed in Mombasa, Kenya, and stayed there for a few days for in processing at the Embassy annex and wait for our little bush plane, which would drop us off on a dirt runway about sixty miles from the Somali border.

We stayed at a beautiful resort hotel, seemingly overrun by Europeans. The water was stunning, the layout exquisite. Our rooms were clean. Each bed had four posts so you could close the mosquito netting. The food was buffet style and definitely Kenyan cuisine. After a while, I noticed some locals giving me strange looks because I was left-handed. (Apparently, in Kenya, the left hand is considered unclean for hygiene purposes.) Wow. What an image! Still, I like to think lefties are "special."

After three days of relative relaxation, the fun was over. The plane was ready to take us to Manda Bay. We loaded our gear into a plane straight out of a movie, and one I had vowed never to fly, but had no choice. Strap in and go. Only thing missing were the chicken coops.

The plane barely held us and our gear, as we flew over Kenya's open fields and villages, Yet, despite the cramped accommodations, Kenya captivated me from the moment I stepped off the plane to the moment I flew low over the landscape. I felt like I belonged there.

The plane delivered us to Manda Bay, landing on a dirt runway where a few SEALs and a full RIB detachment, led by Elmer and Darren from SBT-12, were waiting. I could not believe the squalor they lived in. They told me it was a vast improvement since their arrival. We began turnover and started adapting to the base camp's battle rhythm.

They called it "Camp Simba,". It was literally a base within a base. A Kenya Navy facility with a section fenced off for us to turn into a forward operating base. Army National Guard personnel provided base defense, and civilians from Kellogg, Brown, and Root (KBR) ran the camp operations. They hired Serbians and Croatians to build tents and showers. They spoke little English but were fully committed running the camp like a well-oiled machine. I sometimes wondered if any of them had ever taken an electricity class. Why? Because when you turned on the shower pump from inside the stall, it would electrocute you with 220 volts. I joked that we needed someone to drop-kick us out of the shower! American sailors' screams followed by a resounding "Son of a bitch!" were all too common.

Camp Simba had a Task Unit commander, battle captain, communications team, and others. The tactical operation center (TOC) was the hub of the camp, surrounded by offices and a courtyard with a basketball hoop. Behind the building was a huge tent shading two eleven-meter rigid inflatable boats and a section containing two detachment deployment boxes filled with engines, transmissions, trailer, and truck repair parts. We needed those boxes because there was always something to maintain.

Four new general-purpose tents could sleep six people and store gear for a six-month deployment. A KBR-built shower had four stalls and sinks with mirrors. Water was pumped from a nearby hippo pond into a massive plastic storage container, then super-chlorinated. The result? None of us owned military-issued tee shirts. They all turned pink or tie-dye. Not exactly the look for testosterone-laden tough guys.

As a precaution we moved our weapons box closer to our tents to ensure we could grab heavy weapons and explosive rounds if attacked. Being just sixty miles from the Somali border, a threat could appear at any moment. We had to be ready.

But soon we discovered the terrorists weren't our only danger.

Believe it or not it was the baboons! Among the largest non-humanoid primates, they've roamed the Earth for two million years.

The baboons were terrestrial and territorial. They could find food wherever they could. They even broke into cars and homes. Boy, did they make sure we knew we were encroaching on their territory!

Before we arrived, we had been assigned this location to establish our base camp. The area was abandoned and clearly belonged to the apes. We were the trespassers. Food had to be stored carefully, out of the baboons' reach, and we slept with our weapons close by, just in case one of them decided to pay a surprise visit. When you're literally in a jungle, you have to be prepared for both man, beast and insects.

Being in Kenya often felt like a scene from a horror movie. Rain was rare, but when it came, it lasted only a few minutes. Afterward, every insect larva or hibernating bug with wings would spring to life. It was unlike anything I had ever seen. The base camp would shut off the perimeter floodlights, and we would set up mosquito nets at our tent entrances to trap the insects. We ran full speed from our tents to the main building, holding our breath as we barreled through millions of flying bugs. This spectacle would last about two days, and then it would be over. Bugs and baboons oh my!

As part of our Kenya mission, Elmer and Darren's detachment, along with the SEAL squad, were there to support an exercise with the Kenyan Navy. However, a back-office decision changed the deployment: they were ordered to remain behind and continue training. They were not happy.

Imagine thinking you were finally going back to your ship after completing an exercise, only to be told to remain in the middle of nowhere with baboons and bugs while watching your ship sail away without you.

Up to that point, the four SEALs and eight SWCC had been on the ground for almost three months. Compared to what they were turning over to us; they had endured significant hardships. They wore flight coveralls and Vietnam-era mosquito head nets at night. Duct tape sealed the wrists and ankles of their flight suits to prevent creatures from biting them. They slept with their weapons, ready for any threat since Somalia was so close.

Elmer was the det commander, and Darren was the assistant det commander. They and their team were extremely squared away, and their pride of ownership gave me confidence in taking over their boats and gear. This worked in our favor. On other deployments, leadership was less organized, and we would spend half the deployment bringing the boats and gear up to our standard. Sometimes NSW keeps assets in-country for two deployment cycles to save money and reduce the number of C-17 flights per year. Now, we were taking over Elmer's trucks, boats, and equipment.

Four additional SEALs from the ship worked with Elmer's det to train the Kenyans. They had already run two iterations of training and were making progress in building the Kenya Navy capability. Kris, a SWCC from SBT-20, was the battle captain. We immediately hit it off. He was the senior enlisted in the Task Unit, keeping everything moving and in order. Built like a linebacker,

Kris had the demeanor of a seasoned senior chief petty officer. He volunteered for a deployment into the unknown and made it work.

Kris was serious but showed potential for trust in me and my detachment, despite past friction with Elmer, Darren, and the SEALs. That tension was obvious from my first meeting. Elmer and Darren were not SWCCs who could be pushed around or kowtow to the SEALs. Many times, senior SEALs tried to pull rank, which had previously resulted in lost gear, damaged boats, and injuries. NSW implemented a directive stating that no one could supersede the positional authority of a SWCC patrol officer, regardless of rank.

Kris briefed me on the issues we would need to repair as we took over. On the third day at camp, we assumed control of all boats, gear, and the mission from Elmer and Darren's detachment. Their gear had been packed and convoyed to Mombasa. We were now ready to hit the ground running. Our intense training was about to be tested, and things were about to get interesting.
The SEAL senior chief held a sit-down with me and my LT to discuss the way forward, though it felt more like an ultimatum. He reviewed the mission and progress but omitted the setbacks in their training, which had fueled the bad blood between him, Elmer, and Darren.

The Kenyans that the SEALs trained in weapons using World War II-era 9mm Grease Guns were underway, when one sailor accidentally discharged his weapon, shooting through the engine hatch and striking one of the Caterpillar diesel engines.

After about an hour of briefing from the senior chief, he informed us that we would not be needed for training. Instead, we could focus on what we wanted during the deployment. I was pissed! I was clearly annoyed, and exclaimed, "You mean to tell me, we're not going to do anything on this deployment but sit on our asses, maintain our gear, while you SEALs do all the training?" He simply said, "Yes." I thought he was a pompous ass and now knew why Elmer and Darren were so pissed off. The SEALs tried to run maritime training and marginalized the boat team when the boats and our capability were the focus of training, and this SEAL senior chief hadn't realized he needed to take a back seat and support maritime-centric training. I would love to see them attempt this without maritime experts. So, I rogered up and left the meeting. It was not a happy day.

That night, Kris wanted to introduce my team to the Kenyan senior enlisted by visiting their bar on base. I use the term "bar" loosely because there was nothing but hot beer and bugs in biblical proportions throughout the establishment. Why? There were no screens on the windows. Oh, and no door either.

We drank beer, endured the bugs, and then the fun began. They turned on some music, and I started to break dance. Yes, being from Chicago, you pick up a few choice moves. The Kenyans were mesmerized, constantly asking how I knew how to dance. I was happy to oblige.

My experience in the boat teams, had taught me, that the Kenyans we worked with had rarely interacted with Americans or our culture. That night, it was all about rapport building. Everything went well dancing, drinking, and fellowshipping. When one of the Kenyan senior enlisted, whom I had grown to admire and respect, asked me about "aliens" in our country. I told him they did exist and reluctantly recounted a story from my childhood. He consoled me, saying, "It's okay, Chief Capenta, tell me." So, I told the tale of a flying saucer hovering over a tree between two garages, my brother and I saw shining lights on it before running away. I added that the tree never grew again after that.

Out of nowhere, he punched my arm and yelled, "How come only you Americans get to see the aliens?" We all laughed and started jumping up and down, doing the Maasai Warrior dance. Mark, my LPO, reminded me it was getting late and time to head back to base. The base was about a mile down the road. When he asked about Kris, I said, "To hell with Kris he's from SBT-20." We left Kris at the bar, forcing him to walk back in the pitch-black Kenyan wild crunching millipedes while he walked.

He got back pretty late. But paybacks are a bitch. While I slept, Kris took a five-gallon bucket of water and dumped it on me.

Drenching me, my belongings, cot, and sleeping bag. As he walked out, he yelled, "Carp, you asshole." From that moment, Kris and I became lifelong friends. I joke that I left him in the Serengeti to fend for himself. It makes a great story. Kris remained my buddy for the rest of my Navy career. We deployed to Iraq together and helped build the SWCC Warrant Officer Community. Our bond was unbreakable.

The next day, new SEALs arrived, and the previous senior chief departed for home. I remembered everything he had said about SEALs taking over the training and setting conditions for the incoming SEALs. I didn't mind sitting out and letting the previous chief do all the heavy lifting until the new SEALs arrived.
One, named Oscar, was quite an anomaly. Originally a SWCC, then a SEAL, he knew both boats and SEAL operations. I knew him from SBU-12. Oscar was a tough SOB. He deployed with Pete and Indy.

Knowing how much Oscar would contribute, I had to come out of deployment retirement early. I refused to sit on my ass and let him, and his teammates do all the work without us pulling our weight. Gabe and I recently completed tours at NAVSCIATTS, we had all the curriculum to establish a hybrid SEAL/SWCC capability and schoolhouse. Talk about the difference in attitude and ego when the right people work together, we were going to crush this deployment, especially as the first six-month mission to Manda Bay.

Kris departed for home, having done an excellent job shaping our base camp and improving life in such an austere environment. It was time to get down to business. The SEAL task unit commander at Manda Bay was Tristin Rizzi, and our SEAL LNO in Nairobi was Rob Newsome. They were in the tactical operations center (TOC), discussing the way ahead. I had prepared for this meeting over the past two weeks, even using my own funds to print curriculum and trainee guides. I always believed every day was an interview. Since the previous SEAL senior chief had marginalized SWCC impact in the maritime domain, I was ready to take over and run things like our NAVSCIATTS training department.

I briefed the new plan to create a Hybrid SEAL/SWCC program requiring six to eight weeks of training to ensure knowledge retention and confidence and preventing future accidents like shooting the boats. The training would be followed up with MIO surges. Rob and Tristin were willing to give it a shot and told me to pull the trigger.

The SEALs took over ground tactics and shipboard close-quarter combat, while Gabe and I got to work creating a NAVSCIATTS-style school for the Kenya Navy and their new hybrid SWCC/SEAL capability. My detachment now had the responsibility of training the Kenyans in all things SWCC. You name it we taught them to be experts. We even created a schoolhouse called the Kenya Naval School of Maritime Excellence (KNSOME).

Creating a full-up capability while simultaneously identifying threats, establishing indications and warnings, and attempting to expand our Joint Operating Area (JOA) beyond the local zone was no small task. On top of that, we were trying to change a military culture deeply entrenched in the British system. The enlisted personnel lacked decision-making authority and broad operational capabilities like the ones we were instilling. Our first six weeks of training produced an incredible class, though it began with chaos. On our initial run to the end of the pier, Oscar started pushing Kenyans into the water. The pier jutted into an inlet fed by the Indian Ocean. It was funny looking back, but at the time, the Americans had to jump in and save our new drowning teammates.

We had forgotten the small print: Kenyans generally do not swim, because everything in the water wants to eat them. Training in the pool at base was equally challenging. The water was so green we couldn't see the bottom, and we worried about contracting unknown infections. Still, every day began with physical fitness, followed by swim training. We even spent money to treat the pool and make it swimmable. A caving ladder and climbing rope were secured forty feet up in a nearby tree for confidence and climbing training. I have to say, the confidence of these Kenyan boat operators was second to none.

The Chief of Naval Operations (CNO) officially sanctioned KNSOME, and the first class was ready to operate. They could plan missions using our formats, and we used scenario-driven intelligence to identify potential locations of real threats or terrorists. Concept of operation briefs were sent back to our Task Force Commander in Djibouti for permission to execute missions. Rob acted as our liaison with the embassy, and the Kenyan CNO authorized all missions. We even had the ability to rent large boats to operate along the coastline for training and operations.

We were now ready to unleash our capability from the eleven-meter RIBs, flying both the U.S. and Kenyan flags. I even came up with an idea to use the hippo pond where we drew our shower water to test and adjust all of our night vision equipment. We had everything from thermal imagers to night scopes and helmet-mounted systems. Hundreds of thousands of dollars' worth of gear went into that operation. We drove our Pajero vehicles to the pond and began setting up the equipment as the sun set. We watched wildlife in the dark while everything worked perfectly. It was breathtaking.

That peace, however, was short-lived. Two giant hippos we had been tracking began calmly moving toward us. Hippos are among the most dangerous animals in Africa. They tip over boats, attack swimmers, and charge on land. We hadn't realized the last part. The next thing we knew, the beasts picked up speed and charged. We ran as fast as we could, terrified and laughing even as seasoned operators.

Eventually, we escaped safely, laughing but leaving hundreds of thousands of dollars' worth of gear at the pond's edge. Our team executed a stealth retrieval mission, rifles in hand, and successfully returned the gear to base. I asked them what they thought their small arms could do against those hippos. "Hey, man, we just needed moral support," Chris said. TIA "This is Africa".

After the hippo incident, we averaged between 100 and 175 boardings per mission surge. Our Kenyan Boat Team became so effective that we jokingly called it "harassing the local population." Anytime vessels saw us, the civilian crews would immediately get on their knees on the main deck with their hands on their heads. We became very familiar with lines of operation, operating patterns, and age old rat lines tied to smuggling routes.

We had two jet skis painted in camouflage gray, modified to carry a High Frequency radio and a Tactical Satellite radio. It also had a 7.62mm machine gun mounted between the handlebars. This added two more armed platforms to our maritime capability. We used the jet skis to escort our Zodiacs close to shore, allowing civil affairs teams to reach villages, dig wells, and start schoolhouses. It was our way of piggybacking on their missions to expand the Joint Operating Area (JOA).

It was incredibly rewarding to see our progress and establish a strong training template. We worked out minor issues with our plan but realized we needed two more weeks of training to bring the Kenyans to the level we required and select the best and brightest from each class to begin training as part of our cadre. These Kenyan instructors had to present daily briefs to us over a two-week period, covering every requirement on task, conditions, and standards. They were also graded on VEGA. Voice, Eyes, Gestures, and Attitude in both practical and knowledge-based teaching exercises.

By the time our third class began, the Kenyans were the lead instructors, and we served as backup. This was our greatest challenge yet, because Kenyan officers were now attending the course and had to take direction from their enlisted instructors a stark departure from the British system they were accustomed to. It required intervention from the Chief of Naval Operations and even dropping two officers from the course to maintain order. We encountered a few bumps, including having to pause training when officers refused tasks until formally ordered by the CNO. Gradually, we began to see the fruits of our labor and identified promising officers who would lead this new team.

We designed our mission planning class using actual intelligence that the Kenyans could verify or challenge, knowing we would visit these locations during execution. The collaboration was inspiring, improving our common operating picture. Beyond running the schoolhouse, we conducted solo missions close to the Somali border, driving our RIBs and two jet skis. One operator drove, while the other rode as a passenger, holding a camera with a telephoto zoom lens on the Jet Ski operator's shoulder.

The seas were always between five and fifteen feet. They slammed us so hard at times that the impact would cycle rounds into the chamber of our machine guns. These transits were punishing for everyone, both on the boats and the jet skis. On a single trip, we endured thousands of violent impacts. Our mitigation strategy: swap out drivers for the return trip to base. After missions, SEALs and SWCCs were often completely immobile, taking up to two days to recover from the transit.

After a few of these runs, we got creative. We had KBR contractors build wooden skids to mount atop the engine covers of each boat. The jet skis were then loaded onto the skids, strapped down, and transported on the RIBs instead of being beaten by the waves for 60 miles. Once at the objective, we would launch the jet skis and escort them to the target area.

This was 2004, and out of necessity, we developed tactics, techniques, and procedures for outfitting, transporting, communicating, and engaging the enemy from a jet ski. We even used them to access areas near shore where RIBs couldn't go, escorting suspect craft to deeper water for boarding and search operations. Pretty cool, if you ask me.

By the way: "Don't feed wild animals" means exactly that lest you end up in our situation.

Ironically, it wasn't the locals who harassed us it was the baboons! Every day at 4:00 a.m., they executed a military-style operation. They would sneak into our camp and pilfer anything within reach of their giant paws. Stealthy at first, but by 5:00 a.m., they were running atop our tents. Eventually, the harassment became unbearable.

KBR had erected a large shed for the garbage cans to prevent the baboons from scattering trash everywhere. That slowed them slightly, but the clever primates were not deterred. They quickly learned to pick the lock and access the trash. Soon, they discovered our food pantry, where all our biweekly food shipments were stored: bread, snacks, real meals, Meals Ready to Eat (MRE), and T-Rations which were larger MREs served in aluminum containers.

Nothing was gourmet, but it was sustenance.

One morning, the usual 5:00 a.m. chaos never came. The camp was eerily silent. Too silent. Then we heard the cook screaming. Every operator ran outside, rifles at the ready. Down the road, we saw a baboon sprinting upright, carrying two cases of MREs twenty-two pounds each! It was both hilarious and astonishing. We laughed and debated if baboons might be stronger than humans. It was like a special ops ape mission, planned against special ops humans!"

We assumed the baboons had enough food for a while and let our guard down. What we didn't know was, some KBR contractors were feeding them. In any wildlife environment, feeding wild animals is a strict no-no. Never, ever do it.

One night, we were asleep when the cook yelled again. We jumped up and saw the alpha male bending the thick bars of our food pantry window. Somehow, he had gotten in but panicked when he saw us approaching. In desperation, he started pooping everywhere as he tried to escape. This was serious the alpha was huge. Thankfully, when someone opened the mess hall and pantry door, he bolted.

The aftermath was a hazmat-level mess. Nothing could be saved; everything had to be discarded. In the jungle, this wasn't just inconvenient it was a crisis. Our next resupply wasn't for two weeks, leaving only stove-top stuffing, hot dogs, and MREs. Normally, we'd have one hot meal for dinner and MREs for everything else, but now we were stuck with hot dogs and stuffing for fourteen days straight. To this day, the thought makes me shudder not because the food was bad, but because monotony made it unbearable.

Out of caution, we called the Kenyan game wardens. Our training hadn't prepared us for baboon threats. The warden explained that baboons rarely group this close to humans unless they intend to attack. Seeing the alpha male in the trees, it became soberingly clear: the threat was real.

Here we were, trained to locate and capture bad guys, now staring down a troop of angry, hungry baboons. One winner, one loser and survival wasn't guaranteed.

The warden advised that neutralizing the alpha male was the only way to stop the potential ambush. We were given permission to take him when he entered the camp, and to display him for a few days so the others would understand he was no longer their leader. Evolution hasn't changed this fundamental rule: someone must be made an example.

Shane, our new task unit commander, took the responsibility in case there was any fallout. The baboon was so enormous that three tungsten carbide penetrator rounds were required to bring him down. Sad as it was to kill such an impressive creature, in the wild, it was kill or be killed.

Afterward we hung the baboon on a lumber pile for the ape troop to see. The warden advised leaving him for a few days before burning the wood to prevent disease. His arm size, length and height was remarkable. The message was received: the other baboons stopped attacking, leaving our food stores and tents untouched. Just another day in the jungle. The threat had been neutralized.

After that incident, we finally received permission to expand our JOA toward the Tanzania border. We continued gathering intelligence on a terrorist named "Pate,". He was the man who smuggled explosives into Kenya to attack the Nairobi and Tanzanian Embassies. We leveraged opportunities to rent dhow boats to blend in with local pattern of life. Dhow boats were ancient vessels with slanted triangular sails, common in the Red Sea and Indian Ocean. But our true goal was using the boats to locate Pate. On several occasions, we even went to Pate's girlfriend's house, sitting on her front porch just to let him know we were nearby. It was only a matter of time before we caught him.

We also had permission to visit different bays and marinas to inventory every boat around the clock that was entering and leaving over a seven-day period To accomplish this, we cataloged the vessels and created a target list. We then obtained authorization from our Task Force and the Kenyan Navy to board and search each boat on the list.

My team drove the boats overland to Kilifi, timing our arrival perfectly. We launched at high tide and began boarding the boats on our target list. A few vessels that ran were intercepted by the Kenyan Navy in Mombasa. This was my first deployment as chief petty officer and assistant detachment commander, and it was exhilarating.

I realized that the mentorship I had received throughout my career led me to this moment. When I acted like an idiot, letting my "South Side" attitude surface, I failed, but there were always people who believed in me. Finally, I believed in myself. Leading with honor and courage became my North Star; I just had to get out of my own way.

During this period, we participated in numerous missions with some classified. This was one of the first where we created a surge capability and a targeting package over seven days, identifying individuals and vessels that warranted closer scrutiny. Kilifi and Mombasa were key ports where larger boats went for repairs, so shipyards were also locations of interest. Once our mission concluded, our road crew transported the trucks and trailers back to Camp Simba. Meanwhile, our plan was to check into a hotel overlooking the ocean in Kilifi. We intended to maintain surveillance while taking a break at the hotel. This also served as a deterrent. During our stay, we spoke with shipyards and locals to learn what they knew and what challenges they faced.

No sooner had we checked into the hotel than we began receiving dirty looks from European tourists. Not unusual because they all had opinions about the war. Though we weren't in uniform, some clearly did not want us or our boats at the pier. One couple even told the hotel owner that either we had to leave, or they would. They did not want to see "war boats" at the pier. The owner defended our presence, saying, "The Americans won't be departing. You can have a refund. We appreciate your patronage, but the Americans aren't going anywhere. Them being here is an honor and serves as a warning to anyone that attempts to hurt us and this hotel."

We were astonished by his response, as we weren't even ready to commence our over-water transit back to Camp Simba. The rest of the evening, we enjoyed our meal in peace.
After a few days, it was time to depart. On our last day in Kilifi, we prepped the boats for departure. Our Kenyan operators were well-fed and ready. I consumed my final meal of curry chicken a decision I regretted for the next few days as my stomach rebelled.

Once the boats were ready, we headed to Malindi, to overnight onboard and rotate watches throughout the night. Unfortunately, the curry did not agree with me. I spent the entire night vomiting and felt miserable. It was definitely food poisoning, and to this day, I detest any dish with curry as its main spice.

Thankfully, I recovered in time to carry out the mission. We rotated watches on the boats and couldn't help but notice how pale the Kenyan operators looked. Though it was about eighty-five degrees, they were freezing, so we gave them our operational jackets. Throughout the night, we observed vessels of interest and gathered intelligence before executing any boarding. There was no illumination that night. With night vision goggles and thermals, we could see a fishing boat in the distance with its running lights on. We maneuvered slowly within 500 yards while remaining in the shadows just outside the ring of light cast by the vessel. The boat was roughly forty feet long, carrying ten to thirteen people.

Even though we were supporting the Kenyan SBU "By, With and Through," the mission was inherently dangerous. Our boats were closing in on a contact of interest off the coast of Malindi harbor. This was same area where explosives had previously been smuggled to target the U.S. Embassies in Nairobi and Tanzania.

We all knew our jobs and leveraged P.I.L.E. to our advantage {Push all information up and down the chain of command, Improve your fighting position at all times, Lead at all times, and Exploit all technical and technological advantages}. Now it was finally time to pull the trigger and execute.

Once we closed in on the contact of interest, we used thermal imagers to count the suspects onboard the boats. The Kenyan officer in charge determined the number of operators needed to safely conduct the boarding and search. He decided to send everyone.

As we came alongside, one person ran onto the pilot house. I pointed my rifle at him, yelling in Swahili to stop (Simama Hapo!) and to put his hands on his head (Mikono Ju!). He kept climbing. I took the slack out of my rifle trigger. Suddenly, he pulled down the Kenyan flag. Later, we learned he had thought we were boarding because the flag was flying after sunset. Cultural differences nearly got him dropped. If he had realized how close, he came to death; he might have thanked God for another day.

The Kenyan missions continued, and the schoolhouse became even more successful. Our hybrid SWCC/SEAL unit now fifty strong made a huge impact in their country. The fact that ordinary sailors could become precision operators and maritime experts made all the effort worthwhile. As the school gained notoriety, we conducted more boardings and refined our skills through missions and training.

Maintaining a presence at the Somali border was grueling. Wearing heavy body armor and helmets in the heat took a toll. Many of us suffered heat exhaustion and a drop in performance. Some of us required IV therapy. By the way, SWCC and SEALs are trained to administer IVs to one another in moving vehicles or boats. We needed boats suitable for operating in this climate. Unfortunately, the Foreign Military Sales (FMS) system was stuck in the 1980s. The acquisition offices didn't consider sea state when purchasing boats. They assumed harbor craft could handle ten- to fifteen-foot waves. Later, the Kenyans received boats designed for harbors, not the rough seas off East Africa. If they had more experienced operators in procurement, they could have prevented this.

We began the procurement process to provide suitable boats, with one stipulation: air conditioning. The FMS inventory was so limited that our only option was a cabin boat with A/C, not designed for high seas. It wasn't ideal, but the Kenyans and subsequent SWCC detachments made do.

Our qualified Kenya Special Boat Unit (KSBU) grew with each class. With the cadre expanding, we decided to take the KSBU instructors to the chief's bar on their base, the same one we had visited 16 weeks earlier. Upon entering, the Kenya senior enlisted told us that the KSBU instructors could not drink in the bar. I explained that as a chief petty officer, I was visiting to show them what to strive for in their careers. He was adamant: "Either they leave and you can drink in our bar or take them outside to drink under the Mamba Tree." I kept my South Side attitude in check.

We grabbed our beers, walked out, and sat under the Mamba Tree. Naturally, no one stayed after the first drink. We returned to base, because who the hell drinks under a damn Mamba Tree anyway?

This incident inspired a new Ron Carpenter idea. I sought permission from the base commander to create our own bar, undercutting the others. It became wildly popular, with beer for the equivalent of a quarter and hard alcohol for fifty cents. But fun aside, it was only open on the weekend. The mission remained our priority, and I was working with some of the best special operators I've ever known.

One such SWCC was Eric Mimms, our LNO in Djibouti. He was an exceptional boat operator, seasoned by multiple MK V deployments, and possessed the charisma to get things done. We became close immediately. His mother was Black, his father Italian; whereas my mother was Italian, and my father Black. We were both multi-racial, but he looked Black, and I looked white, and I was apparently much better looking.

Eric was indispensable. If we needed something, he delivered. He drove around Camp Lemonnier, pulling equipment from Army stock, securing treadmills, weights, high-dollar speakers, recreational projectors, and hundreds of movies, some not even released yet. He became the "Tyrone" of our deployment. Whenever we needed anything, we'd say, "Wait, we better call Tyrone."

Thanks, Eric. We are forever in your debt."

So, lo and behold, our task unit commander gave me permission to ask the base commander if we could open our own bar. The base commander authorized it but assigned us a location far from the existing bar, assuming we'd look at it and abandon the idea.

I pulled my detachment and the Kenyan instructors together, then told Gabe that I had to go to Mombasa to brief the Kenya CNO. If they wanted a bar, it needed to be up and running by Monday, the day of the base inspection. Honestly, if anyone saw the place beforehand, they'd have said, "To hell with this nonsense. I'm not doing this."

Gabe, our SWCC, was the perfect man for the job. He was of Latin descent, a patriotic American who had been deported from the U.S. twice but found his way back to join the Navy and become part of the Special Operations Boat Teams. I knew he could pull it off, make the detachment and KSBU shine, and still do it all with a smile. There was nothing he couldn't overcome.

The building we were given was an abandoned carpenter shop, machinery still intact, and sawdust piled twenty by forty feet high. Two days to transform it into a bar? This was going to be a challenge.

The task unit commander and I set off to Mombasa for our brief. It went extremely well, and the CNO planned to attend the KSBU officer graduation. Upon returning to Camp Simba, Shane grabbed me and SEAL Chief Pete and asked us to follow him. He was visibly upset.

"If this ever happens again, I am kicking you and your teams out of the country!" he said.

"What do you mean? I was with you the entire week," I replied, confused.

"Your guys rigged the garbage door with grenade simulators to scare the baboons away. It didn't work, they were too smart, but the Somali garbage men opened the door and took the brunt of the explosion," he said, shaking his head. "Flash Crashes can cause serious injuries." I looked at the door and saw three holes still smoking. I responded. "No problem, sir. It won't happen again." I couldn't help laughing at the sight of the smoking holes. Despite the setback, we completed the bar. Thanks to Eric, it had cool JBL speakers, a TV projector, glasses, and a constant supply of alcohol from Mombasa. The bar had a massive barn-style sliding door. When they opened it to show me the result, it was incredible. The bar was named the "Rattrap," in honor of the boat teams from Vietnam.

The wooden sign had "RATTRAP" etched into it. KBR guys used the dipstick from the generator to paint the letters black with motor oil. The bar itself was huge and immaculate; it definitely looked better than any other bars on base.

The grand opening featured video footage of our training and missions from the previous week. As part of the ceremony, we sang our detachment anthem Brittany Spears' "Toxic." Then the Kenyans and our det formed a circle with the Masai warriors, chanting and jumping. We loved our KSBU brothers.

The bar was a hit, and for about three weeks, all went smoothly. Being close to the piers and out of sight meant the music was loud but we even had a designated driver with the duty van. One night, Gabe reported a Kenyan diver causing trouble. I instructed him to tell the diver to behave and offer free drinks. Fifteen minutes later, Gabe reported that he was still causing issues. I told Gabe to escort him out and to keep it cool.

Gabe politely walked the diver to the door, but suddenly, the man's eyes turned dark and menacing. He punched Gabe in the mouth, splitting his bottom lip. I ran over and stopped Gabe from retaliating.

I told the diver to leave, turned off the music, and ended the party. KSBU and Gabe helped clean up. Gabe was fine, though annoyed I didn't let him get his revenge. It took an hour to tidy the bar. What a night.

Afterward, we opened the barn door to leave and found the diver waiting outside, ready to fight again. Definitely the wrong move.

I said, "Oh, Gabe." Gabe, a former boxer, approached. When the diver punched, Gabe struck him in the mouth, knocking him out. He even hit him again before falling completely to the ground. I ran to the diver.

I lifted the diver, sat him up, and lightly popped him on the back of the head to revive him. He immediately regained consciousness. Remarkably, he still wanted to fight. "Hey man, it's over. Let's just get you a ride". I instructed Meatie, our Masai warrior, to escort him. Meatie placed him in a rear naked choke and began dragging him to the van. I yelled, "Meatie, stop." The diver finally got the message and walked home.

I had that familiar Chicago feeling again but this time, I knew what to do. I was responsible; I didn't blame anyone else. I was the leader, and knowing bad news don't get better with time, I reported the incident immediately .

Back at base, I briefed the task unit commander, who informed the base commander and TF Commander. The diver was thrown out of the Navy due to repeated incidents of bullying and fighting. Clearly, he had deep-seated anger issues.

I briefed my detachment and the KSBU, apologizing for the incident, informing them that the bar was now exclusively for us and our debriefs only. The KSBU warrant officer approached me afterward and said, "The reason this happened is we didn't sacrifice a chicken before opening the bar." I politely declined and asked if I could just bring a bucket of chicken. He said no the chicken had to be sacrificed for the greater good of the bar. Go figure, I participated in my first animal sacrifice. Don't worry, we ate it afterwards.

All things considered, this deployment epitomized why special operations is so critical to national defense. Small teams create strategic effects and lifelong friendships. Yet, the need for manpower in Iraq and Afghanistan allowed KBR to reduce the KSBU size by offering jobs worldwide at twenty times their pay. Turnover was constant. KSBU members took the training we provided and outsourced their capabilities to KBR. One step forward, two steps back.

Our deployment ended successfully. I flew to Djibouti to debrief the task force commander and hand off with Eric, who had supported us all these months. Compared to the Camp Simba squalor and shoestring budget, I was impressed by their massive base camp. I was frustrated that they received hostile fire pay without being in the line of fire, while Kenya did not qualify. As SWCC, we were creative in calculating the exact distance to cross the imaginary line in the open ocean once per month to ensure our guys received hostile fire pay.

Still, being in Kenya was an incredible experience. But as with all good things, it had to end. It was time to go home and with some great news: I had been selected to commission as the ninth SWCC warrant officer in Navy history. I was finally homeward bound, ready to take my own detachment out the door as a detachment commander.

Kenya changed me in so many ways. The lifelong friends I made, for one. The simplicity of living, for another. I learned that being a man boils down to being respected, providing a roof over your family's head and food on the table. Anything beyond that? Just stray voltage.

Soon, I would escape the rat race of competing against other chiefs for promotion. I was about to be commissioned a Navy SWCC Warrant Officer within twelve months. Until then, I would remain in command of my detachment and commence workup for the next deployment.

About three weeks after returning home, I was called into the operations office and congratulated on my selection. The master chief explained that a chief in one of the detachments couldn't deploy due to shoulder surgery, so I was being chosen to take the detachment out. I explained that I had just returned and wasn't fully reintegrated yet. He assured me his mind was made up and suggested I might want one more deployment as an enlisted man before commissioning. I told him I wasn't interested.

The next day, as I walked past the commanding officer's door to say hello, he asked me to come in. Mike Lumpkin, our commanding officer, was exceptional fair, with a deck-plate leadership style I had rarely seen. He knew the truth came from the deck plates, from the sailors actually doing the work.

As soon as I entered, I asked, "Been walking the deck plates again?" He laughed. "Ron, I take it you're aware of this upcoming deployment?"

"Yes, sir," I replied.

"Well, what do you think about that?"

I said, "Sir, I've known you for fifteen years and toured four commands with you. If you tell me I'm the only one that can take this detachment out, I'll pack my bags tonight and depart." He seemed relieved.

Mike then shared something personal. He turned his monitor to show me a list of collateral duties. About seventy-five percent were assigned to the legal man at the command. It highlighted leadership issues tied directly to the chief's mess. I asked, "Do you need me to go?"

"No," he said. "Keep doing great things with your detachment." That vote of confidence moved me.

This RIB detachment was special. All the SWCC I had were outstanding. Gabe, Chris, and Shawn remained from Kenya, and I added Dan, Matt, Sevi, Casey, and Alex, all dedicated and hardworking men. We trained rigorously, operating boats even in the worst sea states, and even did high speed vessel proof of concept testing that damn near killed us. Storms in San Diego didn't even stop us. We would obtain a waiver to get the boats underway regardless. Understanding the maritime environment and performing under extreme conditions was essential to be great Boatguys.

One constant challenge was standing for long periods. To maintain posture and absorb impacts, we constantly squatted thousands of times per night. When fatigue set in, we'd fold down the bolster seat, but any high g-force impact would slam our spines into the seats. This led to many of us permanently injuring L4-L5/L5-S1. We'd jump back up and resume squatting. Bending forward to grab the steering wheel while wearing a helmet with NVGs, also broke many of our necks at C4/C5/C6. No complaints. You do what you have to do. Looking back, submitting operational deficiency reports (ODR) could have helped us demand better equipment, but we simply adapted and the paradigm of injury continues to this day. We just weren't informed enough.

The commanding officer gave permission to for my det to forego driving our boats overland to North Carolina. Instead, we drove them over the water from San Diego to San Francisco, with an over-the-road crew shadowing us. This was to prove we didn't need to haul them across the country to train.

Driving in five-to-twenty-five-foot seas was intense. In the surf zone three miles off Monterey Bay, we had to make an abrupt port turn, then continue five more miles offshore to reach consistent seas. Later, we discovered Pebble Beach had become the new Mavericks, with forty-five-foot waves spilling onto the shoreline.

By this point, the detachment was ready for another deployment. We stayed away from the command to maximize learning: hundreds of hours driving, operating boats, managing communications, weapons, navigation, and engines. They could even conduct blow-by tests to detect a five-second turbo lag, identifying intercooler issues. These guys were a cut above the rest. Part of my training, of course, involved teaching them to drink responsibly. Almost every opportunity, we'd take the boats to San Clemente Island, gather around a bonfire, tell stories, share experiences, and drink just like the old-timers in Panama did for us. I taught them, "You can be drunk, or you can be stupid, but you can't be both at the same time." This leadership style ensured we avoided incidents like the one in Okinawa years ago.

This was literally going to be my final act before turning over RIB Det Bravo to Mike Andre, the incoming detachment commander and future SWCC warrant officer. He was the right man for this det.

A final part of the San Francisco trip highlighted a grim reality of being a Special Warfare Combat Crewman. It was the sheer amount of head trauma we sustained.

We made it to Monterey and stayed for four days to let the seas calm and the storm pass. The mission for that day was simple: transit across the bay from Monterey to Santa Cruz to overnight before the final push into San Francisco. Compared to the previous nights, the seas were relatively mild roughly six to eight feet and we only had to cover thirty nautical miles.

As the detachment commander, it was my job to report back to our team in San Diego and send a proof-of-life photo via our tactical satellite capability. The data burst went perfectly. While picking up speed, I twisted my body, looked down, and turned a knob for boat-to-boat communications and TACSAT.

No sooner did I turn, than the boat flew off an eight-to-ten-foot wave. I was out of a neutral spine position. The boat slammed down at thirty to forty miles per hour, and I pancaked on the deck. My crew looked back and saw me wedged between the communications box and the inflatable sponson. According to them, I looked more like a compressed mannequin than a human being.

It felt as if someone had flipped off a television in my brain an immediate flash of black. Fortunately, I came to fairly quickly. A flash of light caught my eye, and I began assessing my body for injury. I couldn't hear, and a metallic taste filled my mouth. My crew kept asking if I was okay, but all I saw were their mouths moving. It was terrifying. Thankfully, within thirty seconds, my hearing returned. I brushed myself off, conducted a quick assessment, and told my guys I was okay and to Charlie Mike.

Looking back, this type of incident happened more times than I care to remember. We never dwelled on it because the mission never stopped. That's the life of the boat teams. Over the years, we've all come to terms with being knocked out or pancaked in our bolster seats from impact exposure. I had thirteen or more of these incidents. Yet the mission always continued.

After that event, I officially turned over Det Bravo. It was bittersweet. I knew I would miss all those hard-pipe hitters, but I was ready for the next adventure it was finally time to commission as a Naval Officer.

Chief Warrant Officer Ron Carpenter: ready to rock and roll. I could not have done it without Mike Lumpkin and his sage guidance, nor without the many mentors along the way, especially the old salty chiefs and young enlisted who helped shaped me.

Hooyah SBT!

Chapter Eleven

Commissioning as a Naval Officer: Iraq

"The object of war is not to die for your country, but to make the other bastard die for his."

General George S. Patton

The Navy is good at many things, including marking transitions. We love our ceremonies, replete with patriotic music, speeches, and traditions that have endured since the Department of the Navy was established in 1798. So, when I was commissioned as a Naval officer in what we call ascension, compared to my previous ceremony for promotion to Chief Petty Officer, this was different. When I was promoted to Chief Warrant Officer, it was night and day. All of the pomp and circumstance was choreographed with precision and just for me and my family.

My mom was beaming from ear to ear. She knew the struggles we had all gone through and giving her this day and this moment meant everything to me. This was the beginning of my journey as a leader and a SWCC warrant officer. It took this long to expose the gaps in my maturity, leadership, administrative skills, critical thinking and the list goes on. I had to stop thinking like a chief and start thinking like an officer.

There were two moments in my career when it was all about me and my family: my ascension into the warrant officer community and my retirement ceremony in 2019. I could hardly believe how long it took to shed so much of my past thinking always like a victim and blaming others. But I still had much work to do. All the lessons I had learned, often the hard way, now placed me in a position with a steep learning curve, where I would represent all those who came before me and carry their legacy forward. I would also teach the next generation of special boat operators not only how to fight the enemy with guns and grenades but how to be part of a tribe of warrior diplomats. I believed I was more than ready for the challenge.

What most people do not realize about Special Operations, is that while we have a precision kinetic side, it makes up only about five percent of our actual mission. What we were designed for is less glamorous yet often has a higher return on investment. Everyone assumes our main purpose is kicking in doors and muzzle striking people with guns. I'm not saying that isn't part of our mission set, but the majority of our missions involve being "warrior diplomats." And, as you have already seen, that can be a very complex Special Operations challenge.

As SWCC, we can go anywhere in the world and embed with partner forces, providing training through building partner capacity in one of two ways: Security Force Assistance (SFA), which is population-focused, or Foreign Internal Defense (FID), which is threat-focused. Many of our deployments, apart from Iraq and occasional missions as battle staff, JTACs, gunners, and drivers in Afghanistan, involved traveling across the globe to train partner forces to become self-sufficient. The bottom line is simple: the more we build partner capacity, the more they can stand on their own. As a result, we don't have to put our own troops on the ground in these countries. It's cost-effective and saves human capital. 1000 Deployed U.S. Troops cost about $1B usd.

Now, in my new role, I would put all my experience to the test as a commissioned officer. This was what I had trained for my entire Navy career and now it was becoming reality.

I woke up early on my first day as a SWCC Warrant Officer, and it was exhilarating! I met with Mike Lumpkin, my commanding officer, and, believe me, it was a bit intimidating at first. He invited me into his office, sat me down, and asked if I knew the difference between taking the oath as an officer versus as an enlisted sailor. I did know, but I decided to listen to this man, whose experience far outweighed mine.

Here's what Mike said: "Officers have a unique position of authority and influence in an organization that could be exploited for political gain. Swearing an oath to the U.S. Constitution instead of to the President or officers above them ensures that no one in a position of power can manipulate officers to control the military. That's what dictators do."

He also said that, unlike enlisted, we can voluntarily resend our commission at any time. Wow, I never heard that before. But it made me realize that I had a huge learning curve and needed to be open to new lessons and experiences. Titles can only take you so far. I also found myself behaving more like a chief. After all, we stick to what we know and all I knew was how to be an enlisted man and chief petty officer. I had to re-program my brain and stop thinking like a chief, just like I had to shed my Chicago hustle thinking.

In my former role as a Chief, I got away with speaking my mind way too much. This behavior clearly would not fly as a commissioned officer. At least to a certain extent. We were the technical experts in the field that could fill any role when required. And those skills, developed over many years of training and in-country experience would come in handy now as a commissioned officer; however, running my mouth instead of following the commander's intent, had to come to a stop. Officers do not question the boss or tell them that they are wrong in front of their subordinates. These issues were handled like gentlemen and with commensurate respect.

I was thrilled to know that Rob Newsome who was our SEAL liaison officer from Nairobi that had us doing missions well before they were called, "Sensitive Activities, was tasked with setting up a new command called, "Sensitive Activities One" (SA-1). He wanted me to help him build out the command and define the mission. Of course, I said, "Hell yes." I soon received orders that would keep me in San Diego because once you commission as a warrant officer, you cannot remain at the same command. They did not want any risk of undue influence or reset of the culture in which you were involved. So, I was excited about working with Rob. It was a good idea at first. Or so I thought.

Mike Lumpkin had quite a different idea. He sat me down in his office and gave me some advice. "Ron! What the heck are you thinking? You have one professional milestone to hit as a SWCC warrant officer and that is to take a MK V Detachment out the door. Once you go to SA-1 you will be stuck over there with no opportunity to meet this milestone. Now get your butt to Special Boat Team Twenty (SBT-20) and complete your career milestone." Whoa! He was right on the money. I agreed. My orders were changed, and I was on my way to SBT-20 in Virginia Beach, Virginia. SBT-12 and SBT-20 were not very different. They both had the same types of coastal patrol boats. All the SWCC were in super shape, with tremendous operational readiness. The differentiator at SBT-20 was they possessed a capability called "MCADS" where select dets had the capability of launching their eleven-meter RIBs out the back of military aircraft and running out the back of the plane chasing after the boat under free fall parachute rigs.

I was merely a dope on the rope and only qualified as a static line parachutist, meaning to remain qualified, most of my landings came at the cost of a hard PLF landing. Not fun.

It was 2006 and I was tasked with minor missions preparing capabilities for counter piracy efforts. Nothing exciting but I was really excited about standing up my MK V det. This boat was eighty-two feet long and weighed fifty tons. Quite a big boy and a real departure from my riverine boats and small coastal boats in the past. As young SWCC, no one wanted to be on the MK V boats. The amount of education and training required to keep the boat operational was immense. We would say that going to the MK V was like the roach motel; "You will check in, but you will never check out." The MK V SOC had a top speed of forty-seven knots when it was brand new. And it had a range of almost 500 nautical miles. (Of course, that planning range decreased as the boats got older and the high g-force impacts started to deteriorate the hulls, frames, engines and do not forget, our bodies.) The boat when brand new looked like a Black Angus cow, but after the years of impact on the hull, it began to resemble a South American cow with its ribs showing. You could actually see the frame members through the entire hull of the boat. Well fate had another job in mind for me.

Special Boat Team Twenty-Two out of Stennis Space Center in Mississippi, our only riverine capability in Naval Special Warfare, finally picked up a mission in Iraq. It was on the Euphrates River in Al Anbar Province to support a Task Force.

This is what we trained for our entire lives and now we were ready to bring this incredible capability into Iraq to support a Special Operations Task Force; it was a great achievement! Little did I know, things were about to change dramatically for me and thirty other SWCC assigned to SBT-20.

SBT-22 bit off a little more than it could chew when it came to its deployments and workups. There was only enough riverine capability back then to support a 1-0 presence meaning they would be able to support one riverine troop in country while the others were somewhere in their workup cycle. This 1-0 concept had sixteen boats assigned to four riverine troops. Their workup cycle, I believe, was the toughest in the boat teams. Period.

The Commodore of Group Four decided to relieve the pressure off of SBT-22 by forming two new riverine troops from SBT-20 and SBT-12. Each troop required almost fifty personnel. This included thirty SWCC and twenty support personnel. They had diverse responsibilities ranging from administration and weapons to medics (you get the picture).

I finally was on solid ground and was glad to see a former SBU-26 brother, Dave Strachan. He was a qualified MCADDs det patrol officer and well respected. This dirty blond haired, blue-eyed, barrel-chested servant leader was mature, laser-focused, and always had a smile everywhere he went. Dave loved martial arts and was a military athlete. He was even the catalyst behind combat fighting in the boat teams. He had a gift of placing himself in other people's shoes and always had infinite patience even when dealing with me. Of course, I would go out drinking with him and bonding with the SBT-20 chief's mess. It felt great being a part of SBT-20.

Surprise, surprise. My hopes and dreams of taking out a fifteen-man MK V Det with a maintenance support team, went south very quickly. I was informed that instead, I would be standing up a Riverine Task Unit. This was a troop with fifty personnel that can act as a stand-alone entity but fall under a task force.

I had no clue how I would pull this off. Hell, I did not know if I was experienced enough to handle a Task Unit. I only knew that I was a gifted team builder because I created a gang out of all my detachments. How in the hell was I going to pull this one off.

I had to come up with a plan and fast! Working up and deploying with two MK V Special Operations Craft was always going to be a piece of cake for me. But this? I mean I did not sign off for this, nor was I ready as a former chief that only led eleven-meter RIB Detachments. This Riverine Troop with all its complex weapons, gear, ammo, boats, tactics, and personnel had a price tag of over $30 million dollars. Me, Dave and Red Nemeth worked on our strategy like crazy, but I was still scared shitless.

Dave and I knew the riverine training from Panama, but this training that evolved into SBT-22 was on a different level and resembled another SWCC schoolhouse attempting to drop any SWCC that did not cut the mustard.

We received our orders and began coordinating with the operations department to pull SWCC from across the command to form "Riverine Task Unit Five." We had to borrow boats and practice nighttime driving in four-boat formation, along with immediate action drills (LT Green, my apologies for damaging your boats brother). This allowed us to mesh quickly before heading to Mississippi for training at a command that immediately resented us. Why? Because we would be compressing their usual twelve-to-eighteen-month workup into just six months and they made us pay every step of the way.

Dave and I shaped our senior enlisted cadre, assigning each chief to their own boat, essentially forming a fire team. The chiefs were Hank Taylor, Gary Lewis, and Todd English, with Dave as the senior. We pushed ourselves through every conceivable block of training we could access. This even included Dave hiring a former Russian Spetsnaz operative to train us in a fighting system that bordered on human rights violations rather than conventional combat, but it was effective. (Spetsnaz are special forces in the Soviet Union.) Just kidding but it was intense having thirty men lie side by side in full body armor and helmets while taking turns running over the last man at the end in what they called an "Indian sprint" (while we were on our backs). Add shooting and close-quarter fighting on concrete in full battle rattle, and it made for an unforgettable experience.

And of course, there was the infamous "gravity punch" that could instantly knock the wind out of you. The Russians viewed fighting very differently than we did. They knew Americans liked to have gear attached to our bodies and practiced controlling us using our rifle slings. They would even simulate a rifle malfunction, toss the rifle at you, and then draw their pistol while you were distracted.

I made it clear to the guys that no one was tossing our rifles. After all, each rifle fully outfitted with lasers and scopes cost well over $20,000.

Early on, Dave and I with the Chiefs made a commitment to one another: we would start this together, and we would finish it together. I never anticipated those words would be so binding. The SBT-22 cadre and leadership tried to derail this experiment, which was sanctioned by the commodore but lacked full support from their command. I understood why a coastal boat team arriving for abbreviated training could potentially affect their future riverine funding, but we had to follow orders. It would test all of our resolve in Riverine Task Unit Five.

Once Dave and I finalized the budget with the operations department, we realized that running the riverine troop and the task unit in Iraq might be more than we could handle alone. SBT-20 assigned two SEAL officers to the deployment cycle; they would split the deployment. Dave and I handled the day-to-day operations of the troop, while the SEAL officers Red and Marcus, skipped the training workup and assumed the task unit commander role in-country, managing our battle staff and integrating with the task force in Ramadi. This was a huge undertaking for SBT-20.

Once we received our orders, we drove from Joint Expeditionary Base Little Creek in Virginia Beach, Virginia, to Stennis Space Center in Bay Saint Louis, Mississippi, to begin riverine training. I hadn't been to Stennis since leaving NAVSCIATTS in 2003. Training at SBT-22 had evolved. It was more dangerous, more lethal, and more accountable than ever. This command and its mindset are a credit to the senior SEAL/SWCC enlisted, warrant officers, and LDOs who built a capability ready to answer any call at any tier level when needed. Talk about Preparation, Intersection, Opportunity (PIO) this was it.

As troop commander, I had to balance rigorous training with administrative duties: flying back to Virginia to report progress to the commanding officer and commodore, tracking training milestones and funds, submitting evaluations, managing Sailor of the Quarter and Sailor of the Month paperwork, closing out travel claims and the list goes on. Even units preparing for war have mountains of administrative tasks. You can be the best tactical operator in the world, but if you cannot brief or care for your people administratively, you have failed them.

Tactical + Administrative = LEADERSHIP

This effort was two-pronged: Dave oversaw tactical formations underway and communicated with me on our administrative network, while I managed overall troop operations. Hank was a beast; young, skilled, and capable in combat. Todd had a heart of gold; what he lacked in experience he made up for with sheer will and loyalty to the task unit. Gary was one of the smartest chiefs I've ever met; his simple, effective analysis pulled us out of many tight spots during training. Together, we were ready to tackle Riverine Task Unit Five.

Then there was me a newly commissioned Chief Warrant Officer Two, with little experience as an officer. Slightly immature, no filter, and talking more crap than a North Korean radio station, I wondered how I could earn and maintain the trust of so many people. One thing I knew for certain: without Dave, none of this would work unless we were in lockstep. Loyalty was the name of the game.

Training ramped up fast. The zero-defect mentality was exhausting, but necessary when you saw how close the boats were while firing. Everything was scripted. If we executed the sequences correctly, we might be underway for two hours of firing and maneuvering; if not, we could be out there for eight hours until we got it right.

Unlike the coastal teams, where maintenance support often acted as if they had a union, the riverine troop's maintenance teams were committed and loyal. When we returned to base at 03:00 a.m., they were ready to get the boats operational again while the rest of us cleaned and reset the boats, weapons, and personal gear for the next day.

By 5:00 a.m., we were back at the hotel, drinking beer and debriefing at the pool. We called them "Hotwashes," where nothing was left unsaid. You had to get comfortable with hearing someone expose your gaps and blind spots that none of us realized we had. It made us all better operators and leaders. We stayed up until 07:00 a.m., slept until 1:00 p.m., and then reset for the next day. This routine lasted six months. The SWCC in RTU-5 were outstanding; I felt lucky to have this team. They were our tribe, sharing incredible moments and hardships alike. "Shared Pain"

I was proud of them, even when I wasn't proud of myself. One example came the night we were told to swim laps in the river with all of our gear. Earlier, the troop had tested their gear and realized the new slim-line ski vests were not Type III flotation. To fix it, they inserted additional foam into their body armor. I was caught up in briefings and meetings and missed that update.

There I was, swimming repeatedly from pier to shore, fighting to stay afloat with body armor, radios, magazines, rifle, pistol, and other gear. At 175 pounds, my equipment pushed me to 225 pounds. The Mississippi mud held me to the riverbed at times, and fatigue set in quickly. Finally, I lifted my head and yelled, "I need help." My SWCC pulled me to shore. My first thought: Who wants to follow a leader who can't swim without nearly drowning?

Even though the mishap stemmed from an incorrect life vest, I realized I had been pulled too far into administrative work and away from the tasks that would keep our troop alive in combat. I reset my gear and decided: I would risk being chewed out for missed reports or inspections, but I would never half-ass training. This was unlike anything attempted in the boat teams for years. We answered to SBT-20 but also to SBT-22. Two chains of command pulling on us constantly and Dave and I had to stay ahead of both and remained busy the entire time.

The next training phase took place on the Pearl River in Mississippi. We conducted firing sequences with millions of rounds of blank ammunition. Learning the updated tactics was challenging, especially as we worked on setting "Condition One". All four boats had to be ready for a mission locked and loaded within one minute and forty-five seconds.

A particularly dangerous new position was midship. It was the Forward Looking Infrared (FLIR) operator. Each boat had one FLIR operator, sitting on a small stool with gaming goggles to monitor the environment. The drawback: the goggles blinded them to their surroundings, leaving them essentially night blind apart from the FLIR feed. Trust within the crew became critical.

One night, we couldn't get it right. Every mistake frustrated the training cadre. They ordered us to remove all lanyards from night vision and MBITR radios before water drills in the dead of night in freezing cold water, with hundreds of thousands of dollars' worth of gear on four boats. Hank, usually unflappable, became frustrated, and my guys were demoralized. I refused to let this continue.

I directed the troop to stand fast and walked to the top of the dock to confront the senior chief. I told him we were tired of the "reindeer games." Every wasted moment could be a nail in one of our coffins. By the time we finished our discussion, RTU-5 had set Condition One in forty-five seconds. The training for that night was cancelled.

The next morning, I spoke to the training officer, a SEAL officer, who was visibly upset and even got in my face. I made it clear I would not be intimidated. I informed him RTU-5 belonged to SBT-20, not SBT-22, and directed him to have his CO contact mine to resolve the hazing-style interference with training.

That encounter crystallized my role as a warrant officer: protect the team, even if it meant risking being relieved. That incident lit a fire under the cadre, and they assigned us a new training lead Dave McCoy. Hooyah, Dave!

It was getting colder, and training at Fort Knox, Kentucky, would be the culmination of everything we had learned on the rivers in Mississippi. Dave McCoy was in the training department during our workup a seasoned riverine expert who had served in SBU-26 and spent many years at SBT-22. He knew the precision it would take to prepare us for war and dedicated himself entirely to our readiness.

Dave gave us his all, ensuring we completed all repetitions required to move into live-fire exercises. His sage guidance, patience, and understanding of the riverine environment saved our lives in combat countless times. We are forever grateful to my brother from anotha motha Dave for shaping Riverine Task Unit Five into riverine warriors.

Our training intensified. We operated at night, sleeping during the day, firing hundreds of thousands of rounds, and running scenario after scenario to perfect intervals and immediate action drills. It was like an orchestra, every element synchronized to produce precise results.

After each mission, we conducted a hotwash. My leadership would discuss what worked and what needed improvement. In these debriefs, we became comfortable being uncomfortable, accepting responsibility without defending ourselves. It was a pure exercise in "name it to tame it." Then we would debrief the troop, reinforcing growth across the team.

Four-boat tactics were incredibly stressful, requiring hundreds of hours to achieve precision. When a gunner had a "dead man" (the sound of the bolt going forward but no round fired), he would endure a "chilly head" in the freezing thirty five-degree Kentucky water. Either his head was dunked or his helmet filled with water. This was SBT-22's brutal training realignment tool. Despite the cold, we completed the training and transitioned back to Mississippi for even more preparation. No rest for the weary.

December brought the final battle problem at Fort Knox a test of every skill we had learned. This was the last check before deployment. To add pressure, the Group Four Commodore would ride my boat. We had worked tirelessly to reach this point, keeping our leadership intact. It was our moment to shine.

I told my senior enlisted, Dave, to call the ball as if we were already in Iraq. We trusted each other implicitly; we had known each other almost our entire adult lives. We planned the mission using the full process: Situation, Mission, Execution, Administration and Logistics, Command and Signal. For contingencies, we relied on the MDMP process and GOTWA: Going, Others I am taking, What happens if I do not return, Time I will return, and Actions if I am contacted. We had become experts at deliberate planning, capable of executing missions within twenty-four to ninety-six hours or conducting time-sensitive targeting with only thirty minutes to plan. This would become our template in Iraq.

Underway, each boat had a member of the training cadre to intervene only for safety violations. But this time was different: commanding officers from SBT-20 and SBT-22, their senior enlisted, and the commodore were all aboard. We had to get it right.

Our boats were loaded to bear five machine guns and one mini-gun per boat, with roughly 27,000 rounds distributed across the four boats. Fully equipped with body armor, helmets with night vision, M4 rifles strapped with bungee cords for quick release, 9mm pistols, and handheld radios capable of tactical satellite communications, we were ready.

Condition One was set in forty-five seconds. Minutes into the mission, we were ambushed. Dave called the ball on the formation and egress route. We egressed right and broke through the ambush. We conducted a Battle Damage Assessment: personnel status, engine condition, rounds expended, and remaining ammunition. Though TTPs were a lot different, blowing through ambushes and violence of action was second nature in Me and Dave's SBU-26 upbringing.

The training cadre paused the evolution, questioning our egress choice. They asked the troop why no one objected. One shouted, "It was a bad call." I clarified that in combat, any call that gets you out of the kill zone is the right call. I suspected the entire exercise was designed to fail us possibly to disband RTU-5 or replace our leadership with SBT-22 personnel.

Before the exercise, I had planned to give the Commodore a bottle of Jack Daniels. He loved Old Western sayings and always proclaimed, "Sharpen your knives, boys we're going to war, and I am the trail boss on this trail! If you don't like it, choose another trail!" The bottle was my nod to his trail boss ethos.

I walked over to him and said, rather humbly after failing the final battle problem,

"Commodore, I wish it were under different circumstances, but you are our trail boss, and we don't mind being on your trail." My troop and I returned to the boats to pull them out of the water and prepare for a long night of cleaning weapons and prepping for over-the-road transit back to Mississippi. We definitely did not deserve this, but we had to Charlie Mike.

Little did I know that our Commanding Officer Kent Paro and Command Master Chief (CMC) Rich Evans sat in on the training cadre's debrief, not only evaluating our performance but also assessing our leadership. I apparently topped their list.

A few hours later, our CMC informed us that they wanted the command to relieve us, but the skipper and CMC stood his ground: "Our Riverine Task Unit ain't going nowhere. They started together and they will finish together." They also mandated a retake of the final battle problem in the first week of January. This was our opportunity to get our deployment up check. Realistically, we all knew we had to get back to Mississippi to secure our weapons, gear, and boats, and plan the long transit over the road to Virginia Beach. We would have three weeks of Christmas standdown. The Task Unit was temporarily assigned to SBT-22 for almost six months. Maybe eating a little humble pie was good for all of us.

Despite the setback, we finally made it home to spend time with our families and momentarily forget about Riverine Task Unit Five. Jackson was growing fast.

He was now four years old, and I felt a pang of guilt for missing so many milestones. I had chosen to chase honor, brotherhood, or whatever you want to call it, instead of being present for my family. But this job demanded everything we had, for the greater good of the team and the brotherhood. The guilt of missing Jackson's life and milestones weighed heavily, yet knowing Jenifer kept the home fires burning was a comfort. Looking back, I realized something had to give and it was never my commitment to my kids; it was always the commitment to each other, to the mission, to the cause. Hell, who could blame the women in our lives for frustration over constant deployments? We hijacked the best years of their lives. By the time we retired and could stay home, our bodies were worn, our mindset and disposition a shadow of what they married. Sadly, relationships often became ones of inconvenience and obligation; a harsh truth, the Navy's collateral damage was marriage and family. And it's not just the Navy; it's also the baggage we carry from our upbringing and perpetuating that cycle.

After the three-week Christmas standdown, I kissed Jenifer and Jackson and returned to SBT-22 to prepare our gear, weapons, and boats for the over-the-road transit back to Fort Knox, Kentucky, to redo the final battle problem. As we approached Kentucky, the weather turned dramatically colder, with occasional snow flurries. Hard times awaited us to include breaking ice to launch the boats.

We arrived and settled in, and I was finding my footing as Troop Commander, testing my training and leadership skills. I was maturing quickly as a new SWCC Warrant Officer, shedding chief thinking, and compartmentalizing responsibilities one day at a time.

That night, Dave and I met with Training Officer Dean and his Senior Enlisted Kevin. We shared a cigar, whiskey, and beer. Kevin was cut from the same cloth as Dave and me, had served in Special Boat Unit Twenty-Six. He and Dean were straightforward and above board. I asked only one thing: if we were substandard, hold us accountable but if we were ready, let us deploy and crush it.

Our mission planning was precise, and every scenario they threw at us was executed flawlessly. The final phase involved departing the Salt River and connecting to the Ohio River for a concluding mission.

We were returning to base in a snowstorm, maneuvering the boats between objectives. Little did we know, this experience would pay off in Iraq, where temperatures ranged from 100°F during the day to 20°F at night. Our task was to meet a recovery timeline, reset the boats, and prepare for the next mission.

Dave and I checked in with the training cadre for the debrief. Dean and Kevin began by congratulating us that we had passed every line item with flying colors. "Whatever you did at home on leave, you brought it back with precision," they said.

I could not let that slide. "You think we were thinking about SBT-22, the boats, or tactics while home on leave? This troop is the same capability you failed before. Nothing changed except the other cadre cheated us out of a little more family time." I was proud of my candor and restraint, but the point was made.

Hooyah. We had successfully passed our final battle problem. Excitement and fear surged through us. I could not have been prouder of our SWCC from SBT-20. We were about to make history. We reset gear and returned to Virginia Beach for two weeks before deploying to Iraq for five months. This would be the longest continuous time I had been away from home. Six- to seven-month deployments were routine, but eleven months with only five weeks at home was daunting.

Our workup and deployment were a memorable experience that every member of Riverine Task Unit Five will never forget. We traveled home for two weeks, trying to focus on my family while simultaneously ensuring everything was in order for the troop's departure. We also held a pre-deployment meeting with our families to cover last-minute details and ensure that newly married spouses and girlfriends, many of whom had never experienced a deployment, had a support network.

Dave and I learned a lesson the hard way from our last meeting, which had been held at a Mexican restaurant instead of the base. It went south quickly. One of the wives, with a little too much to drink, questioned why her husband had been chosen to deploy and how we could guarantee his safety. I assured her that this was the team our command had put together, and that we would deploy together, doing everything in our power to bring everyone back safely. I assume alcohol amplified her anxiety, but my words were heartfelt. The truth was, at this point in my career, I had never been to war never an all-out shooting war, certainly not

Iraq. After that, the pre-deployment meeting was held at the base. No more dinners in the crosshairs of fearful, tipsy spouses. Now watching our CMC Rich attempt to jump over a fence and fall on his post surgery shoulder was funny as hell.

None of us were sure we would return home.

The next day, I walked into my commanding officer Kent Paro office and asked for guidance. "Sure, Carp, have a seat," he said. I asked him what advice he could give about going to war. To this day, it remains the most profound guidance I have ever received, keeping my mission clear and purpose laser focused. He said, "Carp, make sure you and your men are right with yourselves every night as you lay your heads down on your pillows." I knew exactly what he meant. I thanked him for believing in us and for staying committed while some of SBT-22's leadership tried to derail us. I left his office feeling empowered and energized.

I had only about eleven days before deploying to Iraq, the first true combat experience I would have as a Warrant Officer. Jen's mother was staying with us, which made things pleasant at home. While I had been away training, Jen had hired our neighbor to remodel our kitchen. It wasn't what I expected, but I had little time to intervene. One morning, I noticed a crack in the tile on the kitchen floor. Tapping it with a coin, I realized that ninety percent of it was improperly laid and would only get worse while I was deployed. I wished I had never discovered the flaw.

Annoyed, I fired the neighbor and went to Home Depot to buy new tile. I spent the next week demolishing and relaying the kitchen subfloor, Hardy backer, and tile, an enormous task that took more time than I anticipated. The night before deployment, I was up until 1:00 a.m. finishing the grouting. Think about that: I was about to deploy to a war zone and spent my last days at home redoing the kitchen floor.

In retrospect, I understand why. Jen and I had unresolved marital issues, which I partly blamed on myself. We functioned like a business, with the business being family and a marriage of convenience. I also found myself hiding my fears of deploying as Troop Commander, maintaining emotional distance by staying preoccupied. Redoing the floor prevented arguments and allowed me to leave without tension.

This behavior is common in military relationships with high deployment and training tempos. Jen, a Navy wife, had adapted; she had become accustomed to the operational tempo, often not even rising to say goodbye. She maintained the household and parented Jackson in my absence, which was always comforting.

I left with a heavy heart, but also with excitement. The troop was ready. We consolidated our gear and transported everything to Naval Base Norfolk, where our C-17 cargo plane awaited. The plane could carry 170,900 pounds of cargo, cruise at 28,000 feet, and had deck tracks with rollers to load and unload equipment efficiently. Many of us loved military cargo planes, as they allowed us to roll out sleeping bags on the deck and rest during the flight.

Our first stop was Ramstein Air Base in Germany to refuel. We had a short layover, enough to stretch our legs, grab food, and observe the base. There were so many American service members rotating in and out of Iraq that it felt like watching a Vietnam movie. Every war, regardless of era, likely experienced that same surreal rhythm. What struck me most was how business-as-usual it seemed. Returning soldiers showed no outward signs of recent conflict. I suspected the reality would only hit them once they returned home and lost the protective umbrella of their teammates.

We all go through it and must face a new normal after deployments. That is why many of us chose to deploy often. It was our psychological safety net, our balance, and our sense of identity, tied to a tribe that shared the same pain.

But now, it was showtime. We boarded the plane and took off for Iraq. The journey was about fifteen hours until we landed at

Al Assad Air Base. Our operations officer from SBT-20 was deploying with us for two months, acting as the Task Unit Commander to reduce the administrative burden that would have otherwise fallen on Dave and me as we ran the entire Task Unit and Boat Troop by ourselves.

It was pitch black when we disembarked. Nothing surprised us; many of us had deployed worldwide before, and the routine of unloading gear and consolidating the team was familiar. Thankfully, all our gear was accounted for. We located the tents that would be our accommodations for a few days while we checked in with the country and the Task Force.

Al Assad Air Base was enormous the size of a small city. There was a constant hustle and bustle, and the base offered many conveniences: barber shops, laundry services, gyms, and a five-star dining facility. No joke they even served ice cream and had a bakery. Fitting into a place like this almost made you forget you were at war, but it was only a temporary respite. This base fed the military machine across Iraq, and the soldiers here would defend it at all costs to keep the ground and air logistics flowing.

We met our Task Force Commander and prepared to board Army Chinook helicopters to transport us to Al Taqaddam Air Base (TQ). It was about half the size of Al Assad. I sat on the ramp of the helo with my lanyard secured to the deck. As the blades spun in the night sky, sand particles ignited from static electricity. It was an amazing sight.

Flying in formation, we got our first glimpse of Iraq at night. Out of nowhere, our helo deployed "chaff countermeasures," small strips of aluminum meant to mimic targets on enemy radar. Even though it was a show of force, it scared the hell out of me. I prayed, "Lord, please don't let us die in these helos after everything we went through, especially not on the third night. Amen." Thankfully, we landed safely at Al Taqaddam Air Base, just across from Habbiniyah and consolidated with our C-17 and gear.

We directed the troop to don body armor and helmets, load weapons and chamber rounds (Condition 1). It was a low-level combat mission, just to visit the base for a hot meal or the dentist. TQ had its own chaotic battle rhythm. One side of the base fed the war machine, while the other contained massive firepits to dispose of debris from thousands of soldiers and the Iraqi partners they supported. Sanitation was a constant priority.

Dave and I were ready. We joined the first convoy after meeting Riverine Task Unit 1 leadership. The drive to our Task Unit at Habbiniyah, about twenty minutes away, offered a new olfactory experience. Fine, talcum-like sand blew through the air, and the gunners manned turrets with NVGs flipped down. Everything glowed green through the night vision, with lasers marking potential targets. I flipped down my NVGs and watched as the gunners scanned for threats while convoying to the base.

The Task Force authorized forty-eight hours for us to achieve full operational capability (FOC). RTU-1 had vacated the building we would occupy. Their personnel stayed on TQ at a large facility prepositioned for NSW personnel awaiting their freedom flights home. Inside the same compound was SEAL Team Five NSW Task Unit, including a SWCC Master Chief working sensitive activities. Seeing him there was reassuring. Like Dave and I, Joe had cut his teeth in Special Boat Unit Twenty-Six.

I quickly learned of bad blood between SEAL Team Five and Riverine Troop One, mainly due to different mission sets. The RTU belonged to the Task Force and, in the early days, had to remain on a thirty-minute tether as a quick reaction force to support the operators.

The story goes that one Christmas, a couple of slightly inebriated SEALs from Team Five wandered down to RTU-1 where they had a large inflatable Santa Claus and a turkey outside their building. In a display of drunken disdain, the SEALs stabbed Santa and the turkey. It was a Christmas massacre. Disciplinary action followed, as all adhered to General Order One, prohibiting drinking in Iraq. It was ironic, and somewhat comical, that SEALs trained for precision combat were holding knife fights on an inflatable Santa Claus essentially stealing Christmas from RTU-1.

So, that was the first "fire" we had to put out since we were going to be on deployment together. The Task Unit Commander of the SEALs, whom we called "JJ," was someone I knew from when he was our operations officer at SBU-12 back in the day. I wanted to clear the air and let him know that, since we went way back, I would be in charge of the incoming troop and wanted him to understand that we both needed to find a way to coexist and support each other. He agreed, and we bro hugged. We were happy that we were going to be a team. Networking is everything.

The next order of business was meeting the chaplain. I asked if he could stop by and bless our boats. He agreed. I looked forward to him stopping by, performing the blessing, and making sure God was on our side, providing top cover.

Once we were settled in, we were ready to get underway on day two for our familiarization mission. I asked about the supplemental rules of engagement and was told to "shoot anything that moves or has a gun." That definitely was not what I expected. I was adamant that I would not tell my guys that, remembering my commanding officer's instructions before leaving. He had said: "Be right with yourself every time you lay your head on your pillow."

Those were sobering words, but ones I took to heart. I told Dave to imagine standing in his backyard, smoking a cigarette and looking at the night sky, when four gunboats drove up and shot him because he was out after curfew. Instead, I explained that we would use the primary rules of engagement, which were black and white: hostile act and hostile intent. Our troop would have weapons release authority for any hostile acts, such as rounds being fired at us or an ambush. Hostile intent decisions would rest with Dave and me, to quickly and positively identify threats, like someone pointing a weapon at us, and weather we should fire or not.

It was clear, responsible, and respected the inherent right to self-defense. It worked fine in the interim but quickly reinforced how fast situations could change.

I had my own room on the first floor, along with Dave and our ops boss. Our chiefs and the other enlisted men were on the second floor in bunks. All the mattresses were high-end and comfortable, a far cry from the cramped, miserable berths on the big Pyro.

Near the bunkroom were four phone booths, allowing us to make calls at any time. This is what Special Operations does for its people. They try to give as much as possible, even in harsh environments. It was a welcome amenity in an otherwise hostile and dangerous setting.

We worked in periods of darkness, sleeping during the day and operating at night, exploiting technological advantages. The first mission began with a convoy to the Euphrates River to set security while the boats launched one at a time. Driving past the Iraqi soldiers guarding the back gate was unnerving. A feeling I never got used to.

Once all boats were in the water and beached abreast, we boarded. Our gunners immediately manned their weapons. We were as focused and serious as we had been during our final battle problem in training. We didn't know what the enemy would throw at us.

The difference now was that it was real, and the enemy had a vote on the outcome.

The night was muggy, and the river was pitch black. I still couldn't believe I was in Mesopotamia. Twenty high-powered lasers from four boats swept their sectors, giving me a sense of security because I knew what the boats and gunners were capable of. After all, we had expended 2.5 million rounds during training.

It was interesting to watch RTU-1 get underway by passing in the blind. They could transmit but not receive traffic. As we drove toward Ramadi, Iraq, the RTU-1 Troop Commander explained countless procedures. We learned when and how to use jammers under bridges and choke points, memorized all prowords, and followed an execution checklist. It was like drinking from a firehose, but we got it. We returned to base without incident.

The day ended with pulling the boats, supported by our maintenance team, who displayed unquestionable commitment. Together, we convoyed back to base, reset our gear, and prepared the boats for the next mission.

The next day, we woke at 1300 (1:00 p.m.) and headed to the Marine Dining Facility, a tent with no AC serving the same T-Rations we had eaten twenty years ago in Panama. It seemed like the Marines were stuck in the Vietnam era. These boys roughed it wherever they deployed. Green eggs? Really? Now I understood why the Marines get so much done. They do more with less and maintain a perpetually ready-for-war mentality. From food to sleeping arrangements, they suck it up and keep moving. In my opinion, they are the best of all warfighters. Watching them hold weekly funerals, then proceed immediately to the next mission, living in squalor with food meant only for sustenance, made that clear. They were always pissed off and for a good reason.

Yep, it was obvious that food would suck on this deployment. But I was serious! If anyone offered me a hotdog or stove-top stuffing, I was going off!

No sooner had I returned to the task unit than I heard a massive explosion. I could literally feel the shockwave in the air. I ran back to the unit; everyone was ready to fight. I met Dave on the roof, and he told me a suicide bomber had detonated a car bomb outside the gate, killing a lot of people. This was our new reality, and we were clearly not safe anywhere especially in Al Anbar Province in 2007. Living in Habbiniyah between Ramadi and Fallujah, We were a stone throw away from Lake Habbiniyah and the Ramadi Canal. This was Indian country, and nothing could be trusted except our American forces, the SEAL team, and possibly the Iraqi SEALs they trained.

By day three, we were entering the Period of Darkness and were FOC. We had a SWCC LNO at the Task Force in Ramadi, that coordinated our concept of operations. He was one of the senior enlisted on the battle staff from SBT-22. We integrated all our cells with their points of contact in the Task Force. Medics coordinated with the Casualty Evacuation cell. The JTAC coordinated with the close air support cell. Remaining cells tied responsibilities to a computer system we called "SWAMPS" Special Warfare Advanced Mission Planning System.

We were all connected through a cloud that allowed us to simultaneously work on every aspect of a mission: updating locations, navigation plans, communications plans, call signs, close air support, and CASEVAC within thirty minutes. It was as if the fire department had been called, and there was no time for discussion just mission, fires, CASEVAC, and execution.

It was quite amazing to see how we generated missions and executed them.

I reached out again to the chaplain to bless our boats, explaining that on every deployment, I had ensured our boats were blessed. I insisted he come to the boat barn to perform the blessing, and he agreed. I did not want to waste another minute without divine intervention. I drove him to the boats, but unbeknownst to me, I had authorized our boat captains to name the boats, and I did not anticipate their unusual choices.

When the chaplain walked into the boat barn to begin the blessing, he immediately looked back at me with a "you've got to be kidding me" expression. Why? Because our guys had named all the boats after the four horsemen of the apocalypse from the Bible's Book of Revelation; War, Famine, Pestilence, and Death. I explained that I had allowed the troop to name the boats and that this was their choice. The chaplain took a deep breath and blessed the boats anyway. I often wondered what story he would tell his family and others that he blessed boats with unusual names.

Meanwhile, the SWCC LNO already knew that the boats turned over to us had a major communications issue: we could transmit but could not receive responses. No one knew the cause. The previous RTU had permission to transmit in the blind with the assumption someone would hear the message.

Dave and I were not comfortable with this setup, but it was all we had. This was our first FOC mission on our own. Dave, Todd, Gary, and Hank were ready, and we brought the troop together to brief the mission, which was a familiarization mission with just us "on the hook." We had some operational kinks to work out, and this was how we did it.

The boats were driven every day to a hardened bunker where every machine gun was tested. This was so the enemy would know it was our routine and not a prelude to a riverine mission. All weapon checks passed. It was time to climb into the trucks and convoy to the Iraqi side. We approached the gate; Hank noticed an Iraqi soldier on the phone. He jumped out of the Humvee, walked up to him, and confiscated the phone. Our interpreter explained that we did not want anyone on the phone when we passed through, or we would have to destroy their devices. We were getting battle-focused, and my chiefs were stepping up. We dumped the boats without incident.

Our SWCC, that was my comms and medic passed the start point, and we pushed out to go "condition one" on all weapons. We picked up speed, focusing on our Toughbook computers, which displayed GPS coordinates showing where to go and which areas to avoid. We also used our jammers at deadly choke points. We had a good flow until boat one, with Dave aboard, came to a complete stop. What the hell?

Everyone on the boat slammed forward from roughly thirty miles per hour. It seemed like an eternity; Dave did not respond. The boat was stopped, and we were bunched up. Five Two this is Five One! Nothing was heard. I ordered Hank to move up and check on them, while our other two boats provided security. Dave finally came on the radio and explained what happened.

He said his boat hit a sandbar at high speed. He slammed forward, breaking the two back plates off the 240G machine guns. He also lost his laser and precision site from his rifle rail system. Though we were in shallow water, I decided it was not worth staying. The longer we remained in the area, the more dangerous it would become. I declared it a combat loss and told the team we would fill out the missing/lost/stolen recover report later. Lord knows learning how to complete that initial report would come in handy since it wouldn't be the last thing we lost. We hooked his boat for a tow, pulled it off the sandbar, and returned to base to assess damage to personnel, gear, and the boat.

Fortunately, the boat was a tank and sustained no damage. A couple of our guys, including our UAS pilot, were slightly bruised because Dave had pancaked them from the force of his body slamming forward. It could have been much worse.

I could not believe that we had no way to hear the Task Force. This was terrifying, especially after our first mishap, and we had to assume the TF heard us. We later discovered that when the Iraqis open the dam on the Euphrates River, sandbars shift, rendering previous LIDAR scans inaccurate.

After this incident, the 75th Rangers took over from the SEALs as our Task Force commander. They brought Army precision and accountability to the scene. Our SWCC LNO was no longer the senior enlisted but became just our LNO. We conducted more missions but did not understand how the Army knew so much about our operations or whether we were doing something wrong. I had been in country only ten days and was already taking heavies from the TF Commander. We had major comms issues, and this new TF Commander wasn't having it.

I was growing frustrated with the setup and routine. I was also tired of getting chewed out over comms. We decided to have a standdown on the boats and let Task Force communications experts inspect our boats to determine why we could transmit but not receive.

Immediately, the communications team discovered that all the satellite antennas were installed without an insulator between the boat and antenna. No rubber matting had been installed, grounding the signal. Low and behold! We now had crystal-clear communications. The tides were turning except I noticed that our SWCC LNO was running his mouth too much about our missions, voicing opinions that could make our community look bad. I knew this guy from Panama but could not understand why he was undermining us. Needless to say, he rotated out, and Kris Carini the same senior chief from Kenya became the SWCC LNO.

I felt I could be honest with Kris, so I explained what I thought was going on and asked for a fair shake. If we were screwing up, we would take our licks. Up to that point, we were not screwing up, and I was convinced that Kris was the right guy for the job.

Okay, comms were working, and missions were coming in. We were getting our battle rhythm down pat. When we were not working with the Task Force, we linked up with SEAL Team Five, co-located with us, and started inserting them on missions. We built a relationship with 3/6 Marines and consistently met with them to discuss the common operating picture and their area of operations. I never witnessed anyone brief their battlespace better than a Marine. They knew every inch of it and were always called in when the Army let things go to hell in a handbasket. We supported the Marines when we could, either by inserting them or acting as squirter control during massive troop operations. Go figure, the Marines were the only force that specifically requested a "Hot Insert." We were experts at hot extracts, but these warriors wanted to be inserted even under fire.

I called this "kissing the ring." The battlespace owner allowed us on his base and supported us even as he lost Marines every week. Working with the Marines was to our benefit because we discovered that our radios did not communicate with theirs, and they had a different chat system than ours. We had a great relationship with the Marines. At times, we would have to clear ten to eighteen battlespaces just to reach our objective. Looking back, it would not surprise any RTU-5 member that we accomplished so much.

There were times when we would support the Task Force, return to base, and then support the SEAL Team. We would then return to our recovery point, pull the boats, set them up for convoy, drive them to TQ Base, dump them in Lake Habbiniyah, and support the Marines' major clearing operations. Then we would pull the boats, convoy back to the Euphrates River, and stand by as a quick reaction force. This was not done to set records or receive accolades. If the SEALs and Marines were willing to operate, and we had assets not needed by the Task Force that night, why would we not support our brothers in arms? Even SEAL Team Five, if they were willing to operate during a full moon, we backed them up without hesitation. That's how Dave and I felt. Boats of Glass, Balls of Brass, Boatguys Forever!

I believed every mission was a special operations mission if no other waterborne assets could execute it. "It's SOF until it ain't."

After two months of eating crappy Marine food, KBR opened a dining facility that resembled the one in Al Assad. Hallelujah, we had everything. You could walk in and see stacks of paper plates four feet high. The food was amazing! Many of us started putting on weight, eating three to four times per day, along with Gatorade shakes and other junk that the Task Force always delivered. Suddenly, we had a new enemy. Junk food and carbs making us fat and lethargic. Still, we all worked out and ate to our hearts' desire. Then to my dismay, we learned that every plate of food taken back to the task unit cost $58. During periods of darkness, we would have to grab a second plate, flip it upside down to protect our food from dust and sand while walking back to our task unit. That meant each meal cost $116! There should have been better oversight.

Yet, we needed to eat. Many times, we did not have time to sit down and eat like normal people. After all, there was nothing normal about us. Even the uniforms we wore. During the day, my troop wore desert camouflage uniforms. At night, to blend with the environment, we switched to Vietnam jungle camouflage.

Despite our wardrobe challenges, nothing prepared us for what was about to come. There was a change in Iraq, initially difficult to grasp, called the "Al Anbar Awakening." General Petraeus and General Odierno were implementing a counterinsurgency strategy (COIN). I had read countless times about waging war to keep the peace, and most countries failed. Maybe this time would be different.

It became more dangerous on the river than ever. We saw more people on the shoreline. Even some hiding with goats and cows to conceal their body heat. We were instructed not to shoot anyone wearing a white T-shirt. They were part of the Awakening and the neighborhood watch. Shooting them while they were holding an AK-47 would have set the COIN strategy back six months.

The river was narrow in many sections, and the hesitation over whether to shoot or not was stressful. Identifying hostile intent during a COIN operation could mean the difference between life and death, and that decision rested on my shoulders.

It was time to move to another location in Iraq. The COIN strategy was actually working, and we did not want to be the ones to set it back. But we had no idea how much work it would take to move the boats over the road on a long-distance transit to Ramadi. With the exception of the armored vehicles pulling the boats, our Humvees were garbage; no air conditioning and not armored to Level Three or higher. I sat down with leadership to brainstorm options. Remaining in Habbiniyah full time was too dangerous. Hank Taylor! You badass MOFO, thank you for putting up with my demands to make us safe on the convoys.

Dave, Hank, and Gary would take the brunt of the preparations. This included training our guys in new fire-and-movement concepts to protect the boats, quickly hook up for tow, or disconnect the truck and leave the boat if needed. Red Nemeth our new TU commander was awesome at training our guys in ground tactics. We love you Red and will never forget you. We created plans and procedures for the most likely and most probable enemy courses of action. I will never forget Hank's passion and determination. I had him research run-flat tires for trailers and many other items. Though he got frustrated, I reminded him that Task Force had the money and if spending an extra dollar increased our chances of survival, it was money well spent. We sent Todd ahead to Ramadi Shark Base to prepare a space for our boats and accommodations for us.

Our concept of operations was accepted, and we planned for our first convoy to embed within a larger convoy departing TQ Base to Ramadi. That way, there were more weapons available in case something happened.

We practiced contingency plans and even room-clearing to hold down a house until a quick reaction force arrived. All weapons were mounted and loaded, ready for our gunners to engage anyone impeding our movement or shooting at us. We joined the convoy, and holy cow it was long. Trucks, armored vehicles, and semi-trucks carrying food and water stretched as far as the eye could see. Then there was us with two Humvees and five armored trucks called "MTV."

We departed the base, traveling on a highway that looked like something out of a Mad Max movie. Concrete houses were pancaked from bombings, and the desert landscape offered visibility for at least a mile. Apart from roadside bombs, we had the advantage if attacked. All highway barriers were removed from the center lanes, giving the enemy one less place to plant explosives.

About an hour into the transit, we were extremely hot and nearly out of water in the truck. I spoke to Dave on the radio and explained the tradeoff: either suffer heat exhaustion in the un-air-conditioned vehicles or crack the windows and risk exposure to roadside bombs. We chose to crack the windows. Heat first, bombs second.

The further we traveled, the more the windows were lowered. By the time the convoy stopped for a pee break, we had a radio battery propping up the turret hatch to deflect air down to us, and the windows were all the way down. We agreed to raise them back up as we turned onto Route Michigan and arrived in Ramadi. Driving through town and seeing all the cars, I thought to myself, "Lord, please don't let us die in this shithole".

Suddenly, a vehicle came alongside us with a family inside. The mother wore a burka and nodded at us. The father placed his hand on his heart and nodded, while their little boy waved. Those were the intangible moments American troops witnessed constantly that kept us going. A strand of humanity we saw reignited our resolve that these people were worth it. Still, it was a roller coaster of fear, resolve, duty, anger, and frustration. Rinse and repeat.

The convoy arrived without incident. We made our way to the Task Force compound and prepped the troop, gear, and boats to be FOC before dark. We met Kris Carini, our LNO, as well as Dan Synder, another SWCC who served as the Task Force LNO. Coming to Ramadi felt right because we had some solid SWCC backing us up.

We met the battle staff and the 75th Ranger Colonel in charge of us. He was a very serious man, and his demeanor left no doubt: do not screw with him. He was fighting the war and targeting bad guys in the same way we fought organized crime in the 1920s. He had a system that worked, using information from every enemy combatant caught to expand his common operating picture. Even the bad guys hoping for leniency for providing information were told, "If you killed Americans, you are going to prison." Who could argue with that?

Since Kris took over, miraculously, we were no longer in hot water with the Colonel or micromanaged on our missions. It was a relief not being threatened with termination every night. I now understood that the previous SWCC used the only soapbox he had left in the battle staff. His new soap box was throwing us under the bus. At least that ended, and Kris became our champion.

Yes, things were looking up. By this time, we had completed about twenty missions and were co-located with the Rangers. Our first mission was to take them down the river to gather atmospherics. We honed our skills and compiled lessons learned, ready for anything Ramadi could throw at us. As long as we didn't have to see those damn Humvees that nearly killed us from the heat, we were good.

Period of Darkness Mission Number One in Ramadi went smoothly. We convoyed outside the base, launched all our boats, and gathered atmospherics. This was our first op with the 75th Rangers, creating a breadcrumb trail marking safe water and areas to avoid. These Rangers were squared away, confident, focused, and lethal in their tradecraft.

Their Commander, an Army Major, rode on my boat, while the rest of the force was distributed among the boats, about eight per boat. All was going well until boat number two ran aground. They were stuck in the mud and attempting to back off but failed. Here we go again.

We had to lighten the load. The eight Rangers on the grounded boat got into knee-deep water. I positioned two boats fifty yards out in each direction to set security while one boat attempted to pull the grounded boat free. Remember, this is Ramadi and Indian country. Time is critical. One boat stuck, all boats stopped, eight Rangers in knee-deep water waiting to reboard. This was serious business. The good news is, the boat had two engines.

The Rangers had their night vision flipped up, casting green light everywhere. They talked and laughed, some smoking cigarettes. Go figure I was terrified of what could happen, yet these hard pipe hitters, accustomed to the suck and combat, were enjoying each other's company in a river surrounded by the enemy.

Finally, we used two boats to pull the grounded boat free. One potential crisis averted. We moved to deeper water and heard over the radio, "Hey, you forgot us." The Rangers were cool as hell. We retrieved them and continued down the river, ensuring we stayed clear of the riverbanks where someone could drop something from a high cliff or shoot at us point-blank.

We reached our objective, came to a full stop, backflushed our engines, and passed the proword for exfiltration to our recovery point. As we arrived at the ramp, the ground crew was already there. We pulled boats and returned to base, hot-washed the mission, and reset all gear and equipment for the next mission.

After a good night's sleep, we were on a short tether, but no missions were scheduled. We decided to visit Shark Base and could not believe how the Marines lived and stored their boats muddy, run-down, and dirty. Early on, we committed to helping them maintain their Yanmar engines since their riverine boat engines were identical MTUs engines like ours. It was easy for us to supply parts, but they lacked the same support network. Their mission was far more difficult and dangerous. They protected the dam and patrolled during daylight, nearly a suicide mission. Our safety relied on the night, because we owned it with our technology.

We also met the new Riverine Squadron that the Navy Expeditionary Combat Command stood up. They were about to take over the Marine mission and boats. The Marines seemed eager to leave the water behind. Could you blame em. The base and surrounding area demonstrated human resilience in the darkness of war. No one brings light to war. Our job was to shoot and blow things up. Yet, even in the most difficult situations, traces of humanity remained.

The devastation throughout Iraq was staggering, a far cry from the country depicted in the history books. I often wondered: had the people known their lives would be reduced to mere survival, would they have acted differently? How many had family members supporting the insurgency, and why did they choose not to make this work for their greater good?

It is always a small number of people who push countries to war, while the vast majority suffers. Had this insurgency not started, Iraq could likely have a quality of life similar to Bahrain. War is hell, and inescapable while inside it. The only difference for us was that we would eventually go home upright, prone, or in a body bag, but we would leave Iraq when our time was up.

Mission Tasking Number Two had us driving the boats all the way to the city of Hit. This was a long journey. To ensure safety, we conducted a thorough analysis of the river, using satellite imagery to identify high-threat areas, high banks, bridges, and potential ambush sites. Once the chiefs and I were satisfied, we briefed a warning order to our troop and prepped them for the mission, submitting the CONOP. We already had fifteen miles of the river mapped from our previous familiarization mission.

Our interpreter, a highly educated Iraqi and American citizen, stayed with Hank, who had become the handler for our translators. The Rangers loaded onto the same boats as the previous night. Once everyone was aboard, I gave the ground team the green light to return to base. We went "condition one," meaning all weapons had rounds in their chambers on all boats. We stepped out at thirty miles per hour.

We were on our navtrack with an overlay of LIDAR, showing danger areas in the water and areas to avoid. Red bad, green good. We noticed a few boats in the middle of the river and immediately set security.

Hank and Dave's boat broke off to conduct a boarding and search, while Gary and my boat was at a full stop.

The reeds along the riverbank were massive. I kept thinking anyone could lob a grenade on us. At that moment, a zipping sound came through my headset really load. Out of the millions of rounds we fired during training, no one prepared us for the sound of AK-47 rounds whizzing past our heads. Our alert level spiked instantly.

I was keeping an eye on Squad 1, with Dave and Hank closing in on the suspect boats, while Gary and I addressed an issue on the left riverbank. Then it was showtime.

I called out to Gary, "54, this is 51. I think we are taking fire." Gary responded, "No shit! Move up! Move up!" We edged closer to the opposite bank to blend in with the reeds. The fire increased, so I pointed in the direction I thought the rounds were coming from and checked the FLIR picture. It looked like a building with about ten military-aged males moving around.

I requested a kinetic strike from our Task Force. This is a bombing with the potential for up to twenty-nine casualties. Our TF Commander angrily responded, "You will not drop bombs! That is an Iraqi police station." I replied, "Copy all, but they are shooting at us."

As fire became more accurate, Gary's midship 240G machine gunner, Doc, also our second combat medic opened fire on about ten people shooting from the roof. They scattered and ran to awaiting police pickup trucks. It was a hostile act and a proportional response. Remember, the inherent right to self-defense meant Doc didn't need permission to return fire.

After this incident, Dave and Hank completed their search. We reconstituted in a column formation and commenced our drive to the city of Hit, about thirty miles away. A serious problem emerged: Iraqi police began following us, using loudhailers to announce, "The infidels are on the river." We continued, knowing contact could occur at any moment.

It was comforting to know we had two F-18 Hornets flying overwatch. I always had my JTAC push one long for situational awareness while the other circled above us. The three Iraqi police pickup trucks remained in sight. As we neared Hit, we noticed a low bridge that required dropping our radar arch to pass underneath.

I told Dave to stand fast with his two boats while mine and Gary's boat dropped the mast and drove under the bridge. Looking at the buildings lining the river, I realized that if anyone fired from them, we'd be at a disadvantage. We needed 500 meters safe distance for a strike, and we'd be shooting uphill at buildings. It was a massive choke point.

I informed Dave that I was uncomfortable with the situation, and that we would move back to his side of the bridge to commence exfiltration to the recovery point. We made it as far as possible.

No sooner had we begun moving than the Iraqi police arrived. About eight jumped from their pickups with strobe lights activated, running toward the bridge unaware of the thirty lasers trained on them. My boat was closest.

In those split seconds, my mind raced. I had a weird thought: if they fire, they will be met with thousands of rounds, and being so close, their blood and body parts would be all over us. Then I yelled, "Oh Cough Mechanic! Ana Ismay Na Isabit Carpenter! Shukran!" (spelled wrong, of course). The Iraqi police stopped, turned, and walked back to their trucks.

The ranger commander asked what I had said. I replied, "Stop where you are, I am Warrant Officer Carpenter." That was all the Farsi I learned. The Major responded, "You are one crazy fucker." We laughed hard. Maybe I am but it got us out of a potentially deadly situation.

I took a deep breath, consolidated under the bridge with Dave and Hank, and got underway for the recovery point. This night had countless moving parts and challenges that we successfully navigated. Had we not been a group of professionals, any one factor could have triggered a catastrophic domino effect.

Our troop and the Rangers practiced restraint even when we had the right to neutralize the threat beyond hostile intent. Luckily, the Iraqis backed down, and we all lived to fight another day.

It was our last day of our Ramadi visit. We prepared to convoy back to our Task Unit in Habiniyah. As we departed, We tasked Kris and Dan, our LNOs, to find other locations for us to operate out of. After a few days, they Identified Iskandariyah and as our next bed-down location that met our operational and security needs. One of our next missions was to help locate kidnapped American service members.

After a four-hour transit from Ramadi, we regrouped at the Task Unit to plan the next mission to Iskandariyah. This operation required more planning: four boats over the road while the main body flew via Chinook helicopter. Our prior missions had honed our skills, giving us confidence. Go figure, a bunch of Coastal SWCC turned Riverine Warriors validating everything the commodore envisioned. A SWCC can operate any vehicle, fire any weapon, and function in any environment.

Before departing, we received a new mission request from the SEAL Task Unit down the street. Joe, the advanced special operations lead, briefed us on 125 foreign fighters in the Ramadi Canal. I told Joe there was no way. Our mission the previous night had shown flat ground with only a few structures.

Joe insisted, but we couldn't fathom where 125 people could hide. We decided to conduct a recon of the canal and received permission to execute the mission. As we arrived at Lake Habbiniyah to launch the boats, the radio crackled the Task Force warned of an incoming storm grounding air support and CASEVAC. We delayed the mission twenty-four hours. The lake with our flat-bottomed SOC-R boats had already given us a beating in previous storms, so we knew to listen to the Task Force.

The next night presented another issue: the lake was too low due to the dam being opened. Murphy's Law struck. Night number two's mission was canceled.

We returned to base to learn the Army had been tasked to investigate. They engaged in minor skirmishes, neutralized some enemies, and pushed deeper. But as they returned, the same enemy reemerged, wounding and killing some soldiers.

The firefight escalated, yet the enemy believed they had won. In reality, they only allowed 3/6 Marines to conduct three days of artillery training. Imagine the 105mm and 155mm cannons fired day and night for three nights. The next time we visited the area by boat, nothing remained standing. We were briefed that foreign fighters were hiding in tanker trucks. The sheer endurance required to stay inside those trucks in scorching heat commanded my respect but make no mistake: we would drop them in a heartbeat if given the opportunity.

We finally had the green light to relocate to Al-Iskandariyah, also known as Alexandria an ancient city in central Iraq founded by Alexander the Great. It was a majority Shia district located forty-five miles south of Baghdad, right on the Euphrates River.

We loaded all our primary gear onto Chinook helicopters while the remaining equipment and boats convoyed to Forward Operating Base Iskandariyah. We took off into pitch-black skies with night vision on full.

Our Chinooks approached the base, flying past a massive power plant with four smokestacks. The building was brightly lit, forcing us to flip up our night vision. Landing at the base during the night, I was both impressed and surprised that the FOB was so close to the plant. Apparently, they were protecting the power generation that fed Baghdad, the Green Zone, and surrounding areas. Dan met us and guided us to our tents; the home we'd call our own for the next ten days.

As guests on the FOB, operated by 1st Battalion, 501st Parachute Infantry Regiment, we were anxious. After some sleep, we conducted a meet-and-greet with the FOB leadership and offered support in any way we could both for expanding the Task

Force's limits of advance and for locating kidnapped American soldiers. This meant that while conducting our primary mission, we had a secondary mission: inserting 1/501 behind enemy defensive IED belts in areas usually accessible only by helicopter.

Supporting the Army allowed them to extend their tactical reach. The Operations Officer and Battalion Commander were pleased with our presence. The commander shook our hands and told me we'd likely be contacted by the enemy in three days "all the dumb ones are dead." An interesting comment, to say the least.

Dave and I left headquarters as Humvees were being towed past. The up-armored Humvees looked like Swiss cheese: windows shot out, holes through engine blocks, a junkyard of vehicles destroyed by roadside bombs and EFPs.

Every mission these soldiers went on was essentially a suicide mission. The enemy used not only IEDs but also Iranian-made Explosively Formed Projectiles (EFPs) coffee-can-sized devices with a copper liner that, when detonated, melted into a spear capable of piercing armor and engines. Losing a brother every day and having no immediate way to retaliate hardened these warriors. They were battle-worn, fearless, and trained by Army Special Forces to operate alone in a high-threat environment forty-five miles from Baghdad.

Our main mission was to locate American service members who had been kidnapped from a checkpoint weeks prior Duty Status, Whereabouts Unknown (DUSWUN). These missions took us into areas where even our quick reaction force couldn't reach for support. We recovered bloated, decapitated bodies from the river, transported them on the dive platform, and returned them to base for forensic analysis to confirm they weren't American. All the while, I reminded Dave, "All the dumb ones are dead; it's only a matter of time before they hit us." This was exactly why our extensive training mattered.

Kris and Dan did a phenomenal job establishing a base that even had a boat ramp inside the security perimeter. It was equipped with a forward-looking infrared system J-Lens mounted on a twenty-foot pole capable of detecting heat signatures 1,000 yards out. Though the base was Army jurisdiction, operational and tactical control remained with the Task Force. All our networks and links tied directly to the TF server via our standalone satellite server.

By now, we were efficient at expeditionary moves. Boats arrived the next morning without incident, and we quickly settled into our battle rhythm. The base had a great dining facility, requiring us to fill one sandbag per meal per person as contribution to reinforce bunkers and firing positions.

We planned our first mission: search for the missing soldiers and familiarize ourselves with the area. 1st/501 came along as a possible insertion team. The Euphrates area was eerie. Towns east of the river were populated; the west side had structures but fewer people. Dense foliage, palm trees, and high grass provided natural cover for potential enemy attacks.

Fifteen minutes into the mission, we came across a bloated decapitated body floating in the river. The smell sweet yet rotten was unforgettable. Our small but tough medic, with help from crewmen, hoisted the corpse onto the dive platform and returned it to the boat ramp. That task was the one part of the job we dreaded, but it was a necessary evil.

As we moved south, we observed cultivated fields, walking bridges, fishing cages, and islands with dense foliage creating natural chokepoints narrowing the river. Gunners scanned everything, but we passed without incident. We were infiltrating the Iraqis' pattern of life, able to conduct our mission and return safely. Yet danger remained: the enemy was capable of surprise attacks, and intel indicated that Baghdadi was in the area for meetings. He is the future ISIS founder.

Understanding the local culture and pattern of life proved essential. Quick insert, mission completion, extraction, Exfil to recovery. Anything beyond that exposed predictable patterns and risked compromise. Our single FOB limited our transit options, and missions often required return to the same location, creating constant ambush potential.

By day five, we were firing on all cylinders: gathering atmospherics, inserting Army elements into inaccessible areas, and expanding operational reach. Every time we transported Army soldiers, their risk of roadside bombs decreased. Hank was frustrated, believing we were doing busy work instead of pushing further downriver. I explained that we needed to support the Army element. They had the local knowledge and ability to go inland when we couldn't cover the ground.

Next, we planned a mission to Fallujah from Iskandariyah a forty-mile transit requiring F-18 strikes to clear a couple of bridges. The Army tagged along to extend their operational reach. Communication was a challenge; clearing eighteen battlespaces required interfacing across incompatible Army and TF systems.

Nine SWCC had passed promotion tests. I told Dave we'd pin their ranks after the mission. Definitely a bad decision.

We set out toward Fallujah, clearing river obstacles, including a sunken bridge destroyed by Marine F-18s. One boat at a time, we scraped past concrete jutting from the water. The double-hulled riverine boats were built like tanks.

We were moving down the river at a solid pace, making good time while observing everything within sight and hearing. Anyone in an acquisition role or a program manager who claims that an enclosed boat makes a good riverine platform should not only be punched in the mouth but also fired. Having grown up in the boat teams and learned nearly every secret from the Vietnam SEALs and Boat Guys (now called SWCC), I can tell you: in small boats where you cannot hear, see, or feel what's happening, you are essentially writing your own death warrant. The environment and sounds shift constantly. These cues can mean the difference between returning home upright or in a body bag. Operating a cabin boat in a riverine environment is like conducting combat operations in a fishbowl where you hear nothing. Get the point?

As beginning morning nautical twilight (BMNT) approached, communication among all boats, our Task Force, and the battlespace owners was functioning exceptionally well. We were about four miles from Fallujah when I suddenly heard the radio crackle.

It was the Task Force Commander calling. He informed me that we were now outside the quick reaction force range meaning no one could come to our aid if we contacted the enemy. I told him we were good to go and wanted to push a little further. The Commander responded,

"You are the ground force commander. It's your call. Be safe."

To me, this was transformative. After all, I was the same troublemaker, underachiever, always blaming others. A city boy from Chicago had just been authorized to make a decision that could affect thirty SWCC and millions of dollars in equipment. I was from the South Side, but by this point, I had stopped giving it power and focused on being a teammate and a Boatguy.

We continued toward Fallujah. About two miles from the city limits, we began churning mud and silt. I directed Dave to find a suitable path through the debris. There was none. More debris clogged our strainers, threatening to overheat the engines. I paused and realized: it's better to win the battle than lose the war.

We decided to stop, reverse course, and exfil to recovery point. After reversing, Gary's boat became boat one; I became boat two, Dave was boat three, Hank boat four. It was 0345, and we needed to pass the sunken bridge before locals awoke for morning prayers.

We followed a solid breadcrumb trail back to the recovery point and made good speed to the sunken bridge without incident. At 0415, Gary's boat moved to wiggle through the concrete but got stuck, a major problem with locals waking at 0530 for prayers, leaving the only corridor blocked.

I ordered my boat captain to ram them. He looked at me in disbelief. I repeated, angrily, "Fucking ram him." Our boat slammed into Gary's stern. The boat popped over the concrete, and the rest of us navigated through with no issues.

About six miles from base, on FLIR, boat three detected the enemy digging holes and planting IEDs with an auger. They wanted me to engage immediately, but I knew a town was in the background. I marked the location to pass to the Army later. At 0515, too close to home and with daylight approaching, I didn't want a protracted firefight and losing our night vision.

Returning to base, we spotted a military-aged male on the footbridge holding a phone. Coincidence? Maybe not. I told Dave, and we opened our column by two boat lengths as we continued down the river.

It was brutally hot and dry. I reflected on what our troop had endured forty-three missions under our belt. Pride swelled. I checked my M-79 grenade launcher, noticing a broken trigger guard. Three miles from home, I removed my high explosive round to avoid an accidental discharge. Fatigue does strange things. These long missions kept us on edge, all senses alert. As Troop Commander, my senior enlisted and I constantly reacted to machine gun lasers. Moments of peace were rare. I slipped into a brief trance, feeling love for RTU-5.

Then chaos erupted. A massive explosion near boat one knocked out their radar and FLIR. Heavy enemy fire erupted from the right bank. On the radio: "Contact Right!!!"

As we returned fire, another IED detonated near my boat, knocking me and the JTAC against the armor tub as dirt and debris rained down. I immediately unloaded a magazine from my M4, reloaded, and continued engaging. Shore-side blasts were angled slightly upward, sparing us most of the force, but RPG rounds fired front and rear missed by mere feet.

Having ordered the boats to open formation after observing the person on the bridge likely saved us from the full effects. The enemy had timed their ambush perfectly, using our interval as their guide. Had the thermobaric RPGs landed, they would have inflicted heavy casualties.

Time slowed, almost as if in another dimension. Six Russian DSHK 12.7mm machine guns, PKM 7.62mms, and numerous AK-47s fired at us. Our aft gunner straddled the transom, engaging a concrete pumphouse with armor-piercing rounds. "I love this shit!" he yelled, neutralizing a major threat. One down, six to go.

I stopped shooting to relay, "Troops in Contact," coordinating between lulls in the minigun firing. I requested a battle damage assessment and received confirmation from boats one and three but not boat four.

I watched our SOCM stop firing to check on the soldiers. They were flat on the engine cover, appearing dead. I yelled, "Fuck them, man the weapon on the port side," anticipating the next ambush wave from the opposite bank. The enemy executed a linear ambush, perfectly offset to maximize firepower without hitting their own. I shook my JTAC, who was marking targets with tracers, and ordered him to switch to laser guidance for fighter support. That night, we wished for Marine F-18s; the Air Force F-16s struggled to locate us. A bomb drop might have ended differently.

We also needed 500 meters for safe ordnance release. The enemy had us tightly boxed; 40mm grenades were unusable without minimum distance as well.

This was going to be a knock-down, drag-out slugging match where the side that achieved maximum fire superiority would win. Needless to say, we had the best machine gunners in the world and that's exactly what began to happen. We engaged firing points on both sides of the river while leadership passed critical information back and forth. Dave and I were discussing turning around to rescue boat number four, which was still nowhere to be seen. We were just about to call "execute" on reversing direction when, out of the corner of my eye, I saw a SOCR coming around the bend; everything seemed to move in slow motion.

I noticed the American flag slowly flapping from its Radar Arch in the breeze, and though I was fully present, I could not explain why time seemed to slow. Hank's boat was the cleanup shot and addressing targets on both banks. It looked like a little dragon spewing flames on both sides. We consolidated and, on the fly, decided to blow through. We cleared the kill zone and continued to engage targets for one mile yes, a full one-mile ambush. In total, we fired 5,000-6000 rounds.

After clearing the ambush, leadership and I debated running another pass to neutralize remaining targets, but I judged the risk too high and said, "No" and could not justify returning to the kill zone. We could live to fight another day, knowing the enemy would adjust their tactics for next time. When asked about dropping bombs, I informed my two JTACs that doing so would have hit the village behind the berms.

Leadership can be lonely at the top. Making unpopular decisions in the moment but in the right spirit is part of the job. I wanted our troop to return home with honor, not tarnish that with an impulsive action or let ego override critical thinking. My Medic and Comms asked if I wanted to pass anything to the Task Force, and I said, "We didn't drop bombs." I don't know why I phrased it that way, but it's somewhere in a log.

Back at base, I told Dave to pull the boats, hand out cigars, and promote the boys. Procrastination in a combat zone is never the right strategy. Tomorrow is not guaranteed. We promoted nine personnel. They were ecstatic! Cigars marked the achievement, rewarding the troop for a job well done. My chiefs and Dan shared a few laughs sometimes even dark humor helps mitigate the scariest experiences. Still, it was a great day.

There is no rest for the weary. Knowing the enemy would improve, we reset gear and boats and sent the troop to bed. Dave and I had a second job: generating a storyboard in PowerPoint for the Task Force, creating a Clamshell report summarizing the mission, and producing an executive summary detailing everything that transpired. One thing was certain: our SWCC boat captains and gunners saved our lives. As the older officers, Dave and I were just back-seat drivers. Their courage and skill during this complex ambush contributed to us surviving one of the largest NSW waterborne firefights since Vietnam. Every member of our Boat Assault Force and 1/501st returned unscathed thanks to the entire troop working in sync.

The next day, we reset boats and weapons. Leadership reviewed data to understand how our FLIR and thermal imaging systems missed the one-mile ambush entirely. We had many questions and planned a follow-up sensitive site exploitation (SSE) with the 1/501st.

After mission planning, I looked at Hank and said sarcastically, "I guess you got what you wanted." He smirked; I smacked him on the back. Then I directed him to get the boys ready. The enemy was planning too, and they would not miss us a second time.

People often criticize the younger generation as "softer" or entitled. In 2007, I saw a generation of SWCC volunteers prove the naysayers wrong. These men volunteered for the Navy, then for SWCC. They sacrificed everything. No slackers here. Watching them gear up for another mission in the same area where we had nearly been defeated was inspiring. After the patrol leaders' briefing, they looked like a football team ready to take the field: bro hugs, high fives, and pure focus. They embodied the SWCC creed. It was time to test the enemy's resolve again. On time! On target! Never Quit!

We conducted engine checks and "Go Condition 1" on all weapons and systems. With air support overhead, we began the patrol to the ambush site. Our plan was to insert an eight-man fire team on land at the exact location where the bombs were initiated. On the fly, we adjusted tactics to ensure flexibility in case prebriefed plans failed.

I heard Dave on the radio directing boat positions for inserting the team and for cover positions. The fire team turned on IR strobes and inserted on land. The boats backed off but remained close enough to support. The fire team discovered the enemy's concealment: tunnels through reeds and berms, containers hidden to reduce heat signatures. Tricky little devils.

We understood the linear ambush layout and discovered that two of the 55-gallon bombs had failed to detonate, meaning each boat had been targeted at the interval they first saw us pass. After an hour of SSE, the fire team returned to the boats, and we headed back to base to file reports and pass on intel.

By day nine of our assignment in Iskandariyah, we planned to redeploy to Habiniyah to prepare for the incoming riverine task unit. We had accomplished much, not to set records, but to do the best job possible, return home with honor, and ensure all personnel were safe. We never backed down, nor did we let risk-aversion compromise support for Special Operations partners.

We were asked to evaluate moving to Taji Air Base. After analysis, Dave and I concluded the outcome didn't justify the risk, and the incoming RTU could handle it. We redeployed to Habiniyah, preparing the troop, boats, trucks, weapons, for the journey home after five months. We were different more mature, more experienced, and bonded through countless shared trials.

Forty-six missions. Convoys. Firefights. Casualties. Helicopter operations. Nonstandard missions on civilian dhows. We crushed it. Nothing could take that from us. We returned to the States with honor, setting the precedent for future Riverine Task Units. We were part of something bigger, always ready, never waiting for orders. There were other sensitive missions I dare not describe only they were harrowing, but essential.

Riverine Task Unit Five became family. They helped me grow into a Naval Officer, far removed from my street-smart beginnings. From the bottom to the top, our team became Coastal Warrior River Rats exemplifying performance, precision and persistence. Iraq made us more confident and lethal than ever. The next deployment, to the Philippine Islands, would be less kinetic but equally dangerous, showcasing the full spectrum of Naval Special Warfare capabilities.

Operation Enduring Freedom look out.

Hooyah!

Chapter Twelve

The Philippines

"It follows then, as certain as that night succeeds the day, that without a decisive naval force we can do nothing definitive, and with it, everything honorable and glorious."

President George Washington

Finally, our Riverine Task Unit returned home to Virginia Beach. It's hard for me to believe Jackson was five years old. I had only small snapshots of his life during my absence. Guilt mingled with a sense of accomplishment a double-edged sword familiar to most of us in Special Operations. Our culture breeds competition in everything, including deployments that lead to promotions and reputation, but it keeps us away from home. And when we are home, we know it will be short-lived. I tried to make the most of the little time I had with Jenifer and Jackson.

I know I needed to re-establish my relationship with Jenifer and maximize time with Jackson. Up to that point, Jen and I had been married eighteen years a lifetime by Naval Special Warfare standards. We had our highs and lows, and the strain in our relationship was becoming apparent. I was clearly the guilty one, making her feel as though she were an inconvenience, as if my work mattered more than her. Arguments multiplied, and communication dwindled. Somehow, we always patched things up. Rinse and repeat. But once a warrior, always a warrior, on both sides. I truly believe the military spouse is the biggest warrior.

I was proud that Dave and I maximized our time in Iraq by conducting mid-term evaluations on every troop member, ensuring all maintenance and inventories were complete, and preparing the boats for redeployment to SBT-22 after final diesel inspections. This made the first few weeks at home pleasant and reduced our administrative burden.

Dave and I debriefed leadership on the deployment, recommending that the troop remain intact as a hybrid Coastal/Riverine capability. None of our recommendations were supported by command. As a result, manpower support from other detachments strained Special Boat Team Twenty, and other priorities demanded more SWCC.

I informed our troop that RTU-5 was disbanding. Some members transferred to continue experiencing the kind of work we had done; others were recycled to other detachments. RTU-5 went down in history but did not survive the first contact in intact at home. Early in the Iraq war, many health and mental evaluations did not exist, so we returned to work unaware of the long-term impacts of deployments. It was business as usual.

Our battle captain, Cary, ran the tactical operations center throughout the deployment. He was sharp, experienced, and invaluable returning home with us. Cary's gift to Dave and me was signing us up for Advanced Special Operations course. We weren't even home for two weeks before starting the most demanding, thought-provoking course I had ever experienced. But as a student of war, you can never have enough knowledge or training.

Day one of the course, instructors delivered expectations and handed us a stack of books at least two feet high. Each book represented hours of study and preparation. I grew frustrated and angry at one point wanting to throw the books on the floor and walk out. Three straight weeks of late nights, learning urban and rural operations, drawing diagrams, meeting people, and juggling life after a long deployment with little time at home tested my patience.

Yet, the course was fascinating, enabling us to work in a different capacity. Ross, Harry, and I became the "midnight crew," always the last to leave at night. The good news: we all passed and received our qualification. I had no intention of going to any follow on training because that course had been grueling, but the knowledge would prove useful for the Philippines deployment.

By this point, I was a successful post-deployment SWCC Warrant Officer, preparing to attend freefall jump school before rotating out. My executive officer DJ pulled me aside and asked me to remain at SBT-20 as a MK V Troop Commander. The previous Warrant Officer had been relieved, leaving a manning gap. I accepted immediately; staying operational and shaping a new team of SWCC took precedence over freefall school.

I found myself in a detachment with two MK V Special Operations Craft but only one qualified operator. We were all green. The MK V measured 82 feet long, 17.5 feet wide, 17.5 feet high, with a 5-foot draft, weighed 57 tons, had a 500nm planning range, and could reach 47 knots. A monster of a boat.

Its gray camouflage blended well at night. One forward machine gun mount accommodated a 7.62mm, while four aft deck mounts could fire dual .50 caliber machine guns simultaneously on port and starboard. The MK V carried 6-7 SWCC, sixteen passengers, and up to four combat rubber raiding craft on the back deck and ramp. I'll never forget the expensive STIDD seats, with nitrogen shocks we had to constantly maintain and replace. They mitigated vertical impacts but left us exposed to lateral g-forces from the 100,000-pound boat pounding through waves. Many SWCC and SEALs were pulled from boats due to injuries caused by the seats bottoming out. Operators were sometimes paralyzed for weeks in the hospital. Every SWCC experienced at least one injury from these boats. The impacts sounded like someone crushing a soda can. Why they never improved lateral and vertical protection remains a mystery.

The MK V detachment was the reason the SWCC Warrant Officer billet existed. I now commanded fourteen SWCC and nine maintenance support members. Manning wasn't full, but we had much to learn. I was already a qualified patrol officer but now had to master MK V systems and implement tactics. System qualification for engineers could take six months to a year; we had only one qualified engineer, who became our trainer and mentor.

My senior chief, Jeremy, was my right-hand man and AOIC. Jeremy came from 11M RIB Airdrop detachments and was accomplished. Like me, he had avoided MK V duty initially. We called it the roach motel. If you checked in, you never checked out! But Jeremy was like Dave: accountable, capable, and knowledgeable.

Though I had just completed an RTU workup and deployment, running two MK V SOCs was far more maintenance intensive. Both boats had emerged from overhaul in decent shape, but upkeep was relentless: painting, rust prevention, engine tuning. Maintenance likely cost over a million dollars annually. Our new moniker was "Boat Troop Five (BT-5)." Weeks passed as we got the boats underway and the troop integrated, recognizing Jeremy and me as their new family.

Demand for SWCC had increased pressure on all boat teams to provide personnel. Each detachment "paid a tax," contributing bodies to other programs. My engineer was reassigned by operations; losing him would halt training. I yelled, "Fuck this! It ain't happening!" and escalated to my commanding officer.

Calmly, I requested a moment to speak freely. Chuck Herbert, a servant leader I respected, listened carefully, weighing options and mentoring as always.

My South Side was boiling, but I had learned over the years to temper it with restraint. I unloaded on Chuck, explaining how pulling my only engineer would set back my troop because none of us were qualified and that other unit needs should not trump our team's priorities.

Of course, Chuck tried to talk me down, as he was famous for doing. But I couldn't hold it in any longer. "I don't need this crap, I am done," I said angrily. Then the sage guidance of a commanding officer kicked in. Chuck calmly said, "Ron, as a troop commander, you are holding the umbrella over your guys' heads. If you were to leave for any reason, who would protect them from the rain?"

He was right. I was still fuming because I knew I had lost every point I tried to make. Chuck used his ninja skills and played the loyalty card. These were my guys, my gang, and I wasn't going to desert them. Chuck knew it too. So, our only engineer said goodbye, and we circled the wagons to continue honing our capabilities and tactics. Boy, do I regret letting Chuck use the umbrella story on me. Every time I got perturbed by something, he would ask if I needed to hear the umbrella story. He was a damn great C.O. Chuck you sly dawg.

Our troop received two First Class petty officers, Gary and Will, who had spent a large part of their careers in the MK V program. Between them, they had a wealth of knowledge and were true assets to the troop, especially in instructing young SWCC. Their adjustment to our culture where rank alone did not confer respect would be challenging. In this troop, either you were a leader, or you were not. Either you earned your SWCC pin and respect every day, or you didn't.

Gary became the LPO, with Will as his backup. They were loyal to a fault to each other, while I, as troop commander, had to make decisions in support of the entire troop. They were constantly in the spotlight with the young SWCC because our operators were athletes and fighters who respected those who earned it. I made it clear to Gary and Will that they had to earn the troop's respect. In prior assignments, they may have hidden behind rank and position, but in my troop, competence and leadership mattered most. The cream always rose to the top. Accountability was non-negotiable. Mark Presson would have been proud of me.

During workups, I noticed Jeremy struggling to keep up amid personal issues. I called him in for a one-on-one and stressed the need for full commitment to the troop. Jeremy revealed he was in the process of a divorce. We agreed it was best for him to transfer out. Now I was down a senior enlisted and had to manage alone until a replacement was assigned. This was terrible timing with our final battle problem approaching.

Then we learned our deployment to the Philippines would involve SBT-12 MK V boats, not ours, along with their maintenance support team. Simultaneously, we would take command of the SBT-12 RIB detachment deploying to the Philippines. My saving grace: I knew most of SBT-12's personnel from past assignments. I now had to establish rapport quickly and create a cohesive unit out of many moving parts.

We worked hard to get our boats ready. My troop left no stone unturned; the boats were a direct reflection of the team's dedication. We inspected the SBT-12 boats in San Diego, letting my guys identify discrepancies. They tore into the detachment, presenting a detailed list of what needed fixing. I was proud they made my life easier and spared me from being the bad guy. The MST officer committed to correcting all deficiencies before the boats shipped. Unlike prior experiences, this MST officer was squared away.

Still, SWCC warrant officers always have positional authority, even over more senior MST officers, which created tension. I had to maintain a working relationship while keeping the troop's interests first. I worried about deploying with strangers responsible for our boats, but I suppressed my concern and focused on the mission.

We returned to Virginia just in time to receive tasking from Ryan, our training cadre. He was a senior chief from SBU-12, highly knowledgeable on MK V operations. The first task: a logistical movement within forty-eight hours, over land and water, moving deployment packages to Mayport, Florida, while traveling by water ourselves.

We briefed the troop on their responsibilities: weapons prep, navigation planning, communications, and securing comms. Moving beans, bullets, and bodies over 600 miles by land and sea was far from easy, but we met the deadline. One planned layover in

North Carolina had us battling eight-to-ten-foot seas. Even for elite SWCC, it was harrowing but my team excelled.

By then, my two First Class petty officers acted as crewmen, and the Second Class petty officers, Matt Nowalski and Brian Badder, were now boat captains. They complemented each other perfectly. The crew responded well because they were respected. I watched proudly while they ran the mission, communicated waypoints, and passed updates to command. I felt like a proud father.

The seas worsened, and I decided we needed shelter. I directed Matt's boat to stand fast while Brian navigated our boat toward Oregon Inlet. The inlet was notorious for sandbars, and the buoy marking the channel was missing. Progress was slow, using night vision and FLIR, until our boat ran aground. It was soft, but the stern was hammered by ten-to-twelve-foot surf dangerously creating suction that could trap us. I informed boat two to stand fast.

Brian, a skilled driver, surged forward broaching us in the surf zone. I panicked internally, but reminded myself to stay calm, as in Iraq. I directed him, "Pull off the throttle and use the bow beached in the sand to pivot the stern back out to sea, then slam the throttles as the waves lifted the stern." Timing was crucial; the storm surge slammed the stern, and we slammed the throttles in reverse. The first attempt failed, pushing us further ashore. I reassured him: "Don't worry, Brian, we got this." Eventually, we backed out little by little. To ensure safety, I contacted the Coast Guard for escort through the sandbar, learning that the buoy had shifted and sand had accumulated at the inlet.

We conducted a battle damage assessment: beans, bullets, bodies, and boats were all accounted for. Only one task remained arriving at the layover on time. The seas were still rough but manageable. We arrived at Morehead City, reset the boats, and set a watch.

The next morning, we conducted muster, situation reports, and a navigation brief. I reminded the troop that staying calm under adversity and having Boat Two ready to tow exemplified teamwork and intentional action. Little did we know, this lesson would later save Filipino Marines' lives.

Transiting back through Oregon Inlet, Murphy's Law struck. Toxic fumes filled the cockpit while seas remained five-to-seven feet. A fire alarm sounded the most dangerous onboard MK V. My team executed flawless damage control: engines shut down, status reported, due to impacts, the fuel rack was cracked spraying diesel on the engine. Ventilation cleared the vapors. Thirty minutes later, the boat was running. High seas, engine repairs, and diesel fumes enough to make the toughest sailor seasick but we pushed through and stayed on schedule for Mayport, Florida.

At Mayport, we faced our final battle problem. For eight days, we lived on cots in a hangar, planning and executing mission after mission with precision. Ryan Renner, our training cadre, challenged us by disrupting our tempo, but we worked backwards from the objective and implemented contingencies. I even used TST briefing formats when he made it difficult to deliberate plan the op.

With only one hour to brief the mission, we prepared the boats in thirty minutes while keeping MSTs on board. I used duct tape to lay out phase objectives on the hangar floor, briefing all phase objectives and contingencies from memory. The CO and command master chief observed. Only one question: "What if your comms go down?" I confidently replied, "We have redundant comms, including TACSAT backpacks on each boat. It's nearly impossible to lose comms, sir." I would live to regret those words.

No sooner had we gotten underway than we lost all comms. To this day, I believe the training cadre sabotaged our crypto. Both boats lost communications simultaneously, which was highly improbable. After troubleshooting for a few minutes, I decided to switch to backpack Tactical Satellite radios to execute the mission, while our comms cell worked on getting the boat radios back online. Fortunately, the mission went off without a hitch, and we returned to base safely. We passed our final battle problem and were given the green light to deploy.

I was still short a senior enlisted in my troop and could not deploy without one. The training officer, a fellow warrant officer , pulled me into his office to discuss the possibility of his senior enlisted filling the slot in my troop. He mentioned that Ryan Renner was a little apprehensive because he thought I was a control freak who wouldn't let him do his job. I told the training officer that I preferred to speak directly with Ryan rather than have a middleman discuss another man's concerns. So, I did.

We had a great conversation. I told Ryan that the troop was my troop and that they carried my signature in everything they did. I explained that it was my standard, no one else's. If he could maintain my standard or elevate it while infusing his own characteristics, we'd be in a strong position with no issues. Ryan agreed, and the rest was history. Ryan excelled in the AOIC position.

With our final battle problem behind us, we were tasked with transiting to New York for Fleet Week, followed by a visit to the great City of Philadelphia.

New York Fleet Week was quite an experience. We were in the middle of the procession of ships and could drive wherever we wanted to greet onlookers. We loved that they loved us. It felt good to see them wave and cheer.

We had to split the troop between two different hotels. As a token of respect and appreciation, I gave the maintenance support team the Millennium Hilton, while we stayed fifteen blocks down the road. That didn't sound far until you factored in New York traffic taking us 45 minutes to reach our hotel.

Our main effort was to support the Navy SEAL Foundation and educate distinguished visitors on Naval Special Warfare mission and capabilities. My SWCC were needed more than the MST to drive people to and from the Statue of Liberty.

So, apart from coming to the boat in the morning to assist with maintenance, the MST would actually be the ones enjoying Fleet Week. After day three of working from 7:00 a.m. to 7:00 p.m., it was taking a toll on my guys. One of my SWCC, Nick, got pretty sick, so I had Gary contact the MST officer to ask for one of his guys to replace him. I couldn't believe the MST officer outright refused. I was close to our public relations officer and furious they were having the time of their lives while my SWCC were working non-stop.

Giving them a good deal was our way of saying "thanks," but somehow the "how soon we forget" mentality set in. I called the MST officer. He was senior to me, but I had positional authority that trumps rank. Anyone who knows me knows I never hide behind rank or treat anyone differently. I tried to create a family and a gang out of our troop, but this immature officer wasn't having it. This was the last straw.

I told him that Nick was sick and we needed one of his guys to cover for him. He refused again, saying he was tired of us taking advantage of them. I said, "We have been working more than fourteen hours a day running these boats while you all are relaxing. I am only asking you to send one of your guys to back us up." He still refused. I asked where he was. He said they were in the pool. I was pissed. "If you don't have one of your guys at this boat in twenty minutes, I'm coming to that pool, and I'm going to fucking drown you in front of everyone. We have a sick crewmember here. Get fucking moving!"

The PAO heard my response, paused, and walked away, her face showing disbelief. From that point on, I stopped trying to keep the peace with the MST officer. Yet he would still deploy with the SBT-12 troop to the Middle East. I was hoping the SBT-12 MST team would be different. Boy, did I miss the MST team at SBT-22.

New York Fleet Week ended, and despite that one inconvenient experience with the MST officer, my troop loved the city, the nightlife, and the public accolades. We even staged a counseling on one of my guys that was too drunk to work. It was actually only to promote him to the next rank. He was very surprised. Mission accomplished.

Our next stop was The City of Brotherly Love Philadelphia, where both the Declaration of Independence and the U.S. Constitution were drafted and ratified. I had visited Philadelphia three months prior for a pre-deployment site survey to determine where we could moor the boats and lay our heads. There is a distinct difference between New York and Philly. New York was welcoming but hard and callous, while Philly was warm and genuine. Everyone showed us love, especially those in uniform. Philly's violent crimes unit, the Boots, led by Captain Mike Cochrane, reminded me of our team. They were tough and a band of brothers. I will always remember them and how they served their people. If you ever see these officers in polished boots and leather jackets, you are looking at Philly's finest. Joe Hanson and Joe Moore and many more we love you guys.

This initial visit opened my eyes to how successful people live and interact. Our trip was sponsored by the Benjamin Franklin Global Forum and the Union League of Philadelphia. I was amazed by the history and heritage that the Union League had restored and protected. Here I was, a chief warrant officer, walking around showing off our boats and briefing on NSW capability, thinking I was badass. During that visit and subsequent ones, I realized that everything I had assumed about rich or wealthy people was wrong. Growing up in the hood, I was taught not to trust them; a lie I now know all too well.

Conversely, I met countless people supporting causes and offering a hand up, not a handout. They shared their knowledge and experiences, along with humility. From those visits, I made lifelong friends who profoundly impacted my life. They say, "It's all about who's on the bus," and my bus was about to gain some new passengers.

There was Bob, Cathy, Dava, Ivan, and George, who became my big brothers and sisters. They provided sage guidance, instilled business acumen, and encouraged me to learn and grow. Up to that point, I had only boasted about being a badass, despite having no formal education. Often, I felt like an imposter. I knew I excelled at many things but didn't understand why. Being around these successful people humbled me. They succeeded through business, relationships, and emotional intelligence, not special operations.

Meeting them lit a fire under me. When I returned, I immediately enrolled in college, determined to emulate their wisdom and stay on track. (This was 2007, and I have been friends with them ever since.) Since then, I completed two bachelor's degrees, a master's degree, and an executive coaching certification all thanks to these mentors. It's all about whose on the bus, period!

Each had a distinct pedigree: Bob excelled at networking and hosting impactful events; Cathy an executive coach taught emotional intelligence and leadership; Dava was a PR and marketing expert; Ivan came from Italy and built a business from scratch with money borrowed from his aunt and sold 5 lbs. of nails for $5; George, a Vietnam veteran, discovered his passion for art and runs Mount America foundation with his wife, Michelle, supporting at-risk kids, veterans with PTSD, and Naval Sea Cadets. There was no drama just real men and women doing great work. Their mentorship profoundly shaped my life, filling gaps that the military could not.

In the military, unless you come from a family or community of role models, you often have nothing to compare your progress to. I constantly looked for reference points, but few existed. The military emphasizes "mission first, people always," but eventually, your service ends. If you don't apply yourself early, opportunities after retirement are scarce. To predict the future, you must create it both in and out of the military. Network early.

My past prepared me to endure adversity, pain, hate, and discrimination, but it didn't equip me to elevate my game. The Navy shaped me into a good sailor, chief, and warrant officer, but it didn't provide a roadmap beyond the military. Not that there weren't great examples around me but in the military, we rarely pry into personal lives unless it affects the mission.

However, my Union League family was different. They genuinely wanted to see me succeed not just in the military, but long after my career ended. I was also amazed at their passion for our country's history. The Civil War had necessitated the founding of the Union League to recruit soldiers and raise funds. Since then, the Union League has stood the test of time, supporting our military and law enforcement. Wearing our uniforms in the building was considered as formal as wearing a tuxedo and exceeded their dress code standards.

Visiting Philadelphia and forming lifelong friendships, like Officer Mike Cochran and the legacy he left with the violent crimes unit called "The Boots" before being promoted to Inspector, was unforgettable. "Thanks, Mike, and your team, for all the conversations and the beef soup in Chinatown". Inspector Tony Boil was another remarkable example of sacrifice, having served thirty-five years in the Air Force while also dedicating himself to law enforcement. He was also a badass.

After leaving Philadelphia and the fine people we met, we traveled along the Delaware River back to Virginia Beach. We had roughly two months before deployment when we were informed that we could no longer use our boats. A team had conducted ultrasound testing and discovered thousands of stress fractures throughout the frame members and the mast of both boats. Repairs and reinforcements would be required before Special Boat Team Twelve could deploy them to the Middle East. If these boats were sustaining structural fractures, imagine the forces our bodies endured.

To put it in perspective, the boats had a max speed of 47 knots and weighed over fifty tons. Slamming into waves transmitted extreme forces through our bodies, even though the seats were designed to mitigate only vertical impacts. The seats would bottom out, amplifying the force threefold meaning a 10g hull impact could become 30g on the body and 50g or more on the head. Many of us have severely damaged C3-4-5 and L4-L5/L5-S1 vertebrae, and the list goes on. Still, we would do it all over again. Just with better seats next time.

Unlike the peaceful and inspirational visit to Philadelphia, I had to fly to the Philippine Islands for a deployment site survey and to meet the new task unit commander and his SEAL leadership. Low and behold, it was JJ from Iraq! Having a commander with combat experience reassured me. Many Americans, sometimes intentionally, don't understand life in special operations. One day, we could be on a combat deployment; the next, supporting a partner force and helping them execute missions. "By, with and through". A partner force is the essence of patience. Our metrics of success were based on their performance. If they failed, we had nothing to boast about beyond hours underway and nautical miles traveled.

To prepare, I met with JJ and the team at the U.S. Embassy and Joint U.S. Military Assistance Group, followed by a formal briefing with the Filipino Navy and Marines. We then flew to Mindanao, the southern region of the archipelago. Mindanao is the Philippines' second-largest island, home to over twenty-seven million people, about twenty-three percent of whom are Muslim. Our commercial airline attempted to land before Typhoon Kamaegi arrived but we flew directly into the storm. The plane was tossed violently, circling for hours, and our consolation prize was one Dunkin' Donut per passenger. What should have been a one-hour flight stretched into six hours.

Our base was on Zamboanga Island, where we joined the deployed task unit under operational control of Joint Special Operations Task Force–Philippines (JSOTF-P). Even a small NSW footprint must integrate into an existing base, and this one provided accommodations for JSOTF-P at the top of the hill and our NSWTU at the bottom, closest to the water. We called our compound the "Nipa Huts," with palm-frond roofs and a large outdoor gazebo surrounded by benches.

The tactical operations center was modest, with radios and situation maps feeding information to outposts on other islands. Our area of responsibility included Basilan, Zamboanga, and Tawi-Tawi, an island 450 nautical miles away. The population was predominantly Muslim; with the terrorist groups Abu Sayyaf and Moro Islamic Liberation Front (MILF), a name we often joked about wanting to join. This deployment would be intense.

We had to run training for the Marine Recon and Navy Special Operations personnel, conduct our own missions, and support advanced special operations. Unlike Iraq, where NSW often had free reign in war zones, here we were in a sovereign country with a status-of-forces agreement limiting our authority. We needed to understand the culture, be patient, and accept that the partner force did the shooting while we trained and provided intel. If lucky, we could shadow missions and serve as a quick reaction force.

We traveled to Basilan and Tawi-Tawi to meet commanders, assess friendly capabilities, and receive briefings on enemy forces. These islands were breathtakingly beautiful tourist destinations if not for terrorist threats.

The NSW Task Element stationed there knew their jobs and challenged themselves daily. I was surprised by the local wildlife, giant rodents, baboons, and bats the size of eagles. For the special operators on these islands, adapting to the rural environment was essential, while Zamboanga was more urban. After completing the site survey, we returned to Virginia to prepare for deployment.

Ryan, my senior enlisted, and I had a lot to coordinate. We had a nine-man RIB detachment from SBT-12, led by Jason Galvan, along with two MK V SOCs and a maintenance support team from SBT-12, that we had only met once in San Diego. We also had a 330-foot Mission Support Vessel with fourteen civilians supporting NSW missions. Like Iraq, this deployment could make us rock stars or groupies. I hoped for the former.

This deployment would test my leadership with forty personnel from diverse commands and backgrounds. It was a challenge I never shied away from. I placed us all under Boat Troop 5.

We arrived at Subic Bay, Philippines, awaiting the MK V craft aboard a cargo ship, while our RIB detachment flew into Zamboanga. Once the MK Vs arrived, we transported eighty-two-foot boats, almost twenty feet high, through narrow streets. The MST team creatively used fifteen-foot bamboo poles to lift electric lines as the boats passed.

An aircraft hangar housed the MK Vs for reassembly and installation of removed components. The final step was transporting the boats to the water for testing before the 560-nautical-mile transit to Zamboanga. This sixteen-hour journey required expanded fuel bladders on the back deck.

Ryan checked in with the Task Force and Task Unit at Zamboanga. I arrived at the NSW Nipa Huts. We were accustomed to the third-world environment and local store fronts catering to us. Our compound was surrounded by a larger fence topped with concertina wire. The main gate required a combination to open mainly to control access and protect gear. I noticed rows of Toyota Hilux trucks parked outside and was greeted by our Task Unit Commander JJ, and his senior enlisted Mac.

We were happy to be reunited and eager to get to work. Unlike Iraq, our mission now was to serve as trainers, intel support, boat transport, and anything else necessary to maintain our value to the FILMIL. Once our usefulness waned, so too would our freedom of movement. JJ briefed us on the mission and informed me that the Cross Functional Troop (CFT) had arrived. This meant we might have to supplement their staffing. The CFT was our intelligence-gathering apparatus, providing enemy intel, enhancing our common operating picture, and offering indications and warnings for force protection and mission success. It was critical that we integrate the CFT fully into our battle rhythm.

The Task Force (TF) Commander Colonel Coultrup was an Army Special Forces commander, and a force of nature. He empowered us to be self-sufficient, responsible, and accountable while pushing operational limits. On his second extension as TF Commander, he gave us three days to achieve FOC for all boats, the troop, and the mission support vessel. The Task Force had established a joint operations center capable of targeting, tracking, and locating the enemy while managing daily logistics to support forces spread across the areas of operation. Our SEAL platoon and boat troop would be distributed across NSW-responsible islands.

My boat troop would operate out of Zamboanga and Tawi-Tawi. A few SEALs would accompany us at these locations, while others ran Liaison Control Elements (LCEs) on Basilan Island. These islands had a significant Muslim presence. Most locals were peaceful, but Abu Sayyaf and the MILF were committed to kidnapping, extortion, and terrorism.

Many of the people we worked with, including the Magic Guard, shared a single motivation: to eliminate the terrorists and bring peace to their islands.

The U.S. presence in the Philippines spans decades. I recalled visiting Subic Bay as a young sailor and seeing how American culture had been intertwined with the Philippines since World War II. The U.S. Navy, in my view, had more Filipino nationals serving than any other branch. Historically, Filipinos had a direct path to citizenship through service in the U.S. military. While this path is less prevalent now, the Philippines remains one of our closest allies.

Consider the U.S. government's funding to organize, train, equip, rebuild, and assist the Philippines over decades. Millions of dollars have been spent with limited visible progress. Many times, it would have been simpler to execute a mission quickly rather than embrace the local culture and extend operations that should have taken hours into a week-long endeavor. We jokingly called this "slow island time."

Some programs were baffling. The "Reward for Justice Program," for instance, offered cash for information leading to the capture of high-value targets. Recipients were hooded to protect them and escorted offstage. We joked that the money often went back into FILMIL to build hotels and clubs. When one high-value target was arrested, another inevitably took his place.

Regardless, we had a mission. My troop consolidated, and I brought my two senior chiefs up to speed: Jay, my RIB Det Commander, and Ryan, my MK V Det Commander. We conducted area familiarization and began integrating with Filipino SEALs and Marine Special Operations, even developing our own campaign plan.

Our maintenance support team rotated between Zamboanga and Subic Bay, where the majority of our gear and MK V repair parts remained. We divided into blue and gold teams to operate independently in Tawi-Tawi, each consisting of one MK V and one RIB. Jay and Ryan handled day-to-day operations and could conduct missions independently without my constant oversight. I only assumed direct command if we reconstituted into a four-boat troop, ensuring morale and chain-of-command while maintaining operational tempo and communications.

To support sensitive activities, I reassigned the RIB Det LPO Mitch Spivey from the RIB Det to the Cross Functional Troop. Mitch was charismatic, intelligent, and an operational standout. This decision turned out to be one of the best we made. Teams working across the battlespace became a template of precision in every sense.

The blue team pushed to Tawi-Tawi, while gold remained in Zamboanga. Our campaign plan focused on illuminating threats, supporting FILMIL operations from a safe distance, providing fire support if needed, and offering medical assistance. FILMIL patrol boats were hesitant to navigate a Basilan Island choke point, known as "Ambush Alley," notorious for ambushes. With JJ and me just out of Iraq, it made sense to establish ourselves and send a clear message: there was a new sheriff in town. Our area of operations was semi-permissive, and we could go almost anywhere, but missteps could be catastrophic.

Running a Mission Support Vessel, a MK V Detachment with maintenance support, and a RIB Detachment was demanding, but the CFT gained traction faster than expected. They built a relationship with the Magic Guard, motivated by hatred for terrorists and desire to help their country. Understanding individual motivations was critical for mission success. The Magic Guard operated like any organized gang, led by Sonny, an elder who commanded respect through charisma and fear. Mitch and RIB were too young to relate, so they tasked me with developing rapport with Sonny, creating an information exchange that supported targeting. Though Sonny operated outside the law, our goals aligned. Late nights spent with him became part of my operational routine, alongside report writing, troop management, and my master's degree coursework.

We had Ryan's first approved mission tasking to insert four Filipino nurses on Bahilabong Pier in Ambush Alley to perform circumcisions according to local religious practices. Approval came from the Task Force commander. Ryan's gold team, with one MK V and one eleven-meter RIB, executed the operation.

As Ryan's boats entered Basilan Inlet, a rickety Philippine patrol boat escorted them. MILF rebels opened fire. MK V and RIB crews engaged, but the Remotely Operated Small Arms Mounts malfunctioned, firing rounds high into the air instead of at the enemy. Ryan quickly moved the nurses into the boat canopy, covering them with body armor, then pulled a M240G machine gun to suppress the enemy while passing info to me. The boats exited Ambush Alley without casualties or damage. A close call.

During this "troops in contact" incident, all communications are supposed to go dark. No radio transmissions occurred until after team debriefs, executive summaries, and storyboards were completed. Some members inexperienced in such events, relayed information back to SBT-12, prompting questions from higher command. This was even before JSOTF-P and SOCPAC were aware. Boy did I take heavies from all sides for that.

Although initially pissed, I recognized it as a learning experience. Our operations were often misunderstood by command, who assumed I was looking for firefights. In reality, we merely asserted freedom of maneuver and enemy forces had no say. Ryan earned a Bronze Star for his actions that day.

Being a SWCC meant that, aside from SEAL officers, few understood our capabilities. We had operational freedom provided our Concepts of Operations were approved. Ryan and I communicated with command meticulously, especially given the ROSAM malfunctions. I directed Ryan to conduct extensive at-sea live-fire testing with 10,000 rounds of .50 cal ammo to resolve system gremlins. ROSAMs proved unreliable and were eventually removed from NSW boats; newer versions are now highly accurate.

While Ryan and the boats were gone, I focused on supporting Brandon, RIB and Mitch in their operations. Although I was Mitch's troop commander and a Chief Warrant Officer Three, while Rib was a Chief and Mitch an E6, they held positional authority in this lane. In this role, I reported to them. Mitch was meticulous and would chew me out if reports were late or inaccurate. I jokingly threatened to write him a bad evaluation when I put my troop commander hat back on, but the three of us formed a strong team. Leadership is knowing when to lead and when to follow, and this was Mitch's domain. The tasking I received from him often felt like a scene straight out of an action movie (not The Godfather, thankfully).

The team maintained relationships throughout the Philippine Islands, which required constant touchpoints. Being the older guy allowed me to navigate relationships with Sonny and others who smoked, drank whiskey, and expected a certain demeanor. I drew on my South Side Chicago hustle to blend in with this social sphere. My primary responsibility was maintaining trust with Sonny, leader of the Magic Guard a 150,000-strong organization affiliated with the Chinese Mafia. Sonny carried himself like an old-school Mafia Don, receiving gestures of respect from others, though I limited myself to friendly hug.

Spending hours with Sonny allowed me to gain morsels of intel critical to our operational picture. He despised the Muslim extremists disrupting his country, and we knew that if anyone from our team were kidnapped, Sonny would ensure their safe return within hours. His influence also facilitated the logistical needs of our boats and the mission support vessel. Through Sonny, I coordinated fuel and food, confident that suppliers wouldn't taint fuel or provide spoiled provisions, a problem we often faced on other deployments. Remarkably, we never had a single fuel issue on this Philippine deployment.

Over time, my rapport with Sonny grew, and I worked alongside him to gather intel, illuminate threats and connecting the dots with Mitch and Rib. Their dedication and expertise were astonishing; it was as if they never slept. By the third month, it was impossible to distinguish SEALs from SWCCs or support personnel. We had become a hybrid Naval Special Warfare Task Unit, like family. JJ and Shane fostered this cohesion, pushing our teams while teaching cultural patience.

One Friday, JJ asked me to accompany him to the base admiral's office. Expecting a quick visit, I was surprised when it became a teaching moment. JJ calmly waited for over two hours while the admiral's secretary dawdled. When finally invited in, JJ and the admiral spoke for thirty minutes about family and nonmilitary matters. Afterwards, JJ requested approval to have outhouses pumped and water delivered over the weekend. The admiral granted it. I complained about the long wait, but JJ used the moment to teach me about respecting local culture and taking responsibility for the welfare of our people. He also gave me the book on cultural awareness and influencing outcomes he was reading, which reshaped my perspective.

Later, Mitch called. One of Sonny's men, close to us, had lost $25,000 gambling and was suicidal. Despite my initial reluctance, Mitch's authority prevailed, and I went to him. I spent hours distracting him, laughing, joking, and offering support. This deepened our bond and ultimately strengthened our operational network.

The next morning, boat training proceeded well. The SBT-12 maintenance team kept the MK V and RIB craft in top condition. With enough intelligence to validate a high-value target (HVT) mission, we launched a plane to confirm a signal. It was positive. We scrambled Filipino boats alongside ours to capture HVT #1. However, poor driving skills on FILMIL boats forced JJ to cancel the mission and convert it into boat operations and driver training. It was frustrating to see extensive investment yield minimal capability with training constantly reset to basic levels. The paradigm was vicious: the country remained dependent on U.S. support, and I wondered who was really benefiting.

Following orders, I returned to town to visit Sonny. A man carrying a bag, which immediately alarmed me, approached the lobby where Sonny was sitting. As he laid pistols on the banister, my instincts kicked in. I checked the floor for plastic under my chair a habit I picked up from movies then placed my hand on my Glock. When the man picked up a pistol and fingered the trigger, I drew my weapon and yelled pointing my weapon at him, "What the fuck is your problem? Sonny, what the fuck is going on!"

Sonny laughed. "Ron, calm down. It's okay. People like him bring guns, we give loans, and if they can't repay in three months, we sell them for triple." I relaxed, raised my whiskey glass, and toasted Sonny, reflecting on the life we led edge-of-the-seat, constant vigilance, whiskey in hand.

This became routine for seven months. I maintained oversight of operations while navigating urban life safely. I often stopped for a drink with local police to maintain rapport. Once, a moped T-boned my truck while turning a corner. A new set of police were on duty and rushed the scene, accusing me of causing the accident and demanding money. Recognizing it as a shakedown, I asserted control, I ordered the police to unblock the fucking road, order the moped driver to pick up his fucking moped and get out of the damn street. I reimbursed him $200 USD for bike repair, later checking in and visiting him at his distant village. Such personal investment was common in expanding our network.

The next challenge arose when our Mission Support Vessel (MSV) had a Naval officer from Naval Special Warfare Unit One onboard for six months to act as our liaison between the crew and our task unit. We had 11-meter RIBs in the davits on the MSV, and the RIB detachment didn't mind the better food and living conditions onboard.

Then orders came from our boss in Guam: the Naval officer needed to fly home because his wife was having a baby, and I would ride the MSV for ten days starting in a month. I informed the chain of command that I was running a troop and supporting other activities. Their response? Do all of that from the MSV. Seriously?

The MSV had never anchored. It was continuously cruising, punching holes in the ocean, burning $30,000 in fuel per day, and constantly transiting long distances to replenish food and fuel. I met with the captain to ask why refueling and provisioning couldn't happen in Zamboanga. He said it was too dangerous and would require force protection that the FILMIL refused to provide.

A light went off in my head. I consulted JJ, Mitch, and Rib. We discussed the problem: the MSV would have to leave station for two weeks to resupply. We needed a solution to keep the vessel on station longer and reduce fuel costs. After brainstorming, we devised a plan. We would create our own security company using Sonny's men as guards. We got permission to train the guards, and set up the company.

Over three weeks, our SEALs trained about thirty of Sonny's men in rifles, pistols, and uniforms. Once ready, the MSV pulled into port. The pier was cordoned off with forty-foot shipping containers stacked with concertina wire. Suddenly, four SUVs arrived. I tensed, almost reaching for my gun but Rib got out, smiling.

The security detail was professional, disciplined, and immediately took control of the perimeter. NSW Zodiacs with three guards each also joined the effort. The MSV crew received much-needed R&R, escorted into town by the CFT to grab food, snacks, and cigarettes. Fuel and food had been coordinated through Sonny. Everything ran like clockwork. The MSV remained in port for ten hours, and then we returned to sea. Anchoring off the base with security saved about $375,000 in fuel over fifteen days.

Meanwhile, HVT #1 resurfaced on Jolo Island. A Special Forces Task Unit was already training and supporting FILMIL counterterrorism missions against Abu Sayyaf and MILF. My troop was tasked to consolidate all capability off Jolo to support an interdiction of HVT #1. Once at Jolo, I took a Zodiac to rendezvous with an awaiting military convoy and begin mission planning.

The SF major was squared away and briefed me. Then, unexpectedly, he handed the floor over for me to present capabilities and actions. NSW forces constantly brief, so it was a piece of cake to convince them we could execute the mission. My only request: move assets to the MSV and execute from out at sea to reduce surveillance and pattern of life.

Four Filipino boats and crews, along with Marines waited for three days on the MSV to pull the trigger but the mission was canceled when the boat never showed. Dry holes were far more common than jackpots. I returned to land and sat in on the major's debrief to the general. I watched him navigate culture and politics, agreeing to disagree on numerous topics. Green Berets are amazing at FID.

Upon my return to Zamboanga, the Filipino admiral had ordered a show of force on Basilan Island. Despite existing forward operating bases and SEAL elements already stationed there he placed twenty-nine regular Marines atop Hill 330. Predictably, the Moro Islamic Liberation Front Special Operations Group inflicted casualties. Five Filipino Marines were wounded initially; medevac helicopters attempting to rescue them were almost shot down.

The base admiral informed us of the situation. We went to his backyard overlooking the water and our MK V boats, placed the troop on alert, and prepared gear for CASEVAC operations. Of course, we waited for hours with the Admiral to ask him if we could position our forces. Mario Martin, our Task Unit Combat Medic, prepped equipment for potential evacuation. He was precise, professional, and one of my closest friends.

We were permitted to move the MSV with RIBS two miles off Basilan Island for support. Monitoring the firefight, we learned the five wounded Marines were now KIA with three more injured. After three hours, I consolidated the MK V boats with the MSV, joined by Rib to pass us intel. Filipino boats moored alongside us. Mission planning began in earnest. As always, no plan survives first contact intact. I pulled input from my senior chiefs to create a more sound plan.

Since optics were critical, the Filipinos wouldn't want Americans leading the charge into Ambush Alley, the same site of our recent ambush. My underlying agenda was to keep the Filipino boat unit far enough away to avoid friendly fire. I had them lead 1,000 yards ahead to block reinforcements from the opposite inlet. They agreed.

Our mission: CASEVAC Filipino Marines in vicinity of Hill 330, while being slowed by MILF wounding their personnel. By 04:30, we approached morning nautical twilight, about forty-five minutes before sunrise. Task Force Intel cleared a pier for extraction, but conditions were dicey. Night vision was fading; FLIR was our only surveillance capability. We were thin-skinned aluminum boats and RIBs with no armor like SOCR boats. Nine Marines were now wounded.

I passed a SITREP to JJ that the Filipino boat commander informed me they would conduct the mission. I was furious and told him good freakin luck. I informed JJ that we were standing down. No sooner than I called JJ, Ryan ran in and said Carp we have a green light, to go! The Filipino boat commander in a stern voice, ordered me to take down our American flags, I responded, "Over my dead body!"

Boarding Ryan's MK V, we executed the plan. Rib came along since he was a sniper and coordinated with NISG which was the FILMIL Navy intel. We learned 400 MILF SOG forces were centrally located, obstructing the Marines' path and wounding them to slow them down. Then 105mm howitzers and 81mm mortars targeted the enemy as we approached Ambush Alley.

We rounded a bend and encountered a long rock jetty which was our only landing point. It wasn't a pier. Intel screwed this up bad. A Fifty-ton vessel, five-foot draft with lives at stake. I reassured Ryan, "Fucking beach it Ryan!" Old Chicago me might have panicked, but experience taught me there's always a solution. No victim mentality here. Just mission execution.

Well, no plan survives first contact intact, and we were committed. Explosions still echoed in the distance. The Marines arrived at the jetty, and we pulled them onto the boat one at a time. There were twenty-four Marines in total with nine wounded and five KIA that were left atop Hill 330. It was taking longer than expected, but we finally had everyone. Meanwhile, the MILF SOG was closing in.

We unbeached the boat and transited out to sea, with boats 3 and 4 taking the lead while boat 1 covered our six. No sooner had we cleared about 1,000 yards from the island, both engines shut down. During our time beached atop the shallow jetty, we had sucked in sand through the intakes. The engineers rushed to the engine room and informed us that both engines had overheated and sprayed antifreeze everywhere.

We had to call the other MK V over to cross-deck all passengers and the wounded, while I tasked the RIBs with holding security. Matt, our other MK V boat captain, struggled to come alongside, and Gary, the 1st class, demanded Matt give him the helm. Matt refused, so Gary radioed his complaint. I could not believe that, in a real-world mission, I had to deal with parochial bull shit. I asked Matt if he could figure it out and come alongside. He said yes. I told him, "Then hurry the hell up."

Matt came alongside, and all passengers and wounded were cross-decked. I will never forget seeing our combat medics and SWCC patching up the wounded Marines on the back deck. They were in their element, seemingly in their own world. Our SWCC combat medic Mario Guray, and task unit medic Mario Martin took command of the back deck, delegating orders to everyone. With nine wounded Marines to treat, these men were credited with saving lives. That was a good day.

Back to business. I released the MK V with the wounded to transit at high speed back to Zamboanga base for immediate transport to the hospital. Thanks to the medics stabilizing them, this was possible. I ordered the MSV to come alongside and allow us to moor. Once complete, we commenced transit back to Zamboanga. The journey took an incredibly long time, but we made it safely. It took about fourteen hours for the engines to cool. I had already prepared my storyboard, clamshell, and executive summary. All things considered, it went as well as could be expected except I might be fired for destroying a million dollars' worth of engines. Shit happens. We overcame challenges and successfully executed a dangerous mission.

In retrospect, I believe we threw the MILF SOG for a loop. They probably assumed the waterborne extraction of wounded would occur somewhere more suitable than atop a rock jetty. Those areas they expected might have been booby-trapped. I attribute this to flawed intel. Had we not received it, we might have sought safer extraction points, resulting in a different outcome.

The engineers had to replace sixty-five gallons of antifreeze after the engines cooled. But, lo and behold, they started right up, and I became an avid believer in MTU engine technology.

I dodged another bullet and thankfully was not fired for beaching a MK V on top of rocks.

Our deployment showcased synchronization, collaboration, and a sense of family among the different groups that came together to create successful end states. Thanks to our MST team keeping the boats running perfectly, the usual two shipyard visits to Cebu for repairs were reduced to one on my orders, It was one of the first times a MK V Detachment only did one yard period. We were on our game.

Everything went smoothly until one day; proper hands apparently were not greased. The FILMIL and the base commander (not the admiral) did not like being left out of the loop. Out of the blue, we were informed that the Filipino Navy had boarded our U.S.-flagged MSV, secured our crew, confiscated weapons, and arrested our security detail. This was next level messed up. We informed the JSOTF-P Commander, and the shit hit the fan. The TF commander ordered us to cease training or interaction with the Filipino Navy and find another partner. They boarded a U.S.-flagged vessel owned by Special Operations, and our TF commander was not happy.

Back to the drawing board.

We chose to train the FILMIL Marine Special Operations Group. They were meat eaters, highly professional, and never backed down. Our security guards were released with their weapons, but it was shocking how tenuous things had become due to one incompetent base commander. Consequently, our ties with the Filipino Navy for the remaining two months were severed by order of our TF commander.

Time went by quickly. Five weeks before the end of deployment, one MK V began taking on water due to a deteriorated shaft seal that could not be repaired without a major yard period. The boat had to be pulled from the water, the shaft removed, and repacked. I recommended having the MSV tow the boat back to Subic Bay to prepare all boats for redeployment to the

U.S. That way, the four weeks could be spent overhauling the boats and paying cheap labor to make them shine for pre-deployment inspection. The boats were sent to Subic, while the RIBs remained on call.

Next, it was time for turnover briefs and prepping the incoming team. My only issue: I also had to prep my relief in the cross-functional troop, a junior SEAL officer who had to drink from a firehose quickly, as our op-tempo was picking up. Rib and Mitch were conducting missions and assembling targeting packages elsewhere in the Philippines while I brought the SEAL officer up to speed. From the moment he landed, he hit the ground running with me from meetings to coordinating with Sonny, to missions with NISG and their door-kickers capturing bad guys. He could not believe the level of detail and frequency of missions we executed. It wasn't that they weren't hard; we did them so often that we made them look easy. By the way, I was just a minion, taking orders from Rib and Mitch. The incoming team would have to figure out their own op-tempo. At least we prepared them for success, turning over all contacts and reports. Sustaining this tempo required highly emotionally intelligent operators; they would either rise to the occasion or fail. There was no middle ground. This tempo thrived only with a Task Unit Commander like JJ and his Senior Enlisted Mack.

The new Detachment arrived, and my MK V Detachment in Subic prepped the boats for shipment home as the RIB Detachment loaded boats onto a C-17. Deployment was closing out. The last task: move out of our compound and live in Manila for two weeks to conduct out-briefing with the Embassy, then fly to Hawaii for out-brief with the Special Operations Command Pacific. It was me, JJ, Mack and Mitch remaining to close things out.

This deployment brought out the best in everyone. It showcased the full capability of a Naval Special Warfare Task Unit when egos are left at the door. Members elevates each other in their areas of expertise. Deliberate mission planning and time-sensitive targeting consistently supported the common operating picture, expanding our influence and disrupting enemy patterns of life.

I knew I would miss it. But I also knew I had lost a part of myself in all the activity tied to Sonny and sensitive operations. I had left Chicago behind many years ago; reclaiming that persona made me uncomfortable. It gave me too much power and reminded me how I could have been a dangerous man had my life not pivoted toward the Navy. As the old saying goes, "Face your fears, and they will disappear" most of the time. Sadly, Sonny died a few years later from a major heart attack. He had been a great ally.

My next orders were recommended by my commanding officer. I was supposed to transfer to a special unit, but I opted out to avoid diving deeper into my past and losing the man I wanted to become. In late 2009, I accepted orders to Naval Special Warfare Group Four, headquarters for the boat teams. It was time to diversify, learn to become a training officer, and master admin, logistics, and macro-level planning. This would prepare me to work with theater special operations commands and help build operational strategic plans, including contingency planning and doctrinal alignment. I felt confident in my choice for my family, even though the path ahead was uncertain. As sure as day, there would be bumps in the road on my path to honor.

Mess up, Make up, but Never Give Up.

Chapter Thirteen

Coping with the Stress of Combat: Pakistan

"In the middle of difficulty lies opportunity."

Albert Einstein

Jackson, almost overnight, went from a tiny baby to an active seven-year-old boy. I finally had more time to spend with him and could not believe what a little warrior he was. He had all the piss and vinegar, just like his dad. As a second grader, I was able to wake up at home, feed him breakfast, and take him to school.

Jenifer and I reintegrated into our business-as-usual routine, but this time there were more lows than highs as I worked my way back into our family. But I understood her position and did not blame her for feeling the way she did. Who in their right mind could get used to someone leaving home on and off for twenty-four months, then suddenly returning to the family routine and taking over again?

It is the Achilles' heel of military life. The military goes on, but a large percentage of our families sadly become collateral damage.

I am happy to report that Special Boat Team Twenty, Boat Troop Five was a complete success. We integrated the entire Naval Special Warfare capability into a form of warfare that is, in many ways, harder than combat. Learning patience tied to cultural awareness, is the long game that special operations are experts at and will defeat the enemies of tomorrow with.

We had only been home a couple of weeks and were still turning over gear when I was informed that our MK V Detachment had been chosen to travel to Florida to appear in the movie Act of Valor. They say it is better to lose the battle and win the war, so this was one of those times when I said, "Hell no, we won't go!" They could choose another troop unless they wanted most of us divorced or sleeping on the couch after a seven-month deployment.

I transferred from SBT-20 and checked into Naval Special Warfare Group Four known simply as "The Group". It serves as headquarters for all the Special Boat Teams and NAVSCIATTS They were recently rebranded as Special Boat Training Command. My new role was future operations officer, followed by training officer once the warrant in that position rotated out.

I was surprised and thrilled to see my former senior enlisted, Jeremy. In the time between leaving our MK V Detachment and my arrival at Group Four, he had gone through a complete transformation. He had gotten divorced and was now dating, and as he described it, "the girl of my dreams," and they were even discussing marriage.

Literally every time he saw me, he would slap me on the shoulder and start talking crap. So, I talked crap back. We had a great relationship, as did many others to include Cary, my former battle captain from Iraq.

I had been at Group Four for only one month when I was informed that I had been chosen to lead the Group Four element returning to Iraq in support of another Task Force.

I was pretty pissed. I had finally gotten a breather and was able to spend time at home with Jackson.

It became official when I was ordered to the commodore's office for a check-in. He asked, "So I take it they informed you of the Task Force mission." "Yes, sir," I replied.

I went on to explain that I had been at NSWG-4 for just over a month and was actually enjoying the predictable routine even going to Jackson's school to have lunch with him. Needless to say, my pleading soliloquy did not change his mind.

I carried on, realizing I had absolutely no control. In the military, an order is an order.

Even though I was irritated, I had enough experience to know the deployment was happening whether I liked it or not. On the bright side, the commodore had his desk covered with baseball cards representing operators and support personnel in the Group Four command. Each card listed the individual's capabilities. He told me I could pick anyone on those cards for the team. That part was pretty cool.

I informed the operations master chief that I knew there were others who could have been selected for the deployment and that it might have been worth considering that I had just returned from a workup and long deployment. Though I realized he could have cared less, I still made my feelings known.

I also told him I was taking Cary with me.

"You can't take Cary," he said. "It will leave a gap in sensitive activities."

I felt myself welling up with anger.

"I don't give a shit," I told him. "I'm creating a gap too."

After one month of planning and assembling a twenty-man team that would fall under the deploying task force, the deployment was suddenly canceled. The plug was pulled.

I was able to stay home and finally get my house and my life back in order.

And boy, did I need it.

Life went on as planned, except for a tragic incident that none of us could have imagined.

One afternoon Jeremy, in his usual routine of banter, slapped me on the back and blurted out, "GFY, Carp."

I responded the way I always did.

"GFY, Jeremy."

GFY means Go Fuck Yourself, and many of us adopted it early in our careers as a twisted form of endearment.
Later that same day, Jeremy's lighthearted banter would be silenced.

He had recently started college and was working toward his bachelor's degree. He was sharp, and whenever we talked, he told me about his plans for his kids, his new girl, and the life he was building.

We were all happy for him.

But one night would shake our SWCC community to its core. Jeremy returned home that afternoon and completed his homework assignments as he did every day. According to his girlfriend, he seemed to be in a good mood.

Then the unthinkable happened.

Jeremy placed his homework in the top drawer of his desk, pulled out his .45-caliber pistol, placed the gun to his head, and pulled the trigger.

In an instant, he was gone.

When we heard the news, we were all devastated.

Our NSW culture struggled to understand it. Many simply could not comprehend that one of our brothers had died by suicide. Some even questioned how someone who had not seen combat could suffer from Post-Traumatic Stress. Those statements really pissed many of us off.

As if someone had to go to combat to suffer from PTS, depression, or the countless other challenges that come with the relentless physical and psychological punishment we endure on the boats. Beatings that break our bodies and shake our brains.

Special Operations at that time did not have the answers. The outdated ways of looking at suicide clearly were not working.

The strange thing was that Jeremy had shown none of the typical warning signs. He had not given away his possessions or drastically changed his behavior.

None of us had a clue.

The saddest part for me was that Jeremy had so much to look forward to.

Hell, I still had his Mountain Hardwear jacket that I knew he wanted back someday.

But people rarely take their lives on a whim. There is usually a trigger or an underlying mental health struggle. Many of us in the military wrestle with toxic masculinity, the belief that we must always be tough and silent. Looking back, I realized Jeremy must have been struggling for months, maybe even years.

As I grieved his loss, I had no idea that someday I would face similar thoughts myself. Many of us did. Some, sadly, acted on them. This reality is reflected in the twenty-two to twenty-five veteran suicides that occur each day in our country.

That is the real tragedy.

Jeremy's funeral was heartbreaking, but it was filled with love. Special Boat Team Twenty and personnel from Group Four attended in full dress blue uniforms. I held it together pretty well until his ex-wife walked down the aisle with their children.

Then we heard them ask, "Mommy, where is Daddy?"

Those words shook me and many others to the core.

Losing friends in war was something we had come to accept. But losing a brother to suicide forced us all to question whether we could have done something to intervene.

Jeremy was a great boat guy and will always be remembered.

Hooyah, Senior Chief Special Boat Operator Jeremy Allan Crow. October 20, 1974 - December 30, 2009.

Rest easy Brother. We will all see you in Valhalla.

After the funeral, it was back to business as usual.

It was the spring of 2010. Not only did I take on the role of training officer, but my Chief Staff Officer, Ken Niederberger, assigned me to a special program to operationalize a new capability.

The boat had been built purely as an experiment. It had not been run in years and was never designed to meet military specifications. It was seventy-seven feet long with a three-foot draft and twin MTU engines nearly one thousand pounds lighter than those on the MK V. It was a semi-wave-piercing hull operated from a cockpit that looked like something out of a spaceship. Even the paint scheme had a specific purpose.

The engineers insisted that because of the boat's operating characteristics, shock-mitigating seats were unnecessary. That was not true. And it is never true. Especially when the yahoos making those statements are sitting behind desks with their egos beating the drum for lab testing only.

I should have known better than to listen to non-operator engineers. They had never spent time underway in the environments where we operated.

They would say things like, "Boat guys love to stand."

That was and is a crock of shit.

Its not that we love to stand. Its that we hate to sit.

We hate sitting on rigid seats or poorly designed shock seats that transfer enormous g-forces directly into our spines.

This boat was no different.

A newly re-engineered fast boat and what do you think we sat in? Rigid seats. Really?

You have to ask yourself why the decision-makers remain so disconnected from the actual needs of operators while pushing agendas that force manufacturers to build outdated hull forms that either make us stand for hours or lean so far forward that our heads whiplash violently with every impact.

SOF truth #1 "Humans are more important than hardware"

Then why do we buy hardware that hurts humans?

Our boats were torture chambers. 24ft RIB, 30ft RIB, 11M RIB, MK V, CCA, CCM. Over 30 years of permanent disability and injuries and TBI. We can do better.

This isn't rocket science. There is technology that works. There are hull forms that work. They just need to open their minds to innovation and stop with the as-built specs.

This boat had many issues and nearly killed me and my crew multiple times. We dealt with carbon monoxide poisoning, near sinkings, and constant mechanical failures. Eventually we started carrying emergency oxygen onboard in case we could not escape.

It was up to me and a ragtag crew of Navy Reserve SWCC operators and maintenance personnel to figure it out. This was supposed to be a limited-objective experiment. Instead, we turned it into an operational capability and one that didn't injure us.

The first order of business was protecting our backs by getting rid of the rigid seats. After extensive research, we identified the solution. The CSO denied funding, but while he was away, the assistant operations officer had signing authority. So, the Chicago in me got creative.

I submitted an Unfunded Requirement (UFER), and the assistant operations boss approved it. Our biggest problem was finally solved. We installed Ullman Dynamics Daytona suspension seats while the CSO was gone. Those seats changed everything.
For the first time, we could sit comfortably for extended periods while the seats absorbed both lateral and vertical impacts.
You probably will not hear many people praising suspension seats in a book, but Ullman seats were the only seats that actually worked and continue to protect operators on the boat to this day.

They mitigate impacts in both directions and proved one hundred percent reliable. The CSO was furious at first until the boat became fully operational with zero injuries. Those seats mitigated impacts exceeding twenty g's and even allowed our crew to sleep during long transits. More than a decade later, those same seats were still in use without maintenance or failures.

Yet the people in power kept buying seats that only mitigated vertical impacts even though lateral impacts were just as dangerous and were contributing to traumatic brain injuries.
There is also a surge effect on boats that create a violent whiplash motion, which may be one of the leading causes of operator TBIs.
To reduce this surge effect, we have to keep the bow down, and attenuate lateral and vertical impacts.

One event on that boat still sticks with me. I never slept while underway during missions. But for some reason, during one medium-range test run, I was out cold.

Suddenly my chief, Justin Chivas (The True Pioneer of this program), shook me awake. "Carp, we gotta stop!" Still dazed, I watched Justin bring the boat to a halt and open the hatch.

Fresh air rushed in.

Within seconds our lungs filled with fresh air and our heads cleared. We later discovered a leak from the engine room had pushed carbon monoxide into the cockpit. Everyone except Justin had been moments away from death. Had he not stopped the boat and opened that hatch, we would all be dead. That near-death experience forced us to continue refining the boat.

Eventually we created something remarkable. A boat with unmatched capability, comfort, and reliability. This ragtag crew that helped me accomplish this was credited with operationalizing a platform that later became a program of record with real operational impact worldwide.

Teamwork always pays off.

My next ridgeline was deploying to Pakistan, but first I had to convince Group Four and Special Boat Team Twenty that the boat was reliable.

It was winter on the East Coast, and a massive nor'easter was barreling toward the region. In my infinite wisdom, I decided that the best way to prove that the boat was ready, was to run it directly into the storm. We planned a run from Virginia Beach to New York, City.

Even the Coast Guard warned us they would not be able to rescue us if something went wrong. I briefed our Chief Staff Officer, Ken Niederberger , and he gave us the green light. Ken had an extensive career and had an amazing reputation. He was focused, calm, and a true servant leader. He trusted his people and treated us like professionals. One of my blind spots was constantly feeling the need to prove myself trustworthy even after receiving permission. I would still try to reassure leadership that I was the right man for the job.

Ken cut me off.

"Ron," he said, "you have permission to go. Quit selling the mission, shut up, and get the hell out of here. Charlie Mike."

We both laughed.

The rest is history. Ken had another saying for me "Don't miss any opportunity to shut the fuck up". Which to this day, is an order I still disobey.

We operationalized a boat that had been destined for the scrap yard. This boat was plowing through nine-to eleven-foot waves. It sounded like someone was trying to smash the windows with a sledgehammer. We were five nautical miles off the coast and decided to move onto the shelf about one mile from shore. That reduced the sea height to about six feet and allowed us to pick up speed.

We overnighted in Atlantic City to lick our wounds, then got up early the next morning to drive into New York Harbor during daylight hours. As we transited through the harbor, we could hear ice slamming against our hull. I joked about becoming the next Titanic. The storm was bad, but we were committed.

We pulled into the Hoboken, New Jersey marina and witnessed the devastation from the snowstorm. The pier was iced over, and there were more damaged boats than we could count. It was our intention to remain moored in Hoboken for three days and keep the engines running the entire time. Our mechanic, Sam Pona, was amazing. Though he was our mechanic, we treated him like he was a SWCC. That included forcing him to get underway all the time with me. He was just that damn good.

He resented me for refusing to let him stay behind as part of the ground crew. Even when he pulled his gear off the boat and started walking toward the trucks, I told him to get his ass back on the boat and into his engineer seat. The engineering seat was always the worst seat in the house. Sam had to sit at the console on the starboard side under a vent that constantly leaked seawater directly on top of him. It forced him to wear his exposure suit the entire time.

Sam, Justin, and many other crew members were the true heroes of the effort. They were the ones responsible for operationalizing the capability.

As the boat, engines, hoses, clamps, and everything else expanded and contracted in the extreme cold, we identified leaks and loose fittings that needed tightening. The boat ran for two straight days at the pier without stopping or sustaining a casualty. It was ready.

We returned from the New York trip in one piece after taking a "cool guy" photo in front of the Statue of Liberty following the snowstorm. I was ready to turn the boat over to SBT-20 and to Ryan, my previous MK V senior enlisted. The boat and crew were in good hands, and I could now focus on preparing for deployment to Pakistan.

During that time, I complained about the amount of personal information they demanded from us before allowing us into their country, especially so soon after the Bin Laden raid. I was told either to send the information or not go on deployment.

I knew my role was to relieve a SWCC Warrant Officer, Justin Ackerman, who was dealing with a constantly shifting situation inside Pakistan. The Pakistanis were more than pissed off at us for violating their airspace and killing HVT #1 Bin Ladin on their sovereign land.

By the way, Jenifer also informed me that she was pregnant. We were about to have our second child in nine months. At the same time, my brother from another mother, Bob Daniels, from the Union League knew I was about to deploy to a place that didn't want us there and might kill us just for shits and giggles.

So somehow, he decided to host a dinner in my honor and invited former Pakistani President Musharraf. A South Side Chicago kid raised on welfare, someone who wasn't supposed to amount to anything, was once again, sitting at a table inside the prestigious Union League of Philadelphia. As a kid, I never thought in a million years I'd even walk up those stairs, let alone have dinner with a former president who still had influence over Pakistan and its intelligence agency, ISI.

Bob and the rest of my Union League family apparently had an agenda. They wanted President Musharraf to use whatever influence he still had in Pakistan to make sure I didn't die and that the mission succeeded. Well, maybe it worked because I made it home without a scratch.

Five weeks after Operation Neptune Spear, I deployed and flew into Islamabad to meet up with the task force and figure out how things worked and how I was going to get to Karachi.

My turnover wasn't going to happen with Justin in country. Justin had to fly out, so we learned through trial and error and the playbook he left behind.

One upside was that I had time to learn about the city of Islamabad. I got the lay of the land and couldn't believe the number of houses our task force owned throughout the city. I was able to pull stacks of American cash to pay for everything we needed, including internet service and rental cars. I flew to Islamabad frequently just to pick up cash to pay for operating cost.

That was also when I met Chris Auger, the SEAL officer who would be my swim buddy for the entire deployment. On one of our flights, we couldn't believe how inconsiderate many of the passengers were. As the plane landed and began taxiing to the gate, people were already out of their seats grabbing their bags while the aircraft was still moving. The flight attendants kept yelling at everyone to sit down or the plane wouldn't move.

Then one guy who had to weigh at least 250 pounds plopped down right on my lap. These people were crazy. I mean, what the hell? Who gets up while a plane is still moving and then decides to sit on someone's lap? I shoved him off me with everything I had and threw in a few choice words for good measure.

Believe it or not, baggage claim wasn't much better. Personal space didn't exist. People pushed, bumped, and outright mauled each other just to grab their bags. Chris and I quickly learned to stand back and let them have their WWE match for luggage before we stepped in to grab ours.

Eventually we got our bags and waited for consulate security to pick us up. On the drive to the consulate, we took in the sights and tried to understand the pattern of life around us. Karachi was a city built to support about ten million people, but closer to twenty-five million actually lived there. The smell of sewage, poop and burning trash hung in the air constantly. It was literally jarring to the senses. And the wind sometimes carried fecal matter along with it.

The chaos we saw on the plane seemed to mirror everything else how people drove, how they interacted, and how quickly things could spiral out of control. One minute everything seemed calm and peaceful. The next minute people were burning tires in the middle of the street, climbing out of their cars, and starting riots.

How in the hell am I going to survive this? I thought. Combat was more organized and peaceful than this. We eventually pulled into the consulate but couldn't enter until the steel barriers dropped and allowed our vehicle inside the compound. The walls stood about ten feet high, and the grounds like most U.S. consulates around the world were immaculate.

The place ran like a finely tuned machine using vetted third-and fourth-generation Pakistani employees to carry out daily operations. The Americans working for the Department of State were impressive. Most people assume embassies and consulates are staffed mostly by Americans, but that's not the case. Americans make up only about thirty-three percent of the workforce. The remaining sixty-six percent are vetted foreign nationals.

We were temporarily assigned a two-bedroom apartment on the compound. The State Department employees actually lived pretty comfortably. There were multiple apartments on-site, and even a commissary where you could buy groceries and cook your own meals.

Our problem was simple. We were the problem.

We weren't Department of State personnel. We were Department of Defense. That meant they had no real obligation to house us, protect us, or look out for us even after we had just killed Bin Laden during Operation Neptune Spear.

The question was obvious. If there was space available, why couldn't we stay on the compound, go out to conduct business, and then return? After all, we already had an office there. Why would they send two gringos to live out in town? Well… one white guy and one multiracial kid who could probably blend in anywhere until I opened my mouth.

No surprise, Ron Carpenter came up with a plan to stay in the apartment.

I went to the commissary and bought everything I needed to make authentic Italian pasta. They loved it. I also promised to cook every Sunday if they allowed us to stay.

One thing Chris and I could do was cook.

Apparently, our culinary diplomacy worked. They finally agreed to let us remain in the apartment, though they still suggested we look for a place in town just in case. I guess the old saying is true: the way to a man's heart is through his stomach.

The Karachi staff were incredibly professional, accommodating, and dedicated. It amazed me how this small group of Americans could influence so much and risk their lives working in austere environments around the world. Pakistan was no different.

They worked together for the greater good of diplomacy. The Chargé d'Affaires was especially sharp and incredibly professional. His mentorship helped me understand how to interact with State Department personnel and reminded me that violence and deadly force were not always the best solutions for achieving lasting peace.

Still, finding a place in town was going to be interesting.

We would have to locate a residence, assess its vulnerabilities, and determine how we could reinforce it enough to survive until a Quick Reaction Force arrived assuming the bad guys didn't kill us or cut off our heads first.

After all, this was the same city where Wall Street Journal reporter Daniel Pearl had been lured, kidnapped, tortured, and murdered. That had happened in 2002, but nothing had really changed. Terrorist groups from the Taliban, the Haqqani Network, ISIS, and others were still operating in the area. My job was to take over from Justin. I could only imagine what he and the deployed team had experienced immediately after the Bin Laden mission.

Our mission had shifted from steady-state support of Pakistan to exploiting every opportunity to keep our foot in the door. All formal training and cooperation had basically ground to a halt.

The original U.S. consulate property was still owned by the United States but had been abandoned after the new consulate opened. It looked like an old plantation-style building with several residential houses behind it.

Technically it was still U.S. property, but security was minimal and nobody lived there. The houses were large and we would eventually have to pick one, reinforce it, and build a force-protection plan around it.

It wasn't ideal. If we had to move into town, things could get very interesting especially since a large portion of the population didn't want us there.

Of course, I always carried a ten-inch-barreled M4 rifle and a 9mm Glock 18 pistol. I had been warned that if I were caught in town with those weapons, I could go to jail. There was no Status of Forces Agreement with Pakistan that protected us.

There had been cases in the past where Americans supporting U.S. interests were forced to use deadly force to defend themselves and ended up sitting in prison until some diplomatic deal secured their release.

That wasn't going to be me.

After seeing how volatile things could get, I decided to carry my rifle broken down inside my backpack and keep my pistol in a concealed holster. Everything was now in motion for working with the Maritime Security Agency and helping them get their boats operational. This would help them interdict narcotics moving out of Afghanistan and Iran.

The admiral and his officers were surprisingly pleasant and well-traveled. They understood the Bin Laden incident would eventually pass and that business between our countries would return to normal.

We did everything we could to support the MSA. In fact, we were the only active-duty U.S. military personnel still allowed to engage with Pakistani forces. All other training had been halted.

Whenever we traveled into town, we ran surveillance detection routes the entire time. No matter how creative we tried to be, we always seemed to end up at the same predictable chokepoints.

Driving to the MSA and back to the consulate was always stressful for me and Chris. We had an up-armored vehicle that we intentionally never washed so it would look old and blend into the local environment. We also used a soft-skinned rental car when we wanted to blend in even more.

Driving in Pakistan had a rhythm, but it was absolute chaos. The more I tried to understand it, the more I realized that this system somehow worked for them even if it looked completely insane to outsiders.

I had a few minor fender benders where we refused to stop. The cultural reality was that situations could escalate into riots almost instantly. People seemed ready to light tires on fire in the middle of the street at any moment, as if the chaos had been prepositioned.

I grew my beard out and blended in fairly well especially if I dressed like the locals. I used to joke with Chris that if we ever got caught, I'd jump out of the car, run into a store, change into my Pakistani clothes that I kept in my pack, and come back out and help kick him in the face.

The more time we spent driving around the city, the more paranoid I became about roadside bombs and surveillance.
I would drive and inform Chris, "That guy has a phone."
Or, "Did you see that signal with the hat?"

Sometimes we would pass parked semitrucks or drive over bridges, and every scenario played through my mind. It was exhausting. The hardest part was not letting yourself slip into a passive mindset. Iraq was easy with RTU-5 compared to being in Pakistan with just a swim buddy.

Then there were the protests.

Even growing up in Chicago couldn't prepare me for thousands of people protesting against the United States. At times protesters would park multiple school buses directly outside the consulate gate along the ten-foot concrete wall that surrounded the compound. They climbed on top of the buses and screamed anti-American slogans for hours. It was unnerving.

Another stark reality was that the Marine guards were not considered Department of State personnel. Their job was to protect classified material and the building itself. Between contracted security, the Regional Security Office, Chris, and me, we only had about twenty rifles to defend the compound. That was unsettling especially when a protest crowd could easily be thousands of people. It felt like standing in front of a stampede. All it would take was one person jumping the wall to create a major problem.

We spent hours in contingency meetings discussing worst-case scenarios and assigning defensive firing positions on the roof of the building. During those meetings, the Chargé d'Affaires was always the calm voice in the room. He reminded us that during the hostage crisis at the U.S. Embassy in Tehran, not a single shot had been fired and everyone survived.

In other words, he was presenting another option.

Still, it was hard to imagine not pulling the trigger if a violent faction of the crowd breached the wall and came at us. Our universal rules of engagement always allowed for the inherent right of self-defense. We just hoped it would never come to that.

The protests lasted for hours. Eventually, before nightfall, the crowd dispersed. And we all breathed a sigh of relief.

Another day passed, and we fell right back into the same routine as if a massive protest hadn't just taken place. The city smelled the same every day like a giant burn pit mixed with the constant stench of sewage. Thick smog blocked out the sun. It made me wonder how people could become conditioned to living in squalor and somehow accept it as normal.

Eventually many of us contracted Giardia, an intestinal parasite usually spread through contaminated water or food washed in contaminated water. The way I explained it to people was simple:

"There's a difference between diarrhea and Giardia.

Diarrhea is when you have the shits.

Giardia is when the shit's got you."

Either way, it all came back to poor hygiene and unsafe water.

The symptoms could last anywhere from a few days to a couple of weeks, and they were brutal. Just know that you end up peeing, puking, and pooping through every possible orifice. We got so good at recognizing the early symptoms that the moment they appeared we started a treatment called a Z-Pack cocktail consisting of Azithromycin, Imodium, Pepto-Bismol, and Doxycycline.

We were doing everything we could to kill the parasite, but sometimes it seemed like the damn thing refused to let go. I caught it three different times during that deployment. It absolutely sucked.

Despite everything, it was remarkable that Naval Special Warfare was the only active-duty military element still allowed to train in Pakistan. After the Bin Laden raid, the Pakistani government shut down almost all cooperation with the U.S. military except for our work with the Maritime Security Agency.

Our Special Forces brothers had done incredible work training tens of thousands of Pakistani Frontier Force soldiers before everything shut down. Our mission, like most NSW missions, was smaller but still impactful. We were there to help the Maritime Security Agency (MSA) get their six 42-foot patrol boats operational.

That and a few others turned out to be a major challenge.

The boats had been sitting on the quay wall on skids for over a year. They were brand new, but because they had never been used, all the engine warranties had already expired. Getting those boats operational again was a complex mechanical problem, but we eventually made it happen.

After about three months in country, we finally had all six boats operational and in the water. Now came the next step training the MSA crews to operate, maintain, and fight those boats. I was ready to get started immediately. Training partner forces in maritime capability was something I had done for years. The problem was my boss, the officer running the entire Combined

Joint Special Operations Task Force. He didn't believe the potential payoff justified the risk, which I couldn't blame him. Every concept of operations I submitted was rejected. The only thing I was authorized to do was classroom instruction. That was frustrating because I knew most of the MSA sailors were tactile learners. They learned best by doing, not by sitting in a classroom. Teaching through interpreters, cultural barriers, and PowerPoint presentations was painfully slow. I knew that with the three months I had left in country I could turn the MSA into a highly capable interdiction force, but I couldn't get the approval to do it. At one point my boss even told me, "You've got a child on the way. Why take the risk?"

My answer was simple.

"If it's not here, it'll be somewhere else."

What made it even more frustrating was that the SWCC officer I relieved, Justin, had been authorized to conduct underway training. The only difference was that his commander had been a SEAL captain who actually understood maritime operations.

A few days later we got word that the Deputy Commander of the Office of Defense Representative–Pakistan (ODRP) was coming for a visit. He was a Navy SEAL admiral and known for being a no-nonsense kind of officer. With him it was simple, produce results or have a damn good explanation.

Technically he didn't have operational control over my commander, but he carried a lot of influence within Naval Special Warfare.

We arranged a meeting between the MSA admiral and our visiting SEAL admiral. The two of them immediately hit it off. They seemed to understand that the political tension after the Bin Laden raid would eventually settle down and things would return to normal.

Chris and I were still cautious, though. Living in Karachi had a way of keeping your guard up.

I took the admiral down to the pier to show him the boats.

He was pleased to see all six fully operational.

Then he asked the obvious question.

"When do you get underway with them?"
"I can't," I replied.

He looked at me for a moment and asked another question.

"When have you taken them shooting?"

"Same answer, sir. I can't."

I could see the confusion on his face. Naval Special Warfare partner-force training always involved building capacity through underway operations, tactical training, and live fire. Without those components, the program didn't make much sense.

Still, he nodded and moved on.

Later that evening we hosted the admiral for dinner at the consulate.

During dinner he asked about future plans, so I explained that we could use the same training template we had used successfully in Manda Bay, Kenya. I didn't have the full brief ready, but I could quickly piece together a rough version using older slides just to give him a snapshot of what the program could look like and could execute quickly.

He said he wanted to see it.

By the end of the evening, he was sitting at my desk while our TF commander sat at Chris's desk. It was clear the admiral still had something on his mind. He called Chris and me into the office and told us to sit down.

Then, in front of our commander, he started explaining why SEALs had been chosen for the Bin Laden raid and why Naval Special Warfare was selected for so many high-risk missions. The message was clear: get off your asses and get to work.

Even though he was focusing on Chris and me, we knew it was directed towards our TF commander, who sat there pretending to type. The conversation was uncomfortable, but it was exactly the push we needed.

As we escorted the admiral out, his final words to me were simple.

"Carpenter move the needle."

"Yes, sir," I replied.

Later that day I cut and pasted a quick version of the training brief together. It wasn't polished enough for a fleet admiral, but it captured the basic concept of how we could train the MSA.

Now came the risky part.

I sent the brief directly to the admiral and copied my commander. This absolutely violated protocol, and I knew there would be consequences.

The normal reward for completing a deployment like this was a Distinguished Service Medal. Chris and I were basically guaranteed one because we were the only team still training in the country.

I told Chris what I had done.

"The phone's about to ring," I said. "And it's going to be the colonel chewing my ass."

Sure enough, the phone rang.

The colonel was yelling at the top of his lungs, ordering me to recall the email.

"Who do you think you are sending a brief to a fleet officer?"

I acknowledged the order and pulled the email back.

The colonel angrily hung up.

A few minutes later an email came through.

I was authorized to get underway with the Maritime Security Agency.

I was ecstatic.

Chris couldn't believe it worked.

I told him I wasn't fighting for a medal. I was fighting to do my job.

Still, we both knew what the outcome would be.

We were no longer getting Distinguished Service Medals.

Sure enough, our awards were downgraded to Joint Commendation Medals.

Neither of us cared.

Now we could actually build a real capability for the MSA. One that could help them protect their coastline and interdict narcotics, weapons, and traffickers moving through the region.

Around that same time, I was selected for promotion to Chief Warrant Officer Four (below zone) a full year ahead of schedule. That kind of early promotion was almost unheard of for warrant officers. It moved me from the ninth-ranked SWCC warrant officer to number four and put me on track for potential promotion to CWO-5 within a few years.

They dangled the carrot, and I took it.

I decided to extend my time in the Navy instead of transitioning out.

Hell, maybe I could become the first SWCC CWO-5 in the history of the Boat Teams.

The next step was informing the MSA that we were finally authorized to begin underway training.

Chris and I drove to our usual weekly meeting with the MSA leadership, but something immediately felt off.

This time there was no warm welcome.

Instead, several guards stood there holding MP5 submachine guns in Condition 1. They escorted us into the admiral's office and waited outside the door.

The admiral explained what had happened.

There had been an incident along the Pakistan-Afghanistan border. U.S. Special Forces had called in airstrikes on a Pakistani checkpoint, killing ten Pakistani soldiers. In an already fragile environment, this was about as bad as it could get. Training was immediately suspended. He asked us not to return to the base until the situation cooled down. When we got back to the consulate we learned the full story.

U.S. Special Forces and their Afghan partners had been operating near the Pakistani border when they came under heavy machine-gun fire from a checkpoint. The problem was, operational details shared with Pakistan were rarely 100 percent accurate. For security reasons, mission briefings often showed the location several miles away from where operations were actually occurring. The ground force commander tried everything to identify his team as friendly forces and get the checkpoint to stop firing. Nothing worked.

Eventually he had no choice but to call in an airstrike to protect his men and the Afghan partner force. The strike killed ten Pakistani soldiers and an unknown number of Taliban fighters. Taliban fighters? At a Pakistani checkpoint? Imagine that.

Pakistan constantly walked a tightrope, balancing relationships with multiple factions in order to maintain some form of stability. They played both sides remarkably well. It always frustrated me that the Haqqani Network operated almost freely inside Pakistan while supplying explosives used to kill U.S. and coalition troops in Afghanistan. Pakistan also controlled one of the most critical logistical routes into Afghanistan; the ground access (G-Lock). The deeper I looked into the politics of the war, the more it seemed less like a war to win and more like a system designed to sustain power, money, and corruption.

Someone always got paid.

Soon the protests began.

And they weren't going to be pretty.

The sad part was that many of the people protesting genuinely believed they were defending something important. In reality they were being manipulated by political forces that were experts at redirecting public anger away from the real problems. Clean water. Sanitation. Quality of life. Those issues should have been directed at their own government.

Instead, we were the convenient distraction.

The first protest in Islamabad nearly breached the embassy perimeter.

Everyone knew Karachi would be next.

Our consulate sat next to a strongly anti-American neighborhood, and an ISI building stood directly across the street. By this point our security procedures had become routine. Unless things completely fell apart, protests were just another part of life.

Nonessential personnel were told to stay home while the protests unfolded.

Soon the streets filled with burning tires and buses parked along the ten-foot wall surrounding the compound. Protesters climbed onto the buses and shouted anti-American slogans for hours. It was always tense because it only took one person to turn a protest into a riot. Thankfully this one eventually ended without violence.

When you read about the March 03, 2026, incident at the Karachi, Consulate where the U.S. Marines killed 10 protesters and wound 100. It didn't surprise me one bit. The consulate perimeter was breeched, and the protestors were firing guns. Those marines experienced what would have been our worst nightmare. Hooyah Devil Dawgs for protecting the Consulate.

Over time we realized that most people in Pakistan were good people trying to live their lives. A small number of bad actors created chaos that affected everyone else.

The teamwork inside the consulate improved dramatically during our time there. The Regional Security Officer, the Chief of Base, and their staffs were incredibly professional. Despite being outgunned and operating in a hostile environment, we developed contingency plans that allowed us either to defend the compound or evacuate by vehicle and attempt to reach the water.

Chris and I constantly tried to provide value to the consulate so they would allow us to live on the compound instead of forcing us to move into the city. The threats never stopped. Bomb threats. Suicide bomber warnings. Protesters climbing the walls.

It happened constantly.

Early on Chris and I made one decision. We would fight to survive and let the bad guys meet their God first. Eventually the protests grew to crowds of three to eight thousand people.

That became normal.

Then one day we received an intelligence warning about a planned suicide attack.

The plan was for a car bomb to slam into the consulate barrier and detonate. Immediately afterward a dump truck packed with explosives would drive through the breach and destroy the living quarters where we all slept. It was a nightmare scenario. But all the security work we all put in paid off. The attackers decided the consulate was too difficult a target. Instead, they detonated the truck at the home of the local police chief, killing him and several members of his family. Just another day in Pakistan.

After that incident our TF commander came up with a new plan. Instead of conducting training inside Pakistan, we would relocate the program to Bahrain, rent houses, and run the entire training cycle there. Just like that, the deployment was coming to an end. I would soon be leaving the smog, the sewage smell, the riots, the chaotic flights, and the consulate compound. It was time to go home. Just another neighborhood in another part of the world.

When I returned home in 2012, the reality finally caught up with me. Years of war, stress, and constant deployments had taken a toll that I didn't fully understand yet. The physical pain was intense. My back, neck, and shoulders constantly ached. Sitting for long periods became difficult. I had frequent headaches.

Something wasn't right.

Even though I was home, I didn't feel like myself.

My usual South Side swagger was gone. I joked constantly, using humor to hide what was really going on inside. That had always been my coping mechanism. But now I felt like I was cracking. And I had nowhere to turn without risking my career or looking weak. Thankfully, I eventually found a way out. And it didn't involve pills or drinking Scotch. I needed a way to empty my buck.

I was stuck on the bottom of another river and couldn't escape.

PART FIVE

WHEN THE MISSION ENDS AND THE NEXT LIFE BEGINS

Chapter Fourteen

NICOE Saved my Life: Lessons Learned

"I may be mixed up, but I'm not messed up."

Unknown

As I prepared to leave Pakistan and return home after a very challenging deployment, I received some good news. I had extended my enlistment and received a reenlistment bonus.

Heck, I must have been doing something right. Being selected for promotion as a CWO4 below zone meaning before your scheduled promotion window is extremely rare. Despite that good news, I soon discovered that some serious emotional demons were lurking just below the surface that I would eventually have to confront.

One thing that always surprises you after being away for so long is how much changes at home, especially when you have young children. They grow up fast. When I returned from Pakistan, I wasn't expecting Jackson to be completely obsessed with WWE wrestling.

Of all things.

Watching him jump off the couch and wrestle with me or his best friend Justin was hilarious. I had to admit, the kid definitely had warrior blood in him.

Jenifer, on the other hand, was about to give birth to our second child, and I had made it home just in time for the delivery.

She was not a happy camper. Aside from the issues in our relationship, she had endured severe morning sickness and carpal tunnel syndrome throughout the entire pregnancy. Needless to say, she wasn't jumping off the couch like Jackson.

Our relationship returned to what had become our normal routine one based more on convenience and mutual support than romance. Still, she was the mother of my son and soon-to-be daughter, so I knew I had to step up and be the dutiful husband.

Jenifer decided our daughter's name would be Rachel and gave Jackson the honor of choosing her middle name.
Not surprisingly, Jackson said her middle name should be "The Rock." To appease him, I offered a compromise.

"Son," I said, "why don't we make her middle name Olivia? That way her initials would be ROC, Rachel Olivia Carpenter and her nickname can still be The ROC."

Fortunately, he agreed.

To complicate things even more, Jenifer's mom had come to stay with us for a while so she could be there for the birth of her granddaughter. Jenifer loved her mom, but she also knew it was one more thing she had to manage at a time when she had very little strength or emotional bandwidth.

I often felt out of place in my own house and sensed that I was constantly being judged for whatever I did and rarely in a positive way. My hypersensitivity to judgment concerned me. In truth, we didn't talk much unless it involved the pregnancy or how Jenifer was feeling.

The only time I felt emotionally whole was when I was spending time with Jackson. He became my refuge from a marriage that clearly wasn't working. And honestly, who could blame Jenifer? After years of deployments and training missions, she had carried the burden of raising a family mostly on her own. The resentment she must have kept bottled up just to keep our family together had to be immense. I definitely had something wrong with me as well. Headaches, anger, hypervigilance, you name it.

Jackson, meanwhile, was becoming quite the little warrior.

A "mini-me" I never expected.

He loved building toys into makeshift weapons out of anything he could find. His fascination with WWE only fueled that warrior spirit.

On top of that, he had an impressive collection of Nerf guns almost every model available at Toys "R" Us. Some people might have thought it was too much for a kid his age, but to me it felt natural.

He was his father's son.

My only real escape from the tension at home was taking Jackson to the park or playing with him in the backyard. About a week or two after I returned home, Jenifer's water broke and we rushed to the hospital.

That night, we ended up being the only family in the maternity ward at Portsmouth Naval Hospital. The entire staff focused on Jenifer and her well-being, and I did the same. For a brief moment, the judgment and tension between us faded. The seriousness of childbirth, the reality that so many things could go wrong temporarily overshadowed the problems in our relationship.

With that veil lifted, four hours later our daughter arrived. Rachel Olivia Carpenter.

"The ROC".

I now understand why some men say, "My son gave me character, but my daughter gave me compassion."

Watching another life come into the world was an emotional experience. It also forced me to confront how much I had missed because of my military career.

I had missed Jenifer's entire pregnancy.

Like so many military spouses, she had carried the burden alone and completed the mission. Now the ROC was permanently part of our lives and to this day that girl has me wrapped around her finger. I love you ROC.

Once the excitement of Rachel's birth settled down, life quickly returned to business as usual. I threw myself back into work, continuing to grow into the type of naval officer the community needed especially since I would soon be competing for Chief Warrant Officer Five.

Looking back now, I wish I had been more self-aware about my own well-being and emotional health. But at the time there were simply too many responsibilities both at home and in the Navy.

It felt like a losing battle, and I didn't know how to put on my oxygen mask first.

This is the challenge faced by every career service member trying to balance family life with military duty. Constant deployments, especially in Naval Special Warfare, take a heavy toll not just on us but on our teammates and families. The other side of that coin is having a partner who is willing to grow and evolve alongside you as your career progresses.

None of us stay the same forever.

Life has a way of nudging us toward becoming the people we were meant to be, whether we're ready for that evolution or not. Along the way we also have to confront the generational patterns and emotional baggage embedded deep within us that can derail our progress.

Life, after all, is a complicated roller coaster.

Eventually it was time to move on.

I transferred to another command to make room for the next SWCC warrant officer and received orders to Naval Special

Warfare Unit Four. The unit was small and fell under Naval Special Warfare Group Two. It supported Special Operations Command South (SOCSOUTH), which covered Central America, South America, and the Caribbean. The command was mostly SEALs, with only two SWCC assigned, me and SWCC Chief Gabe who had served with me at NAVSCIATTS, in Kenya, and in Iraq. He was one of my brothers.

Because the SOUTHCOM area of responsibility was heavily maritime, the two of us had a lot of ground or water to cover supporting SEAL teams and acting as liaison officers. This wouldn't be the first time SWCC operators worked inside units where our maritime expertise helped shape partner capabilities. Everyone in the unit understood the mission and worked well together.

We put in long hours trying to strengthen Naval Special Warfare's presence in SOUTHCOM and maintain the funding required to deploy forces. The work was rewarding and a lot of fun. But like many SEALs and SWCC operators, we rarely had time to deal with the emotional baggage that accumulated after years of deployments, combat, and intense training cycles.

Ironically, many of us were injured during the eighteen-month training workups preparing for deployments more often than during the deployments themselves. Over time, though, I started noticing that something inside me wasn't right.

I wasn't my normal self.

The headaches became more frequent. My body constantly hurt. Depression crept in quietly. No one knew.

As usual, I used humor to hide everything.

For months I would wake up around 3:00 a.m. and pace around the house in a hyper-vigilant state. I constantly checked the locks on the doors and stared out the windows. My heart would race as if something terrible was about to happen. A sense of impending doom hung over me. I didn't sleep much either.

I tried to keep my irritation with people under control, but it was always there just beneath the surface.

The only person who regularly saw it was Jenifer.

We argued frequently sometimes about small things, like whether Rachel should sleep in our bed.

I didn't like the idea. I was terrified and would wake up in a panic believing I had rolled over and killed my daughter.

Death was never far from my subconscious.

The lack of sleep only made things worse.

I was living in what I would later understand as a pain-body state, where my ego had fused with my trauma and turned it into my identity.

Going out to restaurants wasn't any better. I refused to tolerate anything that felt like disrespect. If my food came out wrong, I would confront the waitress, the manager anyone who disagreed with me. My temper could be explosive. What I didn't realize at the time was that the anger was masking a deep depression.

At the same time my body was falling apart physically.
My hands and feet were constantly cold. My back and neck hurt constantly.

Doctors prescribed Vicodin and Percocet. During that time opioids were handed out in the military like candy. I started taking them regularly just to make the pain stop. Before long, popping pills and drinking heavily became routine. It slowly turned into a habit I didn't fully recognize. I had no idea I was becoming addicted even though I believed I was simply following the system and the rules.

In the past, the drug of choice for pain in the military was Motrin. We called it "Vitamin M." But now, instead of Motrin, we suddenly had access to large quantities of opiates anytime we wanted them.

These drugs were extremely dangerous, as we would eventually learn. They were nothing like the harmless Vitamin M we were used to. Here's an example of how easy it was to obtain them.

When we went to the dentist, they handed out Percocet. For routine medical appointments, we would get Vicodin. None of the doctors or dentists were acting maliciously. They were simply doing their jobs and prescribing what they were authorized to prescribe.

But the system was insane.

They always told us to take the opiates for a few days, then stop unless the pain continued, in which case we could take more.
There were times when the pain in my neck, the headaches, and the constant back pain were so severe that I would take two or three pills at a time just to dull it.

More pain. More meds.

Sometimes I would be playing with Jackson, and my back would go out just from bending over to pick up a ball. The pain would hit so hard that I dropped to my knees.

When that occurred, the only option was the emergency room. They would give me a heavy-duty painkiller injection and place me on light duty for two weeks. That wasn't the quality of life I wanted or the life I thought I deserved.

And the opiates weren't the only problem.

Alcohol had become my constant companion.

Ever since my time in the Philippines, I had developed a taste for Scotch. I drank heavily to cope with the pain and sometimes just to fall asleep.

Unsurprisingly, the combination of drugs and alcohol pushed my relationship with Jenifer from bad to worse. I made her feel like she was an inconvenience, and deep down I was riddled with guilt. Unfortunately, she often received the worst of it especially when I was drinking. It was never physical, but words often hit harder than fist. Between the constant overmedicating, the heavy drinking, the lack of sleep, the terrible diet, and the endless arguments with my wife, my attitude began to deteriorate.

Outwardly I remained defiant sometimes openly contemptuous of the world around me. But inside, I was collapsing. No one knew. I was silently screaming for help. I prayed constantly about what I should do. Sometimes I would snap out of it for a moment, but before long I would slide right back into what I called

"Franken-Ron."

I began to hate myself.

I felt like a complete failure. Eventually darker thoughts crept in. I found myself thinking, The world would be better off without me. Those thoughts appeared more often than I wanted to admit, as if some dark force was pulling me deeper into a pit of despair where the only logical conclusion was that everyone's life would improve if mine ended. The irony was brutal.

For my entire career I had been the guy others relied on, the positive one, the motivator, the leader.

Now I was the one drowning in darkness. And I couldn't see the light anymore.

No one in Naval Special Warfare wants to admit to thoughts like that.

Even the toughest operators, who seem completely squared away sometimes battle the same demons.

We had what is called "the covenant of silence."

No one talked about it.

No one asked.

The pain existed, but it was treated as something better left alone. My suicidal thoughts became particularly intense during a temporary assignment to SOCSOUTH at Homestead Air Force Base, outside Miami.

The demons were working overtime. Part of it was the isolation. I was living in an old, run-down barracks, and I kept thinking: After everything I've done in my career… this is where I end up? This shithole?

All those years of sacrifice and this is the reward. Of course, I was drinking heavily and alone. In large quantities.

At home there were too many distractions. My family, my kids but on temporary assignment things were different. Luckily, because of the nature of the assignment, I wasn't issued a weapon. In hindsight, that was a blessing in disguise. Because if I had a weapon during those nights, I honestly don't know what I might have done.

My suicidal thoughts became stronger and more frequent. It was a very dark time. Still, I tried to fight them the only way I knew how.

After decades in Naval Special Warfare, my training kicked in. I threw myself into work and treated every task like a no-fail mission, hoping the focus would distract me from my own mind.

But the pressure never stopped.

There was always another meeting. Another deadline. Another request from someone who needed something immediately. One day we had a meeting at U.S. Southern Command. It was supposed to last thirty minutes. Our goal was to convince leadership that SOUTHCOM needed a mission support vessel in its area of responsibility.

The meeting lasted two hours. In the end, the answer was still no. I left feeling defeated and didn't even want to drive back to base.

That's when Mike stepped in.

Mike Lore was a Navy SEAL and one of my closest friends. He worked with me at Unit Four and happened to be in Miami. He told me to come stay at the Marriott he had a room for me. I think he sensed my frustration. Maybe he even recognized the agitation underneath it. That night, things went off the rails.

After several Irish Car Bombs, I completely lost it.

Mike was the only person in all those years who could see what I was becoming. Hell, he saw a lot of us derailing in his career. He was also the kind of guy who told you the truth whether you liked it or not. Sometimes the hardest decisions have the simplest answers when you have a trusted swim buddy willing to say what needs to be said. Mike listened while I vented.

He asked me direct questions.

"How are you really doing?"

"Are you thinking about killing yourself?"

"Do you have a weapon?"

He knew firsthand how combat stress and workups could destroy people. Jeremy had been proof of that. No one had known he was struggling until he took his own life. Mike helped me that night more than he probably realized. He listened without judgment and gave me the space to empty my emotional bucket. For the first time in a long while, I felt like I could breathe. Not because my problems disappeared but because I finally shared them with someone I trusted. I emptied my bucket.

All you out there going through this, you all need to empty your bucket as well. You need one or two close friends in your life.

Of course, once the serious conversation ended, Mike did what any good teammate would do. He busted my chops. But it wasn't cruel it was accountability. That's how brothers talk to each other.

The next day, driving home, I felt lighter.

Like a weight had been lifted.

Unfortunately, I also knew the truth.

The demons would come back.

And they did.

Fortunately, around that time a facility had recently opened at Naval Hospital Bethesda called the National Intrepid Center of Excellence (NICoE).

Many SEALs and SWCC operators I knew had gone through the program and returned with a completely different outlook on life.

I knew I was teetering on the edge.

I needed help.

But the hardest step was admitting that I had a problem.

I couldn't hide behind the tough-guy SWCC persona anymore.

Something had to give.

So, I applied to NICoE.

The screening process began with a series of interviews to determine whether I qualified for their three-week inpatient program.

I was accepted immediately.

That alone confirmed I was making the right decision. If the professionals thought I needed help, then I definitely needed it.

About a week later, in 2015, I packed my bags and drove from Virginia Beach to Bethesda, Maryland. The trip couldn't come soon enough.

NICoE has an interesting history. The center was created through a public-private partnership supported by the Intrepid Fallen Heroes Fund.

To prove the program's effectiveness, the early focus was primarily on special operations personnel dealing with combat stress, traumatic brain injuries, chronic pain, and other invisible wounds of war.

By 2010, the organization had completed a $65 million, 72,000-square-foot facility at Walter Reed National Military Medical Center. The center was designed specifically for conditions many of us faced; traumatic brain injuries, headaches, vertigo, light sensitivity, chronic pain, and severe combat stress. The program's philosophy was unique. Strip everything away, then rebuild a treatment plan where modern medicine meets functional medicine. NICoE would ultimately change my life.

The program lasted three weeks.

The first two weeks were dedicated to evaluations and testing. The third week focused on diagnosis and treatment plans, and spouses were invited to attend. They often say, "You have to name it to tame it." But this experience went far beyond that. On the first day we were divided into groups called "fire teams." Each fire team was assigned a group of doctors who made decisions collectively nothing happened without agreement from the entire medical team. The first rule they gave us was simple but brutal: Stop taking all medications immediately except life-sustaining ones, and no drinking. For many of us, that was incredibly difficult. But we followed the plan.

Our daily schedules were packed.

- Psychiatry.
- Psychology.
- Nutrition.
- Physical therapy.
- Meditation.
- Yoga.
- Biometrics.
- Sleep studies.
- Acupuncture.
- Reiki.
- MRIs.
- PET scans.
- Optometry.
- Audiology.
- Art therapy.
- Fitness testing.
- Memory assessments.
- Traumatic brain injury evaluations.
- PTSD counseling.
- Group therapy.
- Marriage counseling.

And much more.

In just three weeks I attended roughly 117 appointments. My fire team included SEALs, SWCC, Special Forces soldiers, and one Army soldier named Adam. Adam was wheelchair-bound and missing three limbs. During our first group therapy session, the counselor asked us to talk about our most painful experiences. Most of us hesitated. Our problems suddenly felt insignificant compared to Adam's. He looked around the room and said something none of us expected. "I've lived at Walter Reed for three years," he said. "This is my last phase before going home."

Then he smiled. "Don't feel sorry for me. You guys are more fucked up than I am."

The room exploded in laughter.

And from that moment on, we bonded. We stopped holding back and began sharing openly. NICoE understood exactly how to build those teams to maximize healing emotionally and physically.

One of the most important messages they gave us was this: "You're getting a fresh start." That was music to my ears. I desperately needed a reset.

They told us that if we fully committed to the program, we would leave as different people. I wanted that change more than anything. On the very first day I stopped taking all drugs and began confronting my demons with the help of psychiatrists and psychologists who understood the realities of special operations life.

The process was intense. Sometimes painful.

But it worked because healing starts with honesty. The next phase focused on physical therapy. One therapist discovered that six of my ribs had been out of alignment for years. She repositioned them. She also corrected several joint issues in my shoulder and foot that had been causing chronic pain. Instead of opioids, they used acupuncture, reiki, and specialized ear studs designed to relieve pain. To my surprise, the treatments actually worked. For the first time in years, the pain began to decrease.

Biometric testing revealed another problem. My body had been stuck in fight-or-flight mode for years.

That's not healthy.

The fight-or-flight response is the body's automatic reaction to perceived threats. It activates the autonomic nervous system and prepares the body for survival raising heart rate, accelerating breathing, and shutting down normal processes like digestion.

After years of combat deployments and physical impacts on high-speed boats, it wasn't surprising that my nervous system had become permanently stuck in self preservation mode. Living that way is like being chased by a saber-toothed tiger every single day.

That kind of stress can literally shorten your life. The doctors also discovered something interesting about my circulation. The temperature of my hands and feet was only about seventy degrees, when it should have been closer to ninety. It took about a week of training to reprogram my heart rate and breathing so my body could disconnect from the constant fight-or-flight response.

Believe it or not, they captured 48,000 images of my brain and body during the evaluation process. Every morning the doctors met to review the data and discuss the best approach to treating my symptoms, which were still evolving.

One of the best parts of the program, at least from my perspective, was that alcohol was completely off-limits, and no drugs were allowed unless they were medically prescribed. After each long day of appointments, we were encouraged to go to the gym, work out or swim. The more I committed to the program, the more I felt like I was rediscovering the old version of myself.

One of the more unexpected parts of the program was art therapy. We learned to express our emotions through drawing and painting. In fact, the mask shown on the front cover of this book is the one I created in the NICoE art class.

The mask has two sides.

The black-and-white side, with the tear drops, represents my identity as someone born half Black and half white. The tears represent the hardships my siblings and I endured growing up on the Chicago Southside.

The gold side represents my Navy Journey and my belief that "Even a rock, when subjected to extreme heat and pressure, can eventually become a diamond".

I have kept that mask ever since my time at NICoE because it represents the very essence of who I am.

Before the program, I had rarely taken the time to reflect on where I came from. NICoE forced me to examine my life and gave me a baseline for understanding how far I had come. Despite the obstacles I faced growing up, I had achieved milestones that many people once believed were impossible for me. Realizing that was a powerful moment.

The evaluations also revealed several physical issues I hadn't fully recognized before. I had balance problems, back problems, neck injuries, knee and ankle problems, hearing damage, memory issues, and several other conditions that needed attention.

The team of doctors worked together like a well-coordinated commando unit. They focused entirely on improving my quality of life. Their goal was to address as many of my issues as possible. I experienced breakthroughs in several areas, including nutrition, physical therapy, art therapy, meditation, and pain management. NICoE relies heavily on best-practice treatment methods, combining the latest technology with holistic approaches. For example, they used advanced diagnostic tools to quickly identify ongoing medical issues and determine alternative treatment options before turning to pharmaceuticals.

Being at NICoE became one of the most impactful experiences of my life. It helped me understand how the lifestyle we lived in special operations affected both our physical health and emotional well-being. During the evaluations I learned something that changed my perspective.

My suicidal thoughts weren't simply a personal weakness.

They were the result of several factors working together; traumatic brain injuries, combat-related PTSD, and unresolved trauma from my childhood and drug contraindications.

Understanding that, helped me begin learning healthier ways to cope. More importantly, I realized something I hadn't felt in a long time.

I wanted to live.

By the end of the three weeks, I felt like I was firing on all cylinders again. In fact, I dreaded the moment when I would have to leave NICoE. While I was under their protective umbrella, I had finally rediscovered the best version of me that I hadn't seen in a very long time.

The next challenge was waiting for me at home. My marriage. One of the NICoE social workers was very direct with me. She insisted that Jen and I needed to stop allowing Rachel to sleep in our bed because it was triggering my PTSD symptoms.

The marriage counselor and sex therapist also provided me with advice and tools to bring home. Jenifer had chosen not to attend the third and final week of the program. Honestly, I wasn't surprised, and I couldn't blame her.

As my time at NICoE came to an end, I attended my final debriefing sessions with a mixture of excitement and nervous anticipation. The staff fitted me with custom orthotic insoles, new hearing aids, and several other items designed to improve my quality of life.

On my final day, the entire team of doctors gathered around a table to review the results of my tests and evaluations.

As I sat across from them, I realized something important.

My head was finally on straight again.

I was managing pain better than at any time in my life. I had learned meditation techniques. I understood the importance of sleep hygiene. I practiced slow, controlled breathing.

For the first time in years, I felt like myself again.

I actually liked who I was becoming. Whole again.

The self-hatred that had once consumed me was gone, and I realized something that had once seemed impossible:

The world was better with me in it.

When the meeting ended, I felt tears welling up in my eyes.

But this time, I wasn't ashamed of them.

One by one, the doctors stood up and hugged me.

The lead physician became emotional, and I could see tears rolling down his cheeks. At that point, I couldn't hold mine back either. And for the first time in a very long time, it felt good to let them fall. The doctors and therapists at NICoE became my heroes. I truly wish everyone could experience that level of medical care.

On every level, it was one of the most remarkable and transformative experiences of my life.

Hooyah! NICoE.

I am a survivor because of you, and I will forever be grateful. After returning from NICoE, Jen and I began seriously discussing separation. The truth was that we no longer brought out the best in one another, despite numerous attempts at marriage counseling. There is never a good time to have a conversation like that, and unfortunately, I broke the news just as her mother became seriously ill.

Even though we were separating, I did everything I could to support Jen through that difficult time. At the same time, I knew I had to fight for my own sanity and health.

When I finally told Jackson about the separation, his response shocked me.

He looked at me and said, "Dad, you guys should have gotten a divorce a long time ago."

Kids know.

Staying together "for the kids" often creates more resentment than stability. My hope was that by separating we could reset our relationship in a different way, living our own lives while still working together to co parent Jackson and Rachel. Everything was moving forward with the plan; I would get my own place in Virginia Beach and start establishing a new normal. But as the military often reminds us, no plan survives first contact intact.

Around that time, I was selected for promotion to Chief Warrant Officer Five (CWO5). Dwayne and I would become the first two CWO5s promoted in the history of our community.
It was a tremendous honor.

The problem was that Dwayne had just taken his position at NSWG 4, and as a newly promoted CWO5, I could not remain in an O 5 command billet. I know that sounds like a lot of military jargon, but by this point in the book you probably understand how those assignments work.

The choice became simple: transfer to Tampa or retire. I decided to accept orders to Tampa.

Looking back, the greatest decision of my life was joining the United States Navy and letting Uncle Sam raise me. If I hadn't taken that one step in a different direction from many of my friends growing up in the hood, my life and my story would likely have turned out very differently.

It was bittersweet knowing that my time in uniform was coming to an end and that I would no longer be able to jump back into the same Naval Special Warfare swim lane after retirement.

But for the first time in a long while, I felt prepared.

NICoE had given me the coping skills and the confidence to confront my demons and begin the next chapter of my life, and the Navy taught me something even more important.

It taught me how to be a leader. A person of integrity.

A teammate.

A patriot.

And most importantly, to love me as I am.

Here are some of the lessons I learned during my three weeks at NICoE. Lessons that I hope will help you, whether you are in the military or a civilian.

1. You don't have all the answers. None of us do. Accepting that is the first step toward growth.
2. Listen to your Check Engine Light "Robert Wilson" Everyone has a check engine light. Most of us ignore it. I ignored mine for years. Chronic pain doesn't arrive all at once, it creeps in quietly until it touches everything: your relationships, your family, your mental health, even your sense of who you are. Before long, you're living inside a prison you didn't notice was built. Pain wasn't something I stopped for; It was something I drove through. But eventually the check engine light stops blinking and after a while it stays on.
3. Have at least two trusted friends. You need people who allow you to empty your emotional bucket, and who will hold you accountable when things get tough.
4. Acknowledge pain, suffering, and depression. Recognize it. Face it. Breathe through it. Let it pass. Because eventually, it does pass.
5. Your life matters more than you realize. Ending your life removes every future opportunity to pursue new goals, new missions, and new meaning. Charlie Mike. Carry on with the mission. Don't quit.

6. Ask for help and keep asking. If necessary, demand it. Demand the quality of care you deserve and refuse to accept "no" as the final answer. NICoE taught me that.
7. Have something to look forward to. As Viktor Frankl wrote in Man's Search for Meaning, having purpose and future goals gives us the strength to endure almost anything.
8. Build an identity outside the military. Begin developing who you are beyond the uniform so that when the day comes to transition out, the landing will be softer.
9. Learn to love yourself. Look back at where you came from so you can appreciate who you have become and remember there is always a path back to honor.
10. Every day writes a new page in your story. The ink dries daily. You cannot rewrite the past, but you can reset and try to become a better version of yourself today. As I like to say: "Mess up. Make up. But never give up."
11. When you feel lost, look up. God is still flying the plane. As motivational speaker Les Brown says: "If you fall, fall on your back. Because if you can look up, you can get up."
12. Carry on with your mission. Live your life fully and live to tell your story.

Chapter Fifteen

Return to the Civilian World: Chasing Shining Objects and Hugging Icebergs

"What many people see in successful individuals is only the final, visible portion of their journey. Like an iceberg, the greater part of what it takes to become successful remains hidden beneath the surface."

The Iceberg Illusion

It is hard to believe how a thirty-two-year career could end in the blink of an eye.

When I look back, I sometimes struggle to believe that a young Chicago punk with very few role models managed to climb to the top of the Special Boat Team community. Even now, it surprises me that I became one of the first selected for Chief Warrant Officer Five in the history of the SWCC community.

Despite the pride I felt in my achievements and the excitement surrounding my retirement, I still faced some unexpected challenges. Challenges that many career military veterans encounter when transitioning into the civilian world.

At the same time, I can say with complete honesty that without the Navy, I might not even be alive today.

The fact that I could sit at any table, or walk up any set of stairs, in almost any segment of society is a testament to the power and influence that the United States military can have on someone's life. In my opinion, the military is one of the greatest equalizers in our country, especially for underprivilege communities.

Now more than ever, young people can benefit from a tour of service. For many kids growing up in underprivileged neighborhoods, the military may represent the last real opportunity to change the direction of their lives. Like I once did, they want something different but have very few options. The culture now places a stigma on living a life of service, but there are many that step up for our society everyday. If this message tugs at you, take that one step that will change your trajectory. Do a tour in the military and you are guaranteed to become more confident while being rewarded with an awesome GI Bill to continue your transformation.

These kids want to escape the reality that surrounds them, the constant pull toward despair where the only future that seem possible are prison or the cemetery. We are the greatest country in the world, and yet it is painful to admit that for many young people, those are the only outcomes they believe await them. As you know by now, I was one of those kids whose odds were stacked against him. I wasn't raised to believe in success or achievement.

To make matters worse, author and entrepreneur Patrick Bet-David describes a concept called the "Generational Curse" the idea that destructive habits, beliefs, and behaviors are often passed down from one generation to the next. In my case, that cycle was compounded by spending thirty-two years in military life and leaving home at eighteen. My entire adult life had been spent in uniform. In many ways, I had become institutionalized.

Looking back, I sometimes wonder if that structure was exactly what I needed to break the pattern of despair that surrounded my upbringing.

The Navy didn't just give me a career.

It reprogrammed my thinking.

But like all good things, even that chapter eventually came to an end. Being promoted to the rank of Chief Warrant Officer

Five was one of the proudest moments of my life. I accepted the promotion and took orders to Special Operations Command at MacDill Air Force Base. I had worked my entire career for that promotion. It represented decades of sacrifice and effort.

But it had come at a cost. Along the way I had lost many things.

By 2017, my son Jackson was fifteen years old. Together we packed a moving truck, and he accompanied me on the drive to Tampa, Florida, where I would begin the final phase of my career.

It was a significant adjustment.

I was assigned to the program office responsible for overseeing all Naval Special Warfare boat programs. In many ways, the role was perfectly suited to my background and experience.
My job was to advise program managers and help them make the best possible decisions for the operators who would ultimately use those boats in the field. The challenge was, that many of the major decisions about the boats had already been made long before I arrived.

That meant my role often involved putting out fires solving problems that emerged during construction, procurement, and maintenance of the fleet. When a program office makes a mistake in boat design or acquisition, it can take ten years or more to correct it. In many cases, the only way to fix those issues is to spend your way out of them. I remained at PEO Maritime for a little over two years before finally transitioning out of the Navy.

It was a chapter of my career and my life that I will never forget.

Parting is Sweet Sorrow

As the American actress Helen Rowland once said:

"When two people decide to get a divorce, it isn't a sign that they don't understand one another, but a sign that they have at least begun to."

Growing up in a dysfunctional home and in a neighborhood that didn't teach many of the emotional tools necessary to cultivate meaningful relationships things like love, empathy, compassion, and vulnerability, Jenifer and I reached a point where going our separate ways felt like the healthiest path forward. We finalized our divorce and started a new normal.

By no means am I blaming her.

Our divorce proceedings themselves were relatively smooth. We made every effort to handle the situation honorably and respectfully. In fact, I had carefully planned every step leading up to the divorce.

I gave Jenifer the house and allowed her to keep all the equity. Many of my friends who were going through divorce were fighting bitter legal battles trying to keep every dollar of retirement pay and, in some cases, trying to completely destroy their ex-wives in the process. That kind of bitterness was hard for me to understand. I chose a different path.

I gave Jen nearly half of my retirement income.

Why?

Because the truth is that she served twenty eight years of that Navy career right alongside me. She deserved nothing less.

It was simply the honorable thing to do.

Soon after, Jen began moving forward with her life and started dating again. Meanwhile, I found myself staring at the modern dating scene completely bewildered. Dating at my age felt awkward and unfamiliar.

The truth is that I was never really taught how to love or even what love truly meant.

In the neighborhood where I grew up, there was a strange but widely accepted norm: "It is what it is." That mentality bled into everything. We became numb to the same destructive cycles happening over and over again.

Nobody spoke up.

We simply accepted the drugs, the domestic violence, the crime, and the poverty that surrounded us. The only role models we had were our homies, the guys we idolized growing up.

Unfortunately, they were repeating the same misguided ideas and behaviors they had learned from the older homies before them. Women were often objectified, and relationships rarely had anything to do with truly getting to know someone on a deeper level.

Most of the time, we were just trying to get in a girl's pants.

Bip, bop, bam. Thank you, ma'am.

Rinse and repeat.

That kind of distorted thinking shaped much of my early life. It was part of growing up in a system that gave us just enough to survive but never enough to truly thrive.

That was the reality of poverty, welfare, and a social class that sometimes-pushed people toward illegal activity simply as a means of survival.

In the hood, we often ended up preying on one another.

That was a disease of the environment.

And as you've already read earlier in this book, that mindset got me into trouble more than once both in my youth and during my early days in the Navy.

As I grew older and began reflecting on my relationships, I realized that many of my struggles were tied to something I had never truly developed: emotional intelligence.

I had difficulty putting myself in other people shoes.

In other words, I lacked empathy.

At one point, I actually believed that if I gave Jenifer's emotions too much priority, she would become overly demanding or dependent on me. Looking back, I couldn't have been more wrong. Instead, I treated our marriage the way I treated a military mission.

She had her role to play and I had mine.

From the time we met in 1989, when we were both still kids, it was essentially the blind leading the blind. Jenifer came from a background very similar to mine. Different coasts, but the same side of the tracks. Her family life had also been difficult.

There was drug abuse, an absent father, and a lot of instability. Her mother was the rock that held the family together until she passed away.

So, in many ways, we were two misfits who found each other at a time when neither of us had anywhere else to turn. At that point in my life, the only thing I truly had was a three foot by five-foot rack on a Navy ship.

Years of training and deployments meant I was constantly gone. While I was away, Jenifer built her own life and identity back home.

That's the reality for many Navy wives.

They keep the home fires burning. They keep the wheels turning.

Divorcing was bittersweet, but we both understood that it was the healthiest choice. We agreed to focus on co parenting Jackson and Rachel while each of us found our own path forward. To stay connected with Jackson and Rachel, I established a routine of flying back to Virginia for one week every month so I could spend time with them and remain actively involved in their lives.

Fortunately, Group Four was still located in Virginia Beach, which made those visits easier to coordinate. Still, I found myself in unfamiliar territory.

After nearly three decades in the Navy, I was now a divorced man trying to rebuild a life from scratch. One thing never changed, however.

My guiding principle remained the Navy's motto:

Mission first. People always.

Eventually, I met Luz.

Looking back, I truly believe God answered my prayers.

She was everything I had ever asked for in a partner.

Luz had a confidence and calm presence that immediately stood out to me. She was intelligent, capable, emotionally present, and deeply compassionate. Her business acumen was also impressive, and her focus and discipline inspired me. We started dating, and over time she became my light and my north star. For the first time in my life, love was no longer something that felt distant or confusing.

I knew it from the very beginning.

Spending five hours with her felt like spending five minutes.

The experience was entirely new to me and exhilarating. Realizing that I could express a type of love I never even knew I was capable of was nothing short of amazing. It had taken me a long journey to get there. But now, having finally experienced a new type of love and learning how to receive it, this Chicago boy was ready for yet another life changing chapter. For many service members, the idea of retiring from the structured environment of the military can feel overwhelming.

I won't lie.

I was a little scared too.

But with Luz by my side, the transition felt far less daunting.
With that in mind, I officially retired from the United States Navy in September 2019.

Jenifer and I chose to keep the details of our divorce private. Most people had no idea we had divorced.

So, when the news eventually surfaced, many people were genuinely surprised, and you should have seen their faces when I showed up to my retirement ceremony with Luz.

What most people didn't know was that we had quietly gotten married a few months earlier.

We intentionally kept the wedding private.

Neither Jen or I wanted to put friends or family in the awkward position of feeling like they had to choose sides or speculate about why my first marriage had ended.

By that point in my life and after everything I had experienced, I had learned a few important lessons about emotional intelligence and communication.

In fact, I would like to share some of those lessons with you.
They might help you navigate your own relationships a little more effectively.

Life Lessons for Hombres:

Lessons Learned from Divorce and Life Transitions

1. Men have no business talking about women's rights or abortion rights.
2. If you have friends going through a breakup or divorce, keep your mouth shut. They might get back together, and then you become the asshole.
3. Don't lie. If you must, make the lie close enough to the truth so you can recall both. Otherwise, your lies will trap you.

4. Keep your divorce private or share it only with a small circle of trusted friends. Too many opinions lead to collateral damage.
5. Don't badmouth your spouse on social media. It only makes you look like a jerk and closes the door on reconciliation.
6. All women are good. There are only bad situations or incidents. Mothers, in particular, are humanity's blessing. I truly believe they are smarter than men.
7. Keep the financial aperture small. Hiring multiple lawyers just drains the same bank account.
8. Keep it peaceful.
9. Discuss everything like a business negotiation: work together to make ends meet.
10. Remember that the mother of your children sets an example for the next generation. Act accordingly.
11. After the divorce, plan again for the next phase of your life. I didn't do this, and navigating post-divorce felt blind and sloppy.
12. Breaking up is hard sometimes brutally so.
13. Move at your own pace and turn off all the stray voltage around you. Time makes wine.

Transitioning from Military to Civilian Life

So, I had a full plate and hit the ground running. It did take some time to fully release not only the vestiges of my dysfunctional upbringing, but also the safety and security of the Navy. However, what the US Navy taught me over all those years was invaluable. What I needed to learn on my own was independence and the confidence that I could thrive in the civilian world. Believe me it is possible. I am living proof of that. I simply had to learn how to value myself in the civilian world. After all, I was now a newborn in this new world called CIVLANT FLEET.

Now that everyone knew I was out of the Navy, my phone began ringing off the hook. Everyone had a bright idea or business opportunity they could not wait to share. At the time, I believed I could conquer anything and do it all. I chased after so many shiny objects, thinking I could get rich off a single contract, that I started taking unnecessary risks. I worked on everything from transporting and protecting gold from Africa to foundries in Texas to attempting to charter Russian Antonov and 747 aircraft to land in China and Vietnam to pick up surgical masks and hand sanitizer to transport them back to the US during COVID. I know it sounds crazy, trying to set up escrow accounts for money and bringing in the right people to make it happen. But there I was coordinating meetings to support allies with non-lethal gear and equipment using other companies that already had the infrastructure in place.

My wife, once again, was the voice of reason. She recognized the level of risk I was taking and the reality. We could not even get on the ground in most of the countries we were coordinating with because of COVID. That reality check led me to reflect on my transition and quickly come to a more rational decision. I could no longer continue down that path. I had to stop chasing shiny objects. The number of obstacles I encountered, as well as the amount of time and money I invested trying to make one of those ventures succeed, is still mind-blowing to this day. Hitting one dry hole after another will wear you down and knock the wind out of your sails. It is far better to focus on your core competencies than to believe you will get rich off one contract.

So, as cooler heads prevailed, I decided to focus on my core competencies. Maritime training and testing high-speed boats, along with aligning more closely with advocating for prioritizing human factors with Ullman Dynamics. It became my post-military priority. I started saying "no" more often than "yes." I stopped chasing shiny objects and focused on working hard every day to support my family and keep my head straight. My company TMS Group allows me to do what I love, train high speed boat operators, create capability worldwide and capture operator impact data. That combination has produced positive outcomes in training, equipping, and testing. At the same time, I had to face the reality that I am not invincible. Uncle Sam will not come bail me out if I make a poor business decision that loses money. All the risk rests squarely on my shoulders. While that can be a scary thought at times, it is also invigorating. There is no South Side thinking to distract me here.

Transitioning to civilian life definitely has a learning curve. I never imagined I would have to hire bookkeepers, accountants, lawyers, insurance companies, and deal with the many other responsibilities that come with running a business. The funny thing is that as you grow, you naturally follow a path of progress that has already been paved by those who came before you. I also learned that you can build either a quality-of-life company or an exit-strategy company. The risks are all on you, and you must find the right people to work with and for you or you may fail. Fortunately, I knew many outstanding men and women during my military career. Those are the people who want to be part of the team and are willing to roll up their sleeves to get the job done.

In business, I also learned that success depends heavily on who is on the bus with you. That includes your friends, acquaintances, and customers. Coming from a military background and doing business within government swim lanes, it still amazes me how differently some people operate compared to veterans. I am not saying that all civilians have ethical issues or cannot be trusted. But I am saying that veterans often have an instinctive ability to spot those who may not share their same values, and we can choose to work with them or wave them off. Most of the time, I wave them off because it is simply not worth my time. If I am on a bus with five shitheads, I immediately become the sixth. Optics matter. So does loyalty, customer service, and maintaining as many touch points as possible with your clients and partners.

When I dove headfirst into my own business after retirement, I quickly learned that there are energy and time vampires. Here is how to spot them in a business setting, along with some lessons I have learned about transitioning from the military to civilian life and running my own company:

1. Quickly determine whether you are a morning person or an afternoon person and give the best part of your day to the people and tasks that matter most.

2. Quickly determine whether potential clients are worth your time or simply want someone to talk to on the phone. People who never purchase anything can consume a significant amount of time with no return on investment.

3. You cannot go it alone especially within the good-old-boy network of military contracts and business. Build your own network of companies and allies that complement one another rather than compete unnecessarily. Doing so can create a breath of fresh air in the market and allow contracting officers and program managers to view solutions through a different lens.

4. The natural progression and evolution of business:
   - You have to pay taxes and need a reliable pay system.
   - You have to pay yourself.
   - Everyone has opinions but identify who is willing to roll up their sleeves and get their hands dirty alongside you.
   - Who is on the bus? Make sure you are on the right bus and continually bring new people and mentors onto it. This also means sometimes kicking people off your bus.
   - A business is constantly expanding and contracting. I am always adjusting scenarios and business models, so they remain manageable for a specific contract. Lean Canvas principles are extremely helpful in this process.
   - I learned to narrow down my goals each year, and I have discovered that I am very good at achieving them.
   - Be honest with yourself. If you are comfortable building a quality-of-life company, that is perfectly fine. But if you want to build an exit-strategy company, you had better be prepared to put in the work and effort required. I am still working on this one.
   - I had to be very honest with myself about what I am good at in business. I am someone who can move things to the five-yard line but need a downhill runner to score the touchdown. That is simply my reality. Having worked in teams for so long, I thrive in that dynamic. As a result, I am evolving once again by bringing in the right mix of people to help grow the business in the right way while learning how to become that down hill runner.
   - Know your enemy and know what motivates you to wake up and crush it every day. My enemy is anyone who refuses to consider new data and innovations that can prevent injury and fatigue for high-speed boat operators. I am in a

target rich environment. That is why I wake up every day with that mission in mind.

My transition into civilian life has been filled with both success and failure, setbacks and setups for comebacks, and lessons learned through patience and humility. Without my support network and mentors, I would truly be lost. But the most important lesson I carry with me to this day came from an unexpected place.

During my deployment to Pakistan, I often ended my day at the consulate bar having meaningful conversations with an extremely wise woman who worked for USAID. One evening, after a particularly bad day, I listened closely as she shared some of her experiences. She told me about a time when she had to work closely with a Navy captain who initially refused to give her the time of day. She repeatedly asked if they could sit down for coffee or tea, but he always said "no." Eventually, after enough persistence, he agreed. For the first time two people clearly from very different worlds, sat down together for coffee. She worked for USAID, and he was a naval officer.

Over time, they built a lasting bond that transcended those differences. They spent hours talking, sharing life stories, and learning from each other's perspectives.

She told me, "It's like hugging an iceberg. If you hug loosely, you will freeze to death. But if you hug tightly and keep hugging tightly, the ice will eventually melt, and people will begin to see things in a different light and through a different lens."

Her words have stayed with me ever since. They strengthened my determination to fight for change in protecting boat operators and fueled my drive to succeed in business. I hear nine "no's" for every one "yes," so I keep showing up every day, moving the needle just a little bit at a time.

Thanks to her wise words, I will continue hugging icebergs.

Chapter Sixteen

The Power of Emotional Intelligence: God is my Pilot

"If your emotional abilities aren't in hand, if you don't have self-awareness, if you cannot manage your distressing emotions, if you lack empathy or the ability to build effective relationships, then no matter how smart you are, you will not go very far."

Daniel Goleman

Why do we derail? Why do we stumble at the finish line? Why are we so afraid of success? How do we break that cycle? That is where Emotional Intelligence (EQ) comes into play and, in my view, often intersects with faith.

Little did I know, I was high in EQ, but not in IQ.

Dr. Cathy Greenberg, author of Fearless Leaders: Sharpen Your Focus and Emotional Brilliance, put many things into perspective for numerous SEALs and SWCC. Her guidance in 2010 set me on a path of profound breakthroughs and allowed me to "Name it to tame it." I identified my strengths and gaps that led to successful outcomes in both my personal life and professional career. I learned to embrace success rather than fear it while keeping failure in perspective and behind me. I am not saying we shouldn't learn from failure, but I realized it was often tied to generational patterns that I had to recognize and overcome. For years, I kept banging my head against the wall until my emotional intelligence "light" finally turned on.

As you've seen, it was a long road, filled with fits and starts, before I could honestly say I had become a more emotionally intelligent human being. The truth is, I always regretted not learning about EQ earlier in my career. Only later did it make sense why certain people like me weren't the smartest but still influenced positive outcomes and built cohesive, successful teams. My life and career transformed when I became self-aware and learned to self-manage and self-regulate. I would often remind myself: "Ron, they aren't talking about you. Ron, they aren't judging you. Ron, you are great at this you are not a failure." For so many years, I was a work in progress. Learning about EQ has made a huge difference in my life both at work and in my relationships.

EQ is the number one predictor of workplace success. It helped me evolve into a highly emotionally intelligent person through the experiences the Navy provided. Opportunities I never would have received on the mean streets of Chicago. I never understood why the military didn't invest in this type of training earlier; it would have made a huge difference for new recruits. Better late than never. Even today, I cannot comprehend why EQ isn't taught in civilian schools. When I got into trouble, teachers would always ask, "Why did you do this or that?" My standard response: "I don't know." That answer cost me, yet now I understand why it happened. I've learned to reprogram my past and break some generational patterns. Emotional Intelligence is a powerful tool that makes everyone regardless of background better. For example, my EQI assessment revealed that I needed to be part of a team for identity, safety, and validation. Not surprising since I spent nearly my entire adult life in the boat teams.

Reading Dr. Greenberg's numerous books was incredibly helpful. They helped me understand the finer points of emotional intelligence and set me on the path to becoming a professionally certified executive coach.

Here is an abbreviated version of emotional intelligence, gleaned from my experience and reading her insightful books. Emotional intelligence is a set of emotional and social skills that collectively determine how well we:

- Perceive and express ourselves
- Develop and maintain social relationships
- Cope with challenges
- Use emotional information in effective and meaningful ways

As Charles Darwin, the famed biologist and naturalist, observed: "It is not the strongest of the species that survives, nor the most intelligent, but the one most responsive to change."

To clarify and summarize: IQ reflects the relative intelligence of a person, while EQ measures one's emotional intelligence the ability to integrate both emotional and cognitive thought.

EQ gets you through life; IQ gets you through school.

So, what is the difference between happiness and anger and what are the indicators? What if you could identify the traits that make you happy? Would you focus on them?

There is an emotional intelligence assessment called the "EQI" that I used to administer to my clients when I was a practicing executive coach. It is a very powerful tool that highlights their strengths and identifies gaps in emotional intelligence. It also provides a roadmap for improvement. This includes learning not to overuse one's strengths. One subset of the assessment focuses on "Happiness Indicators." These indicators reflect emotional health and well-being rather than measuring any single subscale. They are characterized by feelings of satisfaction, contentment and the ability to enjoy many aspects of life. The four subscales of Happiness indicators are self-regard, optimism, interpersonal relationships, and self-actualization.

But what happens when we derail and lose our cool? Did you know that this is actually called an Amygdala Hijack? The Amygdala Hijack is tied to your fight-or-flight mechanism, and a hijack immediately shuts down the executive functions that occur in the prefrontal cortex of the brain. You might wonder how this small, kidney-bean–sized part of the brain can control so much. There are three signs of a hijack: a strong emotional reaction, sudden onset, and regret for your actions. Stress often suppresses the prefrontal cortex and its executive functioning, which means that many organizations and individuals operate with diminished cognitive resources on a regular basis. In both work and life, the effort should always be to better understand yourself and how you interact with others. We have to be able to identify our blind spots that make us derail.

I have found the best way to practice emotional regulation is through a simple meditation that I learned from Dr. Greenberg.

<u>Mission Tasking:</u>

Close your eyes and think back to one of the worst experiences of your life, such as betrayal, an accident, a death etc.

Stay in that memory for about a minute. Then open your eyes. You have just accessed your amygdala. You will notice that the smile is no longer on your face and that you feel like anything could set you off if you step into the world in that state.

<u>Here's how you reset the hijack.</u> Close your eyes again and recall a happier time one of the greatest moments in your life, such as your marriage, having your first child, graduating, making a team, finishing a race, or being promoted. Remain in this memory for about a minute. Notice the drop in your stress level and the sense of a burden lifted. In most cases, you will have a smile on your face and feel a sense of peace overtaking your mind and body. This is your prefrontal cortex taking charge again and pulling you out of fight or flight mode.

This practice can prevent derailing situations from engulfing your life and reduce the need for constant apologies.

Remember that you are in control and can pull yourself from an amygdala hijack by acknowledging that it is happening, being self-aware, and self-regulating through self-talk. I often told myself, "Ron, you are derailing pull it back a notch. Go to a happy place. Recall a memory that brings a smile to your face, and you will pull yourself from the brink."

As you continue on your journey in life, ask yourself key questions to grow emotionally. It is not your IQ but your EQ that matters, so push through and create a better version of yourself. First, create balance in your life among faith, family, and career. How have we reprioritized these aspects in our lives? Why do we take the pilot seat and state "God is my Copilot", only to hand the keys back to God once we crash the plane? We must sustain our families long after our careers end, but where do we need to shore up the gaps? When is it time to separate and work on a new normal that brings out the best in our lives? How do you stop being a "boat talker" and become a "water walker"?

Bringing God in your life acts as a force multiplier in this process. At least it did for me. Answering these questions is essential to truly becoming an emotionally intelligent person. Some of the questions that have helped me and can help you include:

- Where is the stress in your life, and how do you create equilibrium, eradicate it, and find your center?
- What makes you feel that it is too late, with no way back from a particular mess?
- Why do you worry so much about what others think?
- How do you create trust and transparency that reduce stress and improve job satisfaction?
- How do you become more present?
- What is your purpose? How do you set meaningful goals and objectives that provide purpose in your life?
- How do you stop digging that hole deeper and get back on the path to honor

I believe you can achieve a little with a lot. We call these micro-initiatives for macro impacts. By making small rudder corrections you can develop muscle memory and gradually change your behavior. It will not happen overnight, but I assure you that it will happen over time. The habits you want to change are often the very ones holding you back from becoming the greatest version of yourself.

Taking one step at a time, one day at a time, is essential, because it takes roughly ninety days to change a habit. It is also helpful to openly share the changes you are making, as this creates accountability. Everyone you inform becomes an accountability partner. Micro-initiatives can be as simple as completing the first task of the day, such as making your bed, a suggestion popularized by Navy SEAL Admiral McRaven. Small changes today can lead to large, impactful changes tomorrow. Remember, even though we often say, "live alone, die alone," it is important to have love in your life and maintain it through family and friendships.

Though I am no expert in religion, I want to share what I have learned over a lifetime and through thirty-two years in the military in hopes that it will help you avoid some of the mistakes I made. Even though I am still a work in progress, my life has been enriched by my relationship with God and by a clear understanding of the benefits that emotional intelligence has brought me. I practice my walk with God daily and use emotional intelligence strategies as well. Something as simple as acknowledging someone for three seconds by saying "hello" can be very powerful.

I believe Dr. Greenberg is correct when she says that we need the courage to fail, the resilience to pick ourselves up and keep moving, the consciousness to learn, and a mindset for success.
Your journey is no different from mine. Get up, dress up, and show up every morning by taking that first small step each day. It all starts with the fundamental belief that we are worth it.

I originally began this chapter calling it only "God is my pilot," but the more I wrote, the more I realized that emotional intelligence (EQ) is equally important. It influences everything I think, feel, and act upon. EQ is perhaps the most misunderstood and underutilized weapon in our arsenal. It also helps us become more empathetic, aware of other people's emotions, and cognizant of them in interpersonal relationships. Even highly emotionally intelligent people often receive very little training to understand the traits that shape themselves or others. In my opinion, overusing a strength can quickly become a weakness. For example, if your strength is optimism, always using it during a moment when someone experiences loss or tragedy becomes a weakness because you were not self-aware enough to adjust. This is similar to a SWCC being an exceptional boat driver but not understanding the intricacies of deadrise, chines, strakes, pitch, or roll. One without the other simply will not stand.

You may wonder how I incorporate EQ with God and my everyday life. Here is my explanation which I hope resonates with you regardless of your personal religious beliefs. If God is my co-pilot, then why do I always crash the plane and then hand the keys over to Him? I have witnessed true miracles following harrowing experiences where I should not even be alive today. Somehow, I survived and thrived despite growing up in the hood, with very low self-esteem, and believing that my future offered little beyond jail, gangs or addiction.

There is a quantum field theory in physics that resonates with me, even though I am no physicist. I believe that what we think and envision can create extraordinary outcomes in our lives. Napoleon Hill writes in his consistently best-selling book Think and Grow Rich, "If the mind can conceive and the heart can believe, then you can achieve." I am living proof of those words. Growing up, I watched my mom rely on her faith in God to protect herself against my stepfather. She confronted this evil man with such strength that she effectively neutralized him, yet she never became bitter. She laughed and maintained positivity despite the trauma, which inspired me to pursue a relationship with God.

I have traveled the world and witnessed both the best and worst of humanity. I have marveled at the human spirit and resilience. My faith in God has allowed me to experience a father figure I never truly had on Earth. God can be whatever you need him to be in your own emotional and physical temple. For me, God has always been the father I needed to talk to. Consider that all the DNA on Earth, from billions of people, fits into the size of a sugar cube. If that does not remind us that we are all connected, nothing will. Yet evil in the world often tries to divide what is naturally connected.

I continually work on my relationship with God, strive to be present, and believe in a higher power. This awareness came after

I got out of my own way, let go of ego and arrogance, and began to become more self-actualized and emotionally intelligent. As a young sailor, I often acted impulsively and boarded the wrong "buses," so to speak. When things blew up in my face, I prayed to negotiate a softer landing or to make problems disappear. Clearly, I did not yet have a relationship with God or with my inner self.

There was always a void in my "going it alone" attitude. I only called on God when in trouble, offering lists of promises in exchange for miracles. I was not a bad person, but I did not understand the bigger picture. I tried to fly my own plane, crashed, and then returned to prayer for guidance. My prayers were often answered, yet I remained cocky, thinking I was in control. This cycle repeated until I began to evaluate my life deeply and seek clarity and understanding. In that moment of clarity, we achieve true clarity of purpose.

As I grew older and rose in the military, I experienced true miracles in other countries. There were times when my teammates or I could have been seriously injured or killed during training or real-world missions. I observed that the strength of certain cultures often lies in their communities, frequently tied to religion. I have never judged anyone's faith, and I recognize that while there are roughly 4,200 religions in the world, there is a connection to the one I know. Although the world is divided by religion and politics, I prefer to see the best in people through the accountability their religions encourage. Even those who do not attend church often maintain moral compasses and community responsibility.

As for me, I do not attend church, but my relationship with God is unquestionable and has evolved, allowing me to pray with accuracy far different from my early "get out of jail" prayers. Do not get me wrong. People who attend church experience a powerful energy together. The positive energy and love projected among members and toward the world is a formidable force to counter evil, addictions, hate, and the many challenges life presents. As I grew older, I became humbler and worked diligently to become self-actualized. After attending NICOE in 2015, my relationship with God became even more profound. During those three weeks, I had the opportunity to reflect on my life and realized that I was a miracle; God prevented many bad things from happening to me and my teams. God also provided obstacles and setbacks from which I learned powerful lessons. Without emotional intelligence and my willingness to shed the demons of my past, this would not have been possible.

I also learned that I could pray and put my wants and needs out to the universe, and God would answer. Interestingly, I asked God for many things in my life, and I received them. The Bible says, "Ask and ye shall receive; believe it is done, and it is done." This is the secret ingredient that some people struggle to trust. I have had friends say, "You can't pray to God for that!" My explanation is simple: you can ask with all your heart, and with even a little faith, God will answer.

My journey and relationship with God took on an entirely new meaning when I reflected on the one-mile ambush from which we emerged without injury, despite circumstances that should have caused numerous casualties. I believe that the blessings I requested from the chaplain for my deployed team and our boats served as the real armor protecting us that night. With that spiritual armor surrounding us, our boat operators unleashed hell on the enemy, ensuring their defeat.

I wrote this chapter primarily to express my belief in a higher power. I call Him "God" and identify as a non-denominational Christian. Around the world, this higher power goes by many names: God, Father, Jah, Lord, Elohim, El Shaddai, Jehovah Jireh, Allah, Alpha and Omega, Jehovah, Yahweh, and many more. The American Indians had a Great Spirit, with various tribes calling him Manitou, Wabanaki, Unetlanvhi, and other titles. Regardless of the name or culture, the accountability, self-control, love, community support, charity, and forgiveness that these religions promote are awe-inspiring.

Of course, one must sift through politics and divisiveness to appreciate the true essence of these cultures and their religion. I have experienced the best of human nature through many religions and cultures and have seen extraordinary individuals embodying their faith during the most challenging times.

I dare not walk through this life without God, nor claim to be in charge of anything. I cannot pilot the plane, and I am too old to keep crashing and starting over. So, I pray in a way that provides specific descriptions to receive exactly what I need. In the same way, I prayed for my wife and was blessed with exactly what I asked. Here are a few pointers for effective prayer: describe in detail what you need.

For example: "Dear Lord, please bless me with discernment so that I can evolve into a better mother, father, sister, brother, or leader. Please remove all evil from me, my wife, my kids, our dog, our homes, and cars. Please place a protective force field around us to prevent harm, be it physical or mental. Please bless me with a Pontiac GTO, blue with a Chevy engine, air conditioning, air ride suspension, and low maintenance costs. Dear Lord, please strengthen Ron's heart and lungs so that they may remain in my life longer, instilling a healthy body that lasts another twenty years." The more specific, the better.

Having faith is a powerful tool, intrinsically tied to emotional intelligence. Many people believe that faith alone is enough. I truly believe faith is essential to be empowered in a world determined to crush us. One can be the most God-fearing person yet have no friends, a team that does not respect them, a family that does not like them, and most people thinking poorly of them. It may be difficult to hear, but if these are the facts, God may want us to change. We must ask ourselves how to align our truth with reality. Otherwise, our egos overshadow the humility and forgiveness we should extend to others.

To align our truth with reality, we must examine our upbringing and identify generational curses passed from one generation to the next. We are products not only of our environment but also of the positive and negative behaviors, traits, and examples we inherit. This is the first step toward change: identifying the blind spots that hold us back from success or strain our relationships.

Also, you have to understand that most of us entered the military while our brains and emotions were still developing. Instead of maturing in a normal civilian environment, we were immersed in a culture that demanded discipline, resilience, and mission-first thinking almost immediately.

The military teaches you to compartmentalize. Fear, grief, anger, and personal struggles all get placed in a mental box so you can focus on the task at hand. The expectation is simple: perform now, deal with emotions later. That ability allows service members to function in high-stress environments where hesitation could cost lives.

Over time, this becomes second nature. But when we transition back to civilian life, that same skill can become a challenge. The emotional box we built to survive and perform does not always open easily. Veterans are not broken we were simply trained to prioritize mission and performance during a critical stage of emotional development. Learning when to keep the box closed and when to open it becomes part of the transition and at times very emotional. Consider my past. Everything about my upbringing communicated, "Rich people can't be trusted; it's someone else's fault; white people always exploit us; it is okay not to strive to be great; failure is expected; I am unchangeable," and so on. These factors are identifiable, especially as one climbs the ladder of success, yet they continue to derail you when success is near.

If, like me, you have more time behind you than in front of you, it is crucial to project love into the universe and be present. Our lives can affect those around us if we are emotionally attuned and use EQ, not IQ to bring out the best in everyone we encounter while creating a relationship with God. Have you ever seen someone smile yet want to punch you in the face? Smile back and spread more smiles into the world than frowns. Love is the light that overcomes darkness; even darkness seeks the light. Focus on others and yourself and recognize that meaningful change requires changing attitudes. You are not always right. You must admit when you are wrong, say, "I am sorry," and take responsibility.

You must say, "I love you" and "I will try harder." Most importantly, you must love yourself. By loving yourself, you will love others more deeply and authentically.

Chapter Seventeen

Your Past Ain't Your Prison

"Be such a man, and live such a life, that if every man were such as you, and every life like yours, this earth would be God's paradise."

Former CO, NSWU 10

It has been quite a journey in this thing called life. Though my journey of windmills and treadmills is not over just yet, it has certainly been an experience. Our lives and our legacy speak volumes about who we were on this earth. When I look back at my life, my greatest fear is that I did not do enough to impact people's lives, or that I may have overlooked even one person whose life I could have changed.

As a young man growing up in the hood, I allowed myself to be painted into a corner of underachievement and self doubt. I never believed I was worthy of success and derailed my dreams every time I got close to becoming successful. I was afraid of accomplishing something meaningful in my life. In the process, I let many people down. Yet they never gave up on me. They continued to give me opportunities to return to honor, and that speaks volumes about what they meant in my life. It also speaks volumes about the U.S. military.

No one enters the military and leaves without experiencing some type of transformation. Service members change their behavior, their personality, their confidence, and often their entire outlook on life. They walk taller and carry themselves with greater confidence. They become more situationally aware. They experience moments of achievement they never thought possible and often become addicted to success. They learn how to operate effectively under intense stress. Even people like me who tried to hold onto the derailing behaviors I learned on the South Side were eventually reshaped by the military system and by mentors who helped reprogram us to become productive citizens and dependable teammates.

In life, we are often painted into portraits that eventually stop making sense. Those who accept that picture will remain trapped inside that portrait forever. That image reinforces victimhood, the blame game, and mediocrity. Sadly, those beliefs prevent some people from achieving the success that God placed within all of us.

How did we allow others to shrink the game on us? Why were we playing small? How did we stay on the same bus with five fools and make ourselves the sixth? Whose rules were we playing by anyway? How did we become trapped in political identities and so easily baited by race? When did the United States become a nation defined only by black and white? When did we start forcing our children to pay for the sins of previous generations?

During those early years, I often said to myself, "Damn, I fell into another trap where I let someone else hold my pen and write the chapters of my life." Then I would remind myself, "Ron, don't let anybody hold your pen. You write your life book, and no one else. Period!"

For many of us, it is easier to drink the Kool Aid and repeat the same party line that blames our past for our present situation. But the truth is that many people, me included are living proof that we can break that cycle. When I became more self aware, I realized my past had created a prison of my own making.

Finally, I decided it was time to get off my butt, tie my shoes, and take the first step toward changing my life and creating a new version of myself. You can do the same. That is why I wanted to provide a roadmap for anyone struggling with their identity the way I once did. Inside me, there was always a voice, one moment pulling me down, the next urging me to do something great. I knew I had to change, and if I did, my past would no longer dictate my future success.

At times I felt handcuffed to a wall, like lying on a steel bed in a jail cell shackled in a life without purpose. And as you have seen, even after joining the military, my past continued creeping back in and derailing my progress. I went AWOL, faced captain's mast, lied, cheated, and stole. I was an underachiever and a troublemaker growing up and most tragically, even contemplated suicide.

All of it fits into the larger narrative of playing small and remaining chained to my past. But those chains can be broken. You cannot live your life perpetuating the burdens of previous generations. You are responsible only for the morals and choices of your own time not for the sins of the past.

We must change. And the truth is we can.

I want to share some of the lessons I learned from the hood, the military, and life, to help you along your road of personal growth and achievement. The following gems of wisdom helped me change, and I hope they will provide guidance in your own journey through life.

"As you develop interpersonally, you will naturally inspire those around you. The process begins with one simple question: "What is my future potential?" If you are part of a team, ask: "What is their future potential?" Once you understand potential, follow up with: "What do I or they need to do to realize that potential?" "What preparation or training is required to attain it?" "What attitude adjustments might be necessary?" *"Author Unknown"*

As you mentor your team and conduct debriefs, apply the approach Dr. Terry Borton calls "What, so what, now what."

What? **So, what happened?**
Focus on describing the situation or experience. What actually happened?

So What? **So, what did we learn?**
Examine the meaning of the experience. Why is it important? What did you learn?

Now What? Now what are we going to do about it. Consider the implications for future action. What will you do differently moving forward?

This technique enables you, your family and your team to grow in ways you may not have thought possible. Growth comes not just from what we did right, but also from what we did wrong, so we can constantly improve. Even when the mission is successful, not everything goes exactly according to plan. Focus on the areas that need improvement, not just on patting yourself on the back. As you improve, those around you improve as well.

Three critical bones in your life

Reba McEntire, the country music star, once said, "To succeed in life, you need three things: a wishbone, a backbone, and a funny bone." Over the years, I have expanded on her sage guidance and developed what I call the "three bones theory." Here is my take: on this journey, you will need three bones that must remain with you for the rest of your life.

The first is the **Wishbone.** This includes all your hopes and dreams, as well as your empathy for others. You must dream and wish big, so big that the average person would shudder at the thought. You also need to understand the wishbone of others; this is called empathy. Ask yourself: Do I know the wishbone of your family members or teammates? If not, why? When was the last time you placed yourself in their shoes?

You might ask them directly what their wishbone is so you can assist them in their journey. Even if your support is only moral, by asking, you acknowledge their hopes and dreams.

The second is the **Backbone**. This is what you stand for and where you draw the line. It speaks volumes about your character and contributes to your enduring reputation what others think of you. If an action does not align with your values, you should not do it. If you cannot stand before your parents or leadership team and explain why you did it, then it is not worth doing. If you are unwilling to stand up for something, you are liable to fall for anything. Have a backbone. Remember to say "no" or "stop," and your dignity and moral compass will remain intact. You also won't have to start the path back to honor.

The third is the **Funny bone.** Humor helps you face your fears and the difficulties life throws your way, and it encourages a positive attitude. Today's nightmares become tomorrow's memories. I was often told by those older than me, "If you don't screw some things up now, your stories are going to suck when you get to my age. Don't worry you can mess up, make up, but never give up."

Those were wise words.

So, take a moment to laugh, even at yourself. Self-deprecating humor is one of the highest forms of emotional intelligence. It is okay, the clouds and rain will pass, and the sun will shine again. Remember to laugh at your failures and your near misses.

Tribe

I read Seth Godin's *Tribes* years ago and adopted its principles.
The next step is deciding which bus to get on and who will ride with you. Your tribe includes your team, your family, your friends, your coworkers, and your community.

Humans have a natural instinct to belong to small groups united by a clear purpose and shared understanding. Tribes operate with standards, and within a tribe we are expected not only to uphold those standards but to exceed them. Without a tribe, you are operating alone and going solo is a weak position.

That said, not everyone belongs on your bus. Even some family members may not be part of your tribe. Your tribe is made up of the people who will hold you accountable and support your hopes and dreams; your "wishbone." They do not envy your journey; they embrace it and genuinely want to see you succeed.

Who is on your bus?

The "bus" represents your family, close friends, or your working team. To identify who belongs on your bus, ask yourself a few important questions: Do they know and support your core values? Who truly has your best interests at heart? Who makes you better? Will they step up and step out with you in supportive ways for the right reasons? And finally, do they need to remain on your bus, or is it time to off-load a few passengers?

The goal is always to look for character and commitment in those riding on your bus. This allows you to evolve.

I used to work with a team for six years that visited The Citadel Military College three times a year to train cadets in servant leadership and share our collective experiences. Together, we helped create a cultural shift in the dynamics of their student body and staff because they embraced a positive attitude and were open to change.

One individual who stood out to me was Kevin, an alumnus of the Citadel class of 1974. Kevin always took detailed notes and remained deeply engaged during every session. He was exactly the type of person I always wanted on my bus.

Our sessions and change efforts were led by Command Post Technologies. The mission itself was worthwhile because it made a meaningful difference in the development of future military and corporate leaders. Scott Bisciotti, President of CPT was an alumnus of the Citadel, coordinated and funded the training. He also brought together many former veterans from different service branches. They were truly an outstanding group of men and women. Scott was the epitome of a servant leader, and the experience he created made a lasting impact in all of our lives. We all learned from one another while helping place the school on a trajectory of success, accountability, and leadership excellence.

There were so many remarkable leaders involved in this effort that I wanted to acknowledge them in this book, because they helped make me a better person as well.

Throughout this experience—and in my executive coaching—I've leaned on one of the most powerful leadership truths I've ever heard, from Navy SEAL Master Chief, Russ Munro:

"The most powerful leadership trait is love."

That principle stuck and our team expanded it into something I teach every leader I work with:

Love yourself.
Love your team.
Love your organization.
Because true love never dishonors what it leads.

From that foundation comes humility—the kind earned through failure, reflection, and growth.

And as Big Tony Smith put it best: "Don't let nobody lick the red off your lollipop."

Know your worth. Lead with purpose. And never give away what makes you powerful.

I appreciate each and everyone of you for coming on this journey with me. Life is what we make it, and our time passes in the blink of an eye. It is up to us to make a difference in our own lives and in the lives of others. We are living in the now; the future becomes now. We cannot dwell in the past. Every day, the ink dries. Yesterday cannot be undone, but we can be better today. Take my word for it: you are worthy, you are loved, you are beautiful, you are smart, you are successful, you are healthy, and you are a gift.
Now go out there and crush it with love, strength, and courage.

I am Ron Carpenter, signing off. It shouldn't surprise you that I am from the South Side of Chicago. I am an American Halfbreed, a thirty-two-year Navy veteran with two bachelor's degrees, a master's degree, a professional coaching certification and President of TMS Group LLC. I could have been a drug addict, a pimp or spent the rest of my life in prison. But my past isn't my prison, and yours doesn't have to be either. So, have a little faith, become emotionally intelligent, keep praying, love yourself, and make the world a better place.

I've taken my seat at the table—shaped by time, tested through trial, and tempered by hardship and storm. When your path brings you here, I hope you'll pull up a chair and join me. I won't be alone—we are here, waiting for the return of those still walking the hero's journey. Hooyah!

Epilogue

Growing up in the hood surrounded by gangbangers, drug dealers, and pimps was no walk in the park. Being biracial added another layer of complexity to challenges I was already struggling to overcome. Many times, in my life it felt like I was watching the same movie on repeat. The saying, "What we think about, we bring about," became a catalyst for change in my life. If we repeat the same patterns day after day, we simply perpetuate the misery tied to being products of our environment. At some point, we have to break the rinse-and-repeat cycle.

It all begins with our programming. I could have easily ended up in prison or become a gangbanger, drug dealer, or pimp myself. But something inside me pushed me to take a different path one gargantuan step away from the trajectory many others in my neighborhood were on. That tug in my heart, that yearning for something better, pulled me out of despair. I realized my hustle needed to go the way of the dinosaur. I needed to understand and embrace concepts that once felt foreign: honor, courage, commitment, God, country and, of course, very fast boats. As our SWCC mantra reminds us, we must always be "On Time, On Target, and Never Quit."

My transformation required moving from being "nobody" to becoming "somebody." I had to do it quickly, and I had to learn to live with honor rather than continuing the programming that would have made my road far longer and far harder.

The South Side of Chicago is brutal, and one of the deadliest places in the United States per capita when I was growing up and still is. It was there that I learned to fight, hustle, steal cars, and manipulate people and situations to survive. The older "gangsters" in the neighborhood would offer advice like, "Go to school to beat the white man at the books, and stay on the streets to beat the homie at the hustle." Talk about motivation.

But over time, witnessing the horrors of the hood became unbearable. I watched friends lose their identities and some end up dead or in prison. I witnessed my father and stepfather murder two men. I saw my mother endure rape, beatings, strangling, and relentless abuse. It was far too much for a young kid to carry. Even though I lived in that environment and was shaped by it, I knew deep down that I wanted more out of life than despair, violence, poverty, and misery.

It was the U.S. Navy and specifically its Special Boat Teams that helped turn my life around. My mother's unyielding grit continues to inspire me, and God gave me the faith and courage to keep pushing through the challenges that life inevitably brings. I remain a work in progress, but just as a rock exposed to extreme heat and pressure becomes a diamond, I believe the same process shapes us. That is why I will keep pushing forward, no matter the obstacles ahead and I hope you will too. Hard work will always pay off.

My mission in sharing this story is simple: to help you realize your own potential. If someone with my background can find a path forward, so can you. During my journey, I often repeated an affirmation from Charles F. Haanel that brought me comfort and strength: "I am blessed. I am whole. I am perfect. I am strong. I am powerful. I am loving. I am harmonious. I am happy. I am loved. I am success."

Believing that you matter despite poverty, despite horrific circumstances, despite abuse, despite overwhelming odds, and despite what others may think is a powerful truth. That belief can change the trajectory of a life.

If my story inspires you in any way, then sharing it will have been worth it. My greatest hope is that you never allow someone else to hold the pen that writes the chapters of your life.

Hooyah!

Author Biography

Ronald E. Carpenter Chief Warrant Officer Five (Ret.)

Ronald E. Carpenter Jr. was raised on the South Side of Chicago and went on to serve more than 32 years in the U.S. Navy, including 28 years in Special Operations with the Special Boat Teams. A combat veteran, he led maritime missions in 48 countries and was among the first in his community to be promoted to Chief Warrant Officer Five (CWO5).

His leadership roles included commanding Riverine Task Unit Five in Iraq and Boat Troop Five in the Philippines, earning two Bronze Stars. He supported operations across the Middle East, Africa, and Central and South America.

Carpenter holds degrees in Education and Business, a master's in business, and is a certified executive coach. After retiring, he founded Train Maintain Sustain Group LLC, providing training and strategic support worldwide.

Driven by his own journey overcoming poverty, he also founded Support a Future, mentoring youth and supporting veterans and Gold Star families. Through speaking and coaching, he has impacted over 15,000 individuals.

His philosophy: *"Reach one to teach one—so the next generation can live to tell their story."*

Pre Navy Photos

Me at 16yrs old under the stain glass windows

Tobo, Tommy and me

3rd Grade at DS Wentworth

My mom when she was a teenager

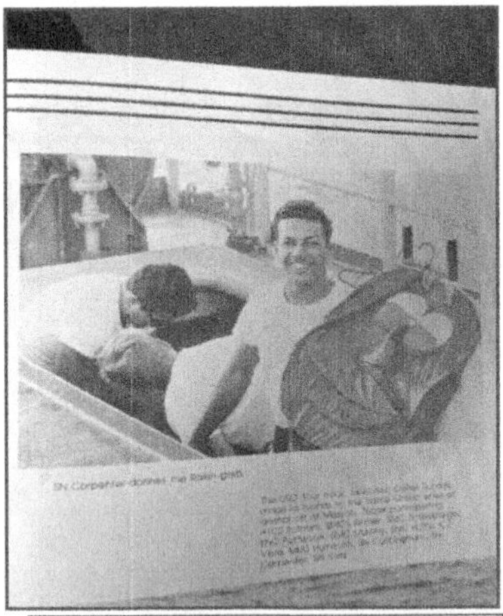

Me being forced to be a California raisin

Ron in his 6th grade Pimp Starter kit

3rd Grade at DS W Our apartment at 100l West 68th Street

Grandma Nellie and Big Tony circa 1950

Cadillac Stan

Mommy Me and Angie...

Mom_ Sheri and Angie

Stan with me and Angie

Ronald Senior (DUSWUN)

My Navy Journey and After

22 Year Old Ron in Jungle School

PB841 at Mc Fall Base Camp in Panama

Me on the Minigun during Hot Extract

CONREP and VERTREP

PB 841 68FT Coastal PB

Panama Canal Transit

SBU-26 Hot extract with Mini-Gun

Patrol Boats High Value Transit with Sub

SBU-26 explosions during Hot Extract

USS Pyro AE-24Canal Transit

Boat Troop 5 in New York

Mama Carpenter at my commissioning

Another day in the Office High Seas

Chato Painting of my career

My Warrant Commission

Nighttime Hook and Climb

My Mixed Up Family 2019

My MK V Craft in PI 2009

Little Jackson and his dad

SEAL Insert

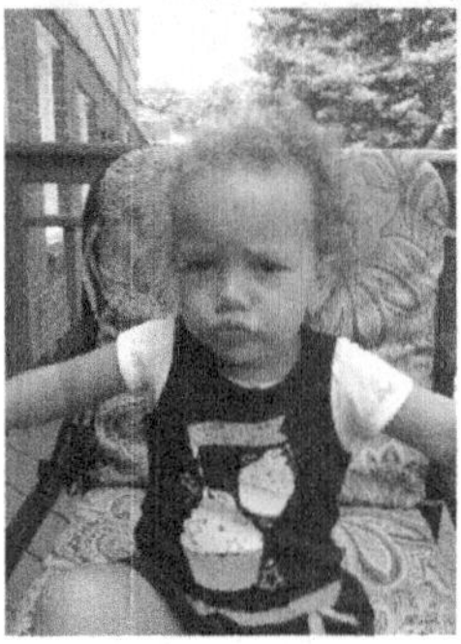

Rachel The ROC

Jackson and ROC with Uncle Tommie

Waiting for darkness to execute

My Boat at the Statue of Liberty

Me Marrying Luz Marina in 2019

Mama Carp still going strong

Made in the USA
Coppell, TX
28 June 2026

82822915R00225